Praise for THE PRISON BOOK CLUB by Ann Walmsley

LONGLISTED FOR THE RBC TAYLOR PRIZE
LONGLISTED FOR THE BC NATIONAL AWARD
FOR CANADIAN NON-FICTION
A NATIONAL POST BEST BOOK

"I loved this book! What a powerful testament to the magic of story-telling."   —Jeannette Walls, author of *The Glass Castle*

"A soulful exploration of men's hearts and minds. *The Prison Book Club* offers a unique window into inmates' lives. Funny and full of insight, Walmsley brings her best to the job at hand, winning us with tenderness. A wonderful read."
          —Ann Dowsett Johnston, author of *Drink: The Intimate Relationship Between Women and Alcohol*

"A lively and warm account of her eighteen months in two prison book clubs. . . . This book is a testament to what reading together can do in prison . . . Walmsley shows how reading and rehabilitation can go hand-in-hand."   —*The Times Literary Supplement*

"Explores the intriguing tension between the lives of incarcerated men and the liberating effects of great books. A terrific read about a world that is at once constricted yet capable of great emotional generosity." —Steven Galloway, author of *The Cellist of Sarajevo*

"Empathetic and insightful."   —*Quill & Quire*

"If you've ever wondered what violent criminals might think about *The Grapes of Wrath*, read on . . . and get ready to be incredibly moved."   —*Elle Canada*

THE
PRISON
BOOK
CLUB

ANN
WALMSLEY

PENGUIN

an imprint of Penguin Canada Books Inc., a Penguin Random House Company

Published by the Penguin Group
Penguin Canada Books Inc., 320 Front Street West, Suite 1400, Toronto, Ontario M5V 3B6, Canada

First published in Viking hardcover by Penguin Canada, 2015
Published in this edition, 2016

1 2 3 4 5 6 7 8 9 10   (RRD)

Author representation: Westwood Creative Artists
94 Harbord Street, Toronto, Ontario M5S 1G6

Manufactured in the U.S.A.

Library and Archives Canada Cataloguing in Publication Data is available upon request.

ISBN 978-0-14-319416-3
eBook ISBN 978-0-14-319417-0

Cover design: Adapted from an original by Kisscut Design
Cover image: Photocase

www.penguinrandomhouse.ca

Penguin
Random House
Canada

For Bruce

Never leave prison with a partly-read book.
You will return to complete it.

—*popular superstition among prison inmates*

CONTENTS

AUTHOR'S NOTE

THIS BOOK IS A MEMOIR based on my experiences as a volunteer in two prison book clubs in 2011 and 2012 and does not represent the experiences of other volunteers in Book Clubs for Inmates Inc., or the role that they may play. The names of people incarcerated in the prisons and the names of people who worked in the prisons have been changed to afford them some privacy. Volunteers' names have also been changed, as have those of the women in my Toronto book club with the exception of Carol's name and my own. In one or two instances, a descriptive detail about the inmates' lives has been changed, to afford even greater privacy. There are no composite characters. Most dialogue is based on audio recordings that the men, the prison authorities and others graciously allowed me to make. In a few instances, the timing of events has been compressed and descriptive details reconstructed for ease of reading.

CAST OF CHARACTERS

All names listed below are pseudonyms except those of Carol and Ann.

THE COLLINS BAY BOOK CLUB

—

The Ambassadors

BEN Serving a four-year sentence for manslaughter, he particularly enjoyed Andrea Levy's *Small Island* but says he has no favourite book. "All the books that I've read have contributed to who I am today and how I look at life."

DREAD Serving a sentence for drug-related crimes, he says Margaret Atwood "transports you like an avatar."

FRANK Serving ten years for aggravated assault and weapons offences, his favourite book is *Alias Grace* by Margaret Atwood.

GASTON Serving a six-year sentence for a series of bank robberies, his favourite book is *The Guernsey Literary and Potato Peel Pie Society* by Mary Ann Shaffer and Annie Barrows.

GRAHAM Serving seventeen years for drug trafficking and extortion, his favourite book is *The Cellist of Sarajevo* by Steven Galloway.

PETER Serving a four-year sentence for armed robbery, the most enduring books for him are *The Grapes of Wrath* by John Steinbeck and Charles Dickens's *A Tale of Two Cities*.

The Other Members

Albert	Grow-Op	Michael	Seamus
Brad	Javier	Olivier	Stan
Colin	Joao	Parvat	Tony
Deshane	Juan	Quincy	Vince
Ford	Lenny	Rick	Winston
George	Marley	Roman	

THE BEAVER CREEK BOOK CLUB

—

The Ambassadors

Graham
Frank

The Other Members

Bookman
Byrne
Dallas
Doc
Earl
Hal
Jason
Jones
Mitchell
Pino
Raymond
Richard
Tom

THE VOLUNTEERS

—

Ann
Carol
Derek
Edward
Tristan

THE TORONTO WOMEN'S BOOK CLUB

—

Ann
Betty
Carol
Deborah
Evelyn
Lillian-Rose
Ruth

THE PRISON STAFF

—

Blair – a chaplain
Clive – a librarian
Donna – an official
Meg – an assistant
Phoebe – an English teacher
Renata – book club leader at a halfway house

THE
PRISON
BOOK
CLUB

I

A WALK IN THE CEMETERY

WHEN MY FRIEND CAROL FINLAY invited me to join a monthly book club that she had started in a men's prison, everything about it screamed *bad idea*. The prison book club's members included drug traffickers, bank robbers and murderers. I admired the work she was doing but I wasn't sure I could do it. Eight years earlier in England I had survived a violent mugging. Two men had chased me down a dark lane beside my London house near Hampstead Heath, strangled me in a chokehold until I lost consciousness and fled with my cellphone.

It had taken me months to overcome the trauma, and during my remaining three years in London I was too frightened to walk alone at night, even with my new ear-splitting pocket security alarm and a weapons-grade, thirteen-inch flashlight with an alarm that mimicked a barking Doberman. I wasn't sure that I could enter the prison without triggering my earlier traumatic response. But then I remembered that in the weeks after the attack in England, and before I was asked to look at a lineup of suspects, I had felt an unexpected maternal impulse as I imagined how distressed my assailants' mothers must have felt about their errant sons. Something my father once said to me also came to mind: "If you expect the best of people, they will rise to the occasion." He had been an Ontario Court judge and had seen people at their worst. By the slimmest of margins, my curiosity began to outweigh my apprehension. I couldn't resist seeing for myself what the convicts would say about the books.

It's a journey that began in a cemetery.

Toronto's Mount Pleasant Cemetery is popular among walkers for its winding routes past nineteenth-century obelisks and sorrowful statues, overhung by unusual species of trees. Carol was an avid walker, and I had invited her to join me there for a stroll. Before setting off, we stood at my father's gravesite, taking a moment for reflection. The grave lay beneath a catalpa tree on a grassy path between two rows of monuments. I had spent many happy hours in my childhood climbing a catalpa, so I found the spot easily among the larches and yews, copper beeches and magnolias. The tree's heart-shaped leaves fanned us and the long bean pods clacked in the wind as we contemplated the slightly sunken rectangle of grass still waiting for its marker. My family had commissioned a sculptor to chisel a bas-relief of a bird rising up from tall grasses on a round disc of black granite. The shafts of the feathers and the midribs in the blades of grass would mirror each other, as would their capillaries: the feather barbs and the leaf veins. All living things pattern themselves on each other and become one. Dad, a naturalist, would have liked that thought.

Turning away, Carol and I adopted an exercise pace and made our way through the headstones to the paved road that snaked through the plots. She was a new friend, but was already unreserved and candid in the way old friends are.

"Did you know that you walk with a forward tilt?" she asked.

"No," I said. "I didn't." Why had no one told me that before? I consciously pressed my shoulders back and my abdomen forward in an attempt to be more vertical.

I looked sideways at her and saw that she stood ramrod straight. Her father had been in the military. Her mother had been a headmistress in a private school. "Plus they were British, so they were frozen in aspic," I once heard her say. She was ten years older than I was and still beautiful—with lively blue eyes and a wide smile of perfectly straight white teeth. She was dead smart too, and sprinting to make her mark on the world because she had a keen sense of her own mortality.

As we walked past the cemetery office, she asked me if I had any good book suggestions for the book club she had started at Collins Bay Institution. It was a medium-security federal penitentiary for men, in Kingston, two hours east of Toronto. She'd been running it for a year and had exhausted her best picks. Now she was deputizing a book selection committee and wanted me to be on it.

We had already talked several times about her project. It fascinated me that she was so brave and so entrepreneurial at the same time. I knew that she had the men reading good literary fiction and non-fiction and that they met once a month to discuss a chosen book. It was in some ways just like the book club that Carol and I belonged to on the outside, except that we were women and not in jail.

"Why me?" I asked.

"I don't know. You're bookish."

Maybe she sensed I was also in a bit of a rut. A year earlier I had lost my job as the senior writer at an investment management organization. At the time I'd been on a leave of absence to care for my twenty-three-year-old daughter, because her struggle with anorexia had taken a life-threatening turn. A few weeks before I was due to return to work, my department had let one-quarter of its staff go. Somewhat disconcertingly, my supervisor emailed me in advance to ask that I meet her on the HR floor on my scheduled first day back. My husband, who is a lawyer, told me what that meant: I was about to be sacked.

On my first day back, my supervisor said exactly what my husband had predicted she would say (word for word!): "As you know, the department has been going through a reorganization, and I'm so sorry but we're going to have to let you go." To ward off an emotional reaction, I had rehearsed a humorous response, but in the end I just sat there trying to look composed.

After that job ended, I had returned to my long-time career as a freelance magazine journalist, while ramping up my assistance to my daughter, who was seeking intensive treatment for her illness, and to my mother, who was dealing with Alzheimer's. I was in my mid-fifties and suddenly more caregiver than writer. Maybe Carol was on to something. I did need a change.

I told Carol right away that, of course, I'd help choose a long list of books for the inmates at Collins Bay. It was an opportunity to help a friend, and my husband and I enjoyed our friendship with her and her husband, Bryan, on many levels, not the least of which was their empathy for our daughter and their efforts to help her find health care resources since we'd moved back from England.

As Carol and I continued along the cemetery paths, we talked about the men's reading level and the books they had read so far. *Angela's Ashes* by Frank McCourt had been the first. I could see how a memoir of a miserable Irish childhood would be perfect for inmates, many of whom likely had experienced hardscrabble upbringings. Cormac McCarthy's post-apocalyptic novel, *The Road*, had been a hit. Carol could barely get a word in edgewise during that book club meeting. And they'd liked Joseph Boyden's novel *Three Day Road*, about two Cree hunters who enlist to serve in World War I, and Barack Obama's memoir *Dreams from My Father*.

I asked her what other sorts of books they enjoyed.

"Well," said Carol. "The thing is, you really can't tell what works unless you come into the prison and sit in on one of the book club meetings." That was when I felt my chest tighten and a hole open up beneath me, like my own ready-made grave right there in Mount Pleasant Cemetery.

In my mind, I was back in England in 2002. We had moved to London from Dallas two months earlier for my husband's work. It was a Saturday evening in early September and I had just dropped off my sixteen-year-old daughter at a birthday party for one of her new school friends in St. John's Wood. I was driving a Mercedes fleet car supplied by my husband's employer and was focused on not damaging it. I had grown confident about driving on the left, but still had difficulty parallel parking in Cannon Lane up against the nearly two-metre-high brick garden wall that surrounded our rented property in Hampstead. Our small "maisonette" occupied one wing of a Victorian pile called The Logs. The '80s pop star Boy George occupied the grand south wing. Fans would write in chalk on the brick of his garden wall, plaintive messages like *Looking for love* and their telephone number. On our side of the house, very few pedestrians ever wandered down the lane.

That evening, I came at the parking spot the easiest way. I drove up East Heath Road from South End Green, with the darkness of Hampstead Heath on my right, turned left on Squire's Mount, where cannon barrels were mounted like bollards in the sidewalk, and drove down the walled single-lane chute of Cannon Lane. A jasmine vine spilling over the wall was emitting an exotic, citrusy perfume and as I passed, the scent wafted into the open car window. I inched by the few parked cars in the lane, found the designated parking spot in front of our house, and focused on manoeuvring the car as close to the wall as possible so that other vehicles could squeeze by. Back, forth, back, back, forward a pinch, back again, straighten the steering wheel.

It was only when I stepped out and closed the door that I noticed two tall black men with unusually long coats and tweed flat caps walking toward me. They were staring at me intently. I hesitated for a second and then saw them break into a run—straight toward me. I ran too—as fast as I could with my osteoarthritic left knee—and managed to press the doorbell by the garden door, knowing my husband was in the house on a business call with colleagues in the U.S. and the U.K. Then I felt a hand over my mouth and an arm around my neck, hoisting me into the air.

The feeling of being strangled was not what I expected. Yes, there was the lack of air. But, oddly, no fear. And my lungs weren't bursting. Not yet. I was hanging by my throat from the crook of one man's arm, suspended in a chokehold, strangling under my own weight. The other man tried to grab my feet, which I flailed about in an attempt to kick.

I looked up and saw the light still on in my daughter's bedroom window. I thought of my husband, safely inside, and of my son, safely at university in Canada. *You have to survive for your family* ghosted in as a thought.

What did they want? They had said nothing. They had just silently set upon me. I had instinctively thrown my purse containing my house keys over the garden wall during the pursuit. In my left hand, my cellphone's screen and numbers glowed pale green in the darkness. In my right hand, my car key was clenched tight. I opened my hands to present both as offerings. No takers.

If they didn't want a Mercedes and a cellphone, then they wanted something else. My mind went to other possibilities. Rape. I was perhaps too old: forty-six. Murder. I was only forty-six—too young to die. From where I was struggling, it was about fifteen metres to the densely thicketed and treed border of Hampstead Heath. They would have to cross the two narrow lanes of East Heath Road to get me there. But at that time of the evening, there would be long gaps between passing cars. It was possible to cross and be unseen by anyone.

Then terror set in. I felt panic rising in my chest and my heart slamming against my rib cage. If my throat had been open I would have vomited. My lungs grew hard. I dropped the phone and pulled at the arm around my throat. I kicked, but there was no leverage. My eyes closed and the image of my daughter's window, and the outline of the fuchsia bush against it, remained imprinted on my eyelids.

I pulled once more, and then my husband's voice came through on the garden gate intercom saying, "Ann, is that you?" There was no way to answer. And then I was out of ideas, and surrender to death came floating in like a lazy impulse, as insignificant a decision as looking up from work for a moment. It was my last thought.

I told the story to Carol and she stopped walking, turned to face me and brought her hand up to her mouth. "Oh, Ann. But what happened? Were you just unconscious or did someone resuscitate you?" she asked, her brow furrowed.

I could still see it so clearly. I came to, lying on the road in the darkness, and heard the sound of feet running away. They must have dropped me hard because there was a sharp pain in one elbow. The garden gate was open, so my husband must have remotely released the gate lock and the sound must have scared them off. I stumbled along the pea-gravelled garden walk, hoarsely calling my husband's name. "I've been mugged," I croaked. He ran up the path to pursue them, but I stopped him. "They're huge. They'll kill you, they'll kill you."

He hesitated, then, thankfully, turned back. Within five minutes, my husband's boss, who'd been on the conference call with him, and who also lived in Hampstead, arrived at the house. He must have called the police, because they arrived five minutes after that and interviewed me in our living room amid the many moving boxes that we hadn't yet unpacked. I have no recollection of how my daughter got home from the party or how I got to the hospital but those things happened.

"I'm okay these days," I said to Carol. "It's just that going into Collins Bay might spark the fear again."

"What was the fear like?"

I was embarrassed sometimes to relate how acute my response had been compared to that of some other women in the neighbourhood who'd been attacked in the same way after driving home alone in a Mercedes. I'd heard of an American woman who'd had her emerald ring stolen in a strangulation robbery in front of her house, just a few blocks away, with her children nearby. Like me, she'd been unconscious, but upon opening her eyes, she stood up, brushed herself off and said, "I've got to get these kids to soccer."

In contrast, my reaction was intense. I cried unexpectedly and often and didn't leave the house for a week, spending much of it in bed. My husband took that week off to comfort me. My voice was an unrecognizable rasp from the strangling. On the night of the attack, I'd sat in the emergency ward of Hampstead's Royal Free Hospital sobbing, until I had to stop long enough for the specialist to peer down my throat. A detective had been in and taken a DNA swab from my mouth and collected my clothing as evidence. He hoped to match traces of my DNA to that on the clothing of the suspects. I kept thinking one thought: Why wasn't someone *good* in the lane just then? If someone *good* had been in the lane, they would have intervened.

Finally, I decided it was time to get out of the house. I couldn't walk up the lane, the natural route to Hampstead High Street. Even in daylight. So my husband walked with me down a busier set of streets. On the High Street I scanned the faces of the passing men for signs of kindness, needing reassurance that there was goodness in human beings, not evil. Most faces were emotionless, busy. Then I saw a man in his early sixties with wire-rimmed glasses, gentle eyes and greying hair, carrying a book. His gaze was intelligent and open. I pictured him in the lane outside my house, which comforted me. I clutched my purse less tightly then.

We walked home along Well Road, and I looked up the southern end of Cannon Lane. Then I stopped abruptly. I had forgotten that this stretch of our lane contained a tiny one-cell 1730s jail built into the side of a brick wall. Unused now, of course, but still with its original heavily barred lunette windows. It was constructed as a parish lock-up when the adjacent house, known as Cannon Hall, served as a courthouse. An ironic twist, to be accosted at the very doorstep of a jail. Almost as ironic as the security camera mounted on our house: it pointed directly at the crime scene, but was not operational.

I soon discovered that I couldn't walk at night or park in underground parking garages, which made it hard to attend my evening writing classes. Walking home from book club at friends' houses in the neighbourhood was terrifying. I couldn't set foot on Hampstead Heath without a walking companion.

In the weeks that followed I saw an ear, nose and throat specialist in Harley Street, a psychologist in Welbeck Street in Marylebone and an art therapist in Hampstead. The ENT said that no permanent damage had been done to my throat. My voice was still hoarse, though, and I had lost the upper octave of my singing range. He assured me that at least my speaking voice would return to normal, unlike another recent strangulation robbery victim I'd read about who had been rendered permanently mute. The psychologist heard me out and said that I was experiencing post-traumatic stress disorder symptoms and would have a peripheral startle response for months to come. Anything approaching me from the left or right would trigger it. It was true. I once opened the garden door to step into the lane and the postman was approaching on my right, a few feet away. I screamed involuntarily and slammed the door. I can't imagine what he must have thought. As for the art therapist, she brought oil pastels and paper to the house and encouraged me to deal with my feelings through drawing.

My husband's employer, concerned about an attack on one of its new expats, sent its global head of security, a sympathetic fellow formerly with the London Metropolitan Police, to provide me with a security briefing. It felt like a scene from an early 007 movie. He arrived with a briefcase full of gadgets. First, he pulled out a heavy thirteen-inch aluminum flashlight that could be used as both a defence weapon and an alarm. There was a button for the barking-Doberman sound and another for a police siren. For weeks I was inseparable from that flashlight. For my purse and pockets, he handed me square pocket alarms triggered by grenade-like pull strings. They were eardrum-piercing. The strings tended to catch on things, so I was forever setting them off and frightening people. A spray canister was next. Not mace, but invisible marking spray that only became visible under ultraviolet light. If the police later picked up the marked assailant, he might not even know he'd been tagged.

The security expert also taught me to read and memorize the licence plates of any cars following mine and to take evasive routes home if the same vehicle remained in my rear-view mirror for too long. He coached me to avoid being boxed in by cars at stoplights and warned me never to occupy the middle lane of a three-lane thoroughfare—both standard anti-kidnapping operating procedures. A friend taught me self-defence techniques, including how to scrape the heel of my shoe down the shin of a chokehold robber. And I visited a rescue kennel in search of a Belgian shepherd dog because I had heard that Belgian shepherds would leap walls to come to their owner's defence. I was well equipped for danger and remained on high alert through the remaining three years of our stay in London.

"And did they get the men who did it?"

"I can't talk about that right now," I said. I hated talking about it still: the fact that they found one man but not the other, that he was charged with numerous similar assaults and pleaded guilty to several, including mine, and that the judge at London's Middlesex Guildhall court, in sentencing him to eight and a half years in prison, had characterized the assaults as having been carried out with "utterly callous and ruthless efficiency," saying it was lucky that none of the women he attacked had died. I couldn't tell her about the police lineup or the visit to victim services. It made me sick to remember it and for long stretches of time my memory of those experiences, and even of the name of the convicted man, lapsed.

"How dreadful," she said with empathy in her voice, and we walked in silence for a while, pointing out blue jays and cardinals. "Given all of that, what do you think? Do you think you could come into Collins Bay and visit the men in the book club? Maybe it would even help you."

"Let me think about it, Carol. In the meantime, I'll get you some book suggestions." We were back at the car near my father's gravesite. I looked over at his spot. "Bye for now, Dad," I said softly, and opened the car door for Carol.

2

PROMISES KEPT

ALTHOUGH CAROL AND I had been friends for more than a year, I still didn't know a great deal about what motivated her. When she and Bryan invited my husband and me to visit them at their Amherst Island holiday property, a rural retreat of sheep pastures and hayfields near Kingston, one element of her story emerged. She was a serial entrepreneur. One of her former businesses involved buying and selling primitive Canadian antiques, and the couple's 1830s limestone house was a Noah's Ark of folk art animal sculptures. Rustic life-size representations of a Dalmatian and a plump white sheep stood in the south sunroom, along with a robin and a crow, all hewn from wood and painted. In the library, other birds filled a high shelf, and a tall carved figure of a Mi'kmaq man in full headdress guarded the entrance to the laundry. A stylized black cat with green eyes sat on a dining room windowsill and a small church occupied one alcove.

The church was a clue to her other previous start-up. After working as a high school English teacher, she had followed her mother into the Anglican priesthood in the 1990s and then founded an Anglican Church parish west of Toronto called Church of the Resurrection. "I've always loved to do stuff from scratch," she told me.

Carol's view was that she might have inherited her combination of entrepreneurial drive and the sense of a calling to help others from her great-great-grandfather Sir George Williams. Williams was a successful businessman in the drapers' trade in Victorian England and was the man who founded the YMCA movement "to save young men from dissipation," as Carol put it. Williams set an example that appears to have trickled down to generations of Williamses, expressed through a family culture that placed great value on service to others, and a genetic predisposition to starting businesses and being competitive. Carol mentioned that other Williams family descendants included London mayor Boris Johnson and Colin Williams, the highly successful London-based titanium trader. "The spectre of Sir George has always hung over some of us," Carol said. "It's this thing about carrying his genes. I seem to have it."

Over dinner, it became apparent why Carol chose books as her vehicle for helping others. She was born in 1945 in Ashburton, England, just an afternoon's hike across moorland from Dartmoor Prison. Ashburton is a town on the edge of Dartmoor, a wilderness of peat bogs and granite tors where ponies and sheep roam freely. Her mother, Patricia Williams, a young British war bride, had moved there with her two oldest children to escape the Blitz. Carol's father, David Wilson Blyth, was an army spotter during the war whose job was to identify targets for bombing sorties. Her mother was passionate about reading. When the six Blyth children were underfoot, their mother would tell them not to go outside and play, but to "go away and read."

Carol was six when the family finally settled in Canada. "There were long, long summer holidays at lakes where we would just sunbathe and read," she recalled. Their mother was influential in her children's lives, guiding four of her five daughters, including Carol, into the study of English literature at university, encouraging them to teach. Her brother, like her, became a serial entrepreneur. I sensed that Carol was partly motivated by a need to succeed in a high-performing family and to leave her mark. We talked and laughed long into the evening, with Carol telling stories about her mother and Bryan guffawing heartily. I knew then something about where her courage came from. Now I had to marshal my own.

In the end, the decision to go into the prison was made for me. While turning it over in my mind, I had filled out the Correctional Service Canada (CSC) volunteer application form, just in case, because there was a long lead time for approvals. When the prison system granted my clearance, I felt I had to follow through with it. I have difficulty walking away from sunk costs and I lack a reverse gear. Just go in once, I said to myself. You can handle this.

What I didn't know until my first visit to the prison was that Carol and I would meet the eighteen or so heavily tattooed book club members in a remote building within the prison walls, with no guards present and no visible security cameras. Carol's idea was to put the men at ease. Our only protection would be a chaplain wearing a personal security alarm that would alert guards in the main building on the grounds, some eighty metres away. *Great*.

Locals know Collins Bay as "the Red Roof Inn," a play on the name of the discount North American hotel chain. The red metal roof and Gothic turrets are the prison's most distinguishing features. Built of local limestone in the 1930s, it's a grey castle fronting a vast square of limestone rampart, with red-capped guard towers at each corner. In my childhood, when my mother drove me past it for my annual eye exam in Kingston, from our home in Prince Edward County, I would ask her if that was Disneyland and whether it had a drawbridge and moat.

So it was strange to finally approach this building as an adult, in October 2010 for my first visit to Carol's prison book club. A warm Indian summer breeze was blowing the tall grasses of the surrounding meadows, and red-winged blackbirds called out from the marshy lowlands that stretched down to the St. Lawrence River where it meets Lake Ontario. The prison farm was barely visible at the rear. Just two months earlier, cattle trucks had removed three hundred Holstein cows from the farm buildings, as the federal government ended the forty-eight-year-old dairy operation that had provided milk to local prisons and farm skills to inmates. I was surprised to see how the city had filled in across from the prison since my childhood. There were car dealerships with metallic pennant streamers and rundown malls with pawnshops selling paintball guns in the shape of AK-47s.

That day I had followed Carol's instructions to downplay my curves and eliminate showy jewellery. I was wearing a breast-flattening sports bra, a turtleneck, a buttoned-up stiff tweed jacket and pants. I'd left my emerald engagement ring in the city, and wore only a gold wedding band and simple pearl stud earrings. I was also wearing my nerves. My hand shook as I signed the official guest logbook at reception. Through the one-way glass to my left I could see the outlines of heads, where guards operated the mechanized gates into the core of the prison.

From that moment on I remember only brief impressions. I was fearful to the point of shock. My peripheral vision closed down and I felt like I was looking through a zoom lens, catching only concentrated bursts of images. After the double set of metal doors at the entrance slammed in sequence behind me, I remember being hit by the smell—an unpleasant yeasty odour that I couldn't quite identify, as though decades of hardship, hate and regret had condensed on the walls. I recall walking down the main hallway with Carol and her co-facilitator Edward, a retired English professor with an upper-class English accent. A prison chaplain, Blair, was escorting us because the book group met in the prison chapel. Blair was explaining something about the building. I remember passing the health clinic with its posters about HIV and hepatitis. Then we passed lots of men in white waffle-weave long-sleeve shirts or blue T-shirts and jeans, some pushing carts or carrying mops, and I recall thinking, gosh, they have a lot of staff here.

The chaplain was saying something about the "telephone pole" design of the prison—a main corridor known as "The Strip" with cell units branching off on both sides. He led us along a sidewalk to a secondary building inside the walls of the prison that looked like a parish hall. And then somehow I was sitting on a wooden chair, waiting for the inmates to arrive, wondering whether to peel off my name tag, which announced to them all that I was ANN.

The men who walked in the door were dressed in white and blue like the ones I had seen walking freely on The Strip—the guys I had thought were cleaning staff. I was confused. Those were the inmates? Why were they walking around freely like that? Where were the guards and why was the chaplain, the only one wearing a security alarm, leaving the room briefly? And why did Carol look so relaxed? Then one man came toward me with his arm extended and a large smile. "Hello, welcome," he said. I stood up and grasped his hand and thanked him. Then many of the others followed suit, gracious and non-threatening. For some reason, the black men gravitated toward one side of the circle and the white men sat in chairs closer to me.

Carol introduced me as the head of the prison book club's Book Selection Committee, saying that I was an award-winning magazine journalist who had majored in English literature at university. I was just sitting in to get a better sense of which books might appeal to them. After that she led them in a discussion of Dave Eggers's wonderful non-fiction book *Zeitoun*, about a Syrian-born landlord and house painter in post-Katrina New Orleans who is swept up by Homeland Security after disobeying orders to evacuate the flooded city. It's a book I had read and loved, but I have no recollection of what the men said about the protagonist's good and bad choices or anything else for that matter. Instead I was rehearsing in my mind the self-defence manoeuvres that I had learned in London. I was sure we were about to be taken hostage. It was the first time I had been so close to criminals since the police lineup in London.

The men seemed equally baffled by my choice to drive such a distance to risk sitting in a room with them, given that I wasn't proselytizing religion and I wasn't being paid. After the meeting, a man with dreads and reflector sunglasses, flanked by two other black inmates, approached me and asked, "Miss, why would a nice person like you want to spend time with bad guys like us?"

That's a very good question, I thought. But I said, "I'd like to help find you some good books."

Another inmate, who I learned later had killed a man and felt profound regret about it, also approached. "I was thinking you look like that movie star," he said. "What's her name? I know, Nicole Kidman. You must get that a lot."

I felt a chill. "Actually, no one's ever said that before," I said, mentioning that she was much taller. Perhaps it was my curly hair that struck him as similar. It was exactly the kind of attention I did not want.

On my drive back to Toronto I asked myself what I had learned in that meeting that would provide new insight into my book recommendations for the men. Almost nothing, because I was so pathetically scared. I could see that they liked non-fiction, and that Carol challenged them to put themselves in the shoes of the protagonist and question characters' choices. But I would need to attend several monthly meetings if I really wanted to understand their reading level, their reaction to different types of fiction and non-fiction and what kinds of narrative engaged them. I thought back to the book list that my colleagues on the selection committee and I had composed two months earlier without ever having entered a prison. It included Margaret Atwood's novel *Alias Grace*; *The Curious Incident of the Dog in the Night-Time* by Mark Haddon; *Don't Let's Go to the Dogs Tonight*, Alexandra Fuller's memoir about her wild Rhodesian childhood (a kind of African *The Glass Castle*); and *The Woman Who Walked Into Doors* by Roddy Doyle. They were all books I had read and enjoyed. With the immediate threat of being inside the prison behind me, I was now feeling a familiar tug: curiosity. What would it be like to hear the men talk about Roddy Doyle's Paula Spencer—the abused alcoholic woman that he so brilliantly conjured up, and Charlo, her abuser? Would literature change the men's lives in any way?

But curiosity about the unknown is so often paired with fear of the unknown. And I needed to consider what it would take for me to return on a regular basis and get to know the men. It wasn't just my own safety I was worried about, but that of my family.

I drove past the highway sign marking the exit to Prince Edward County—the beautiful peninsula of farms and sand dunes on Lake Ontario where I had grown up, partway between Kingston and Toronto. It had been a happy childhood. An image of my father came to mind. In 2000, to mark the millennium, he and I took a father-daughter driving trip in California. At one stop he approached some menacing-looking men to ask for directions. I tried to dissuade him, but it was then that he reassured me, "If you expect the best of people, they will rise to the occasion."

Fear is judgment. I knew that. It is at the heart of some of the worst social injustices. If the men were bringing their best selves to a book club and trying to live a different life for a couple of hours, I should honour that effort, just as Carol was doing. And then it just came down to a decision not to spend my life living in fear and to adopt some of Carol's bravery. I thought if Carol could walk through the doors of Collins Bay, so could I. Sometimes we borrow our courage from others.

At the same time, I thought about that other well of courage I could draw upon: my creative drive. I was a relentless diarist and note-taker. If I could write about Carol's idea to run a book club in a prison and depict the men's reactions to the books' themes of loss, anger, courage and redemption, I might gradually forget my fear. I approached the prison officials with a request for broader access in 2011 and 2012 to write a book about the prison book club. And then I made plans to return to the book club meetings to observe from the point of view of book selection and to bring a writer's perspective to the book discussions that Carol was leading.

It was March 2011 when I returned to Collins Bay, and some things had changed in the book club. The old meeting space was being torn down and the club was now convening near the northeast perimeter guard tower in a nondescript building whose corridors smelled strangely of smoke. Later I learned that the smoke emanated from the aboriginal programs wing, where First Nations inmates were permitted to burn sweetgrass and sage in traditional smudging ceremonies designed to cleanse away negative thoughts or feelings. Smoke in a prison? I couldn't quite fathom how the guards handled the fire needed to light the grass, but it was a progressive policy.

I felt better about the new meeting space. The guards were now in the same building—about twenty-five metres down the hall. And the officials hosting us—the prison chaplains—had a glassed-in office overlooking the book club meeting area, so they and their panic buttons would always be within reach. But it was still a depressing environment. Newly consecrated as a chapel, it was little more than a spartan mid-century school classroom with cinder-block walls painted an institutional shade of sky blue. A wooden cross and altar stood at one end of the room and a few religious books from different faiths filled a bookshelf at the other. The book club had to meet at a time when the chapel was not needed for faith gatherings of Catholics, Anglicans, Wiccans, Jews, Muslims, Rastafarians, Salvation Army or other groups. Like some parts of the prison I'd passed through, the air there smelled of organic decay—sour and fungal—despite its daily cleaning, and the lighting was harsh.

As I walked in, the men were setting up a circle of metal folding chairs in the centre of the room. Soft furniture was discouraged because it could conceal contraband. As the inmates straggled in from lunch, they poured themselves coffee from a Bunn-type coffee maker and looked around for the store-packaged cookies that Carol bought for each meeting. Home-baked pastries were forbidden because they could contain files, saws and weapons. (A year later I learned that British chef Gordon Ramsay had set up a baking program *inside* the British prison HMP Brixton, and though the point was primarily to provide work experience and to produce baked goods for sale to *outside* cafés, some treats were destined for inmate consumption.)

The volunteer contingent had also changed since my last visit. Derek, a former CBC Radio classical music host, and a neighbour of Carol's on Amherst Island, had replaced Edward as Carol's co-facilitator. Derek had been born into the Mennonite faith. The Mennonite Central Committee's social justice causes include prison visits. He was a natty dresser, with smart leather loafers, tortoiseshell glasses and designer jackets. I could tell that his style would make a big impression on the men. And his sonorous radio voice would be ideal for reading passages of the books aloud, which, in time, he did as a way of introducing the next month's book.

That time, I was able to relax enough to absorb the book discussion. We were reading *Three Cups of Tea: One Man's Mission to Promote Peace ... One School at a Time* by Greg Mortenson and David Oliver Relin, a book that Carol had chosen. Published four years earlier in 2007, it was a feel-good non-fiction account of how Mortenson, a destitute American mountain climber, built schools for girls in Pakistan and Afghanistan through his charity, Central Asia Institute. It and his 2009 sequel, *Stones into Schools: Promoting Peace with Books, Not Bombs, in Afghanistan and Pakistan* were both *New York Times* bestsellers, and by the time we sat down to discuss *Three Cups of Tea* in March of 2011, Mortenson had gained a kind of pop cult status as a humanitarian. The book had become required reading for U.S. troops deployed to Afghanistan. U.S. president Barack Obama even donated one hundred thousand dollars of his 2009 Nobel Peace Prize winnings to Mortenson's cause.

According to his book, Mortenson lost his way while descending K2, the second highest mountain in the world, on the border between Pakistan and China, and wound up in the village of Korphe in northern Pakistan, where the villagers nursed him back to health. In thanks, he promised to return to build a school for the girls in the village. He had seen that boys who were educated tended to migrate to the cities for higher-paying jobs, and he had an idea that educated girls would be more likely to stay in their villages and impart their learning to others. Given that back in the United States, Mortenson lived out of his car for a year in order to save money while trying to raise funds for the school, his focus on helping others really caught my attention, just as it had intrigued thousands of other readers.

I recognized a few inmates from the first meeting: Dread, a tall man with a corkscrew moustache and beard who had three tiny dreadlocks dangling from under a black wool tam; Ben, a slow-speaking but eager book enthusiast whose heavy-lidded eyes drooped at the outer corners, giving him a slightly hurt look; and Marley, who wore a long black crucifix around his neck and wove his hair into cornrows that sprayed out from a central part and were gathered on each side by a tiny clip. Another familiar face was Frank, a middle-aged Italian-born inmate with a deep dimple in his left cheek and glasses; he was a key contributor to the discussions. Frank had brought a new member to the book club: Graham. Blond, big-boned and about six feet four, Graham seemed immediately at ease, rocking back in his chair and gripping the armrests whenever he laughed, which he did often. Also new to the group was Grow-Op, a shy, stringy young man wearing sunglasses, who apparently was doing time for growing marijuana. Sunglasses were popular among the inmates, partly as a way of avoiding direct eye contact and confrontation. Sitting next to Grow-Op was a fellow with a scar on his upper lip, who wanted to talk about his prison time in Southeast Asia for drug trafficking. His name tag read RICK.

Carol opened the discussion by giving the floor to Derek, who asked what we all thought about the central figure in the book, Greg Mortenson.

Dread said how impressed he was that Mortenson had remained selfless and endured so many hardships in his determination to build schools for girls. Several of the other men praised Mortenson's perseverance, despite crippling setbacks. The first time he sent funds for building supplies to Pakistan, many of the supplies disappeared. Later, the villagers said they would take the funds to build a bridge instead.

But the book club members also took note of his flaws. "My impression is he was a big klutz," said Frank.

"And he bumbles through life in a Forrest Gump–like way," said the man from the Southeast Asian prison.

Derek agreed, pointing out that Mortenson, like Forrest Gump, managed to show up at key moments that would become historical milestones. "He has tea with the Taliban, meets generals in Pakistan and pays his respects to Mother Teresa after her death," he said.

But Dread saw it differently. "What I liked is that usually people make promises and never follow through on them," he said. Broken promises. Dread had put his finger on it. The villagers never expected to see Mortenson again after they nursed him back to health. The men in prison likely had seen plenty of broken promises in their lives, and broken a few themselves.

I then asked the men why they thought Mortenson focused on educating girls as opposed to boys.

"Because women have a big voice in any community," said Frank. "Women are nurturers, and men are more likely to leave the village once they're educated." Frank had a wife and children waiting for him.

Ben reminded us that Mortenson had another reason: a gesture in tribute to his sister, Christa. Mortenson had originally dedicated his attempt to climb K2 to his sister, following her death at age twenty-three from an epileptic seizure. But when he saw the eighty-two children of Korphe practicing their lessons on an open ledge with no shelter and no full-time teacher, he resolved that he could honour her memory in a more meaningful way.

Carol said she wanted to think about Mortenson as a hero. "He is so committed," she said. "What does it take to be one of these heroes?" As on my first visit to the book group, Carol was keen to rally the men's moral selves to see whether the protagonist might be a role model for them. Frank was immediately onside, describing Mortenson as a humanitarian despite his klutziness, and suggesting that his name should be put forward for the Nobel Peace Prize. In fact Mortenson had been nominated for the prize in 2009.

But Graham had a different take than his buddy Frank on Mortenson. Speaking for the first time in the book club, he questioned why Mortenson took advantage of his wife's patience by travelling up to four months at a time. "Nice that she's patient, but he has neglected his family and his personal health, and his relationship with his board members has broken down." Graham saw someone who had failed his family and was failing on the accountability front too. When Derek mentioned that Mortenson's daughter now travelled with him on his school-building trips, Graham responded tartly: "Is she only going because she wants more time with her father?"

I studied Graham's prominent brow. He had identified that something was wrong with the way Mortenson ran his life and his charity. His acuity caught my attention, as did his facility with words and his confidence to voice a contrary opinion on his first day at book group. Every comment in a book club is coloured with the reader's world view. We were getting Graham's world view and I was guessing that it contained a strongly held belief about family. I wondered if Graham's own father had been as unreliable as Mortenson. It would be months before I got an answer to that question.

"What do you think about his parents?" asked Dread. "They set the stage." They had been Lutheran missionaries and teachers in Tanzania. While there, they built a school and a hospital on Mount Kilimanjaro. When Mortenson's father died in mid-life, Mortenson's fear of losing his sister too compelled him to step in to care for her.

Graham answered Dread's question by saying that Mortenson's parents, Dempsey and Jerene, were no more balanced than their son, even when they were setting up the hospital. His comments sent me back to the book in my lap and I scanned the chapter on his parents. I saw that Dempsey often travelled abroad for long stretches to fundraise and recruit hospital staff and Mortenson had to stand in as the dad. Perhaps Graham was talking about Dempsey semi-abandoning his family. I looked at him with more interest. But the passage also talked about Dempsey going against the wishes of the many expatriate members of the hospital board by offering medical scholarships to local African students instead of to expat offspring. Dempsey's heart was in the right place, but perhaps he was too much of a loose cannon for Graham.

Carol asked how many of the men had come from families that did some volunteering. One new member was the only one to put up his hand. "My family had a lot of involvement with library work," he said. But in a strange segue he began talking about his grandfather, who was involved in crime and "got murdered." We waited, but no one else had a tale of volunteering to offer. I felt a sharp pang of empathy for these men, whose childhoods were so different from my own.

"I'd like to make a pitch for his driving desire to help other people," said Carol. "The most meaningful thing for me is being here with all of you. I would not have met Marley, for example. I know that fills me up." She turned to look at Marley and he nodded back with a big ear-to-ear grin. "I encourage you when you're out to see when and where you can help. Be mentors to help kids who might get into trouble." The conversation lulled briefly.

Then Frank said, "We're afraid to help others, like panhandlers, because they might be scammers." We sat with that thought for another moment. And then I told the men the story of my father urging me to expect the best of people. And that seemed to inspire Frank. He referenced Malcolm Gladwell's argument in *The Tipping Point*, that if you fix broken windows in a derelict neighbourhood, the crime rate will drop. "Just one window can make a difference," said Frank.

Graham had nothing to say on that subject, but he wanted to add one more thing about Mortenson. He said that Mortenson's story about being kidnapped by the Taliban didn't add up. Mortenson claimed that AK-47-wielding Wazir tribesmen held him for six days and then freed him and thrust donations into his hands after he talked about wanting to build schools for neglected Wazir children. Graham argued that Mortenson's story boiled down to being extorted by thugs to build schools in their villages. The part about the money—Graham just rolled his eyes. Later, I learned that Graham had some familiarity with the subject. A former Hells

Angel, he was serving a seventeen-year prison sentence for drug trafficking and extortion.

After the meeting, Marley walked over to me, his crucifix swinging, and sat down beside me. "God is everything," he said, his black eyes sparkling. "I believe in Christ." I think he was imagining that I might share his views because we were meeting in the chapel. I nodded to show my respect. I told him I believed in goodness. Unlike Carol, I was not religious.

The men said goodbye and I gathered up my things, thinking that the book had worked well, even though it wasn't one that our selection committee had suggested.

As we walked out past the main guard station on The Strip, that day's "Strip Boss," the correctional officer in charge of the guards on The Strip, said that he was reading *Three Cups of Tea* because he'd heard from book club members that it was good and he wondered if he could join the book group. He laughed in a way that made it hard to tell whether he was serious or not.

On the drive back to Toronto with Carol, she told me the story of how the book club was born. It was the summer of 2009 and she was weeding the arugula in her vegetable garden on Amherst Island. She was thinking about her recent trip to Trosly-Breuil, France, to visit the noted Canadian humanitarian Jean Vanier and his L'Arche community, where developmentally disabled people live with their caregivers. Vanier told Carol that whenever she travelled to a new city, she should visit people in hospitals for the mentally ill and those in prison because they were the most marginalized and lonely people in society. Those institutions, he said, were where the greatest suffering in society resided. She looked up from her weeding and sat back on her heels, looking across the water to the town of Millhaven, home to the maximum-security penitentiary through which every federal inmate in Ontario was processed and at which some remained to serve their sentences. Then she thought: *There are thirteen other penal institutions in the area. I should get my sorry you-know-what over there.*

Carol, then sixty-three, initially imagined that she might visit men in segregation. But when she met with Blair, the first prison chaplain to answer her call, she suggested casually that maybe instead she could lead the men in reading good literature and discussing their reading in circles of civil discourse. After all, she had helped launch a number of book clubs in her community already. Her idea was to encourage a love of books and to offer the men heroes and heroines worth emulating. She also hoped, as she put it, to "hoist them into the middle class through reading." The phrase was her metaphor for helping the men connect to a broader culture. It was also code for redemption through the development of greater literacy, empathy and social skills. Blair invited Carol to sit in on his Roman Catholic spirituality group and he spontaneously put the idea to the men. The men said, "Miss, when can we start?"

Thus it happened that the original core members of the Collins Bay Book Club came from the Catholic group plus a few mates they'd brought along from their "ranges." (A range is a row of cells within a cellblock.) Despite its origins, the book club was strictly secular, and I was glad that Carol's religiosity was not part of it. Carol and her husband bought about twenty copies of Frank McCourt's *Angela's Ashes* for the first book club meeting that August—in 2009. Since then, she had started book clubs in four other federal prisons, including Grand Valley, the only federal women's prison in Ontario. Many of those books the Finlays had also paid for out of their own pockets.

As I looked sideways at her at the wheel of her SUV, I could see that she was a smart, creative, determined woman and that five prisons likely would not satisfy her. She complained to me about how hard it was to juggle everything. From the set of her lower lip, it was clear that complaining was part of her process. It was the step just before impatience, where change could happen. In the months to come, I would see that volunteers who didn't measure up would be gently encouraged to apply their skills elsewhere, prison staff who didn't return her calls would be phoned back—repeatedly, assistants who bungled book orders would be replaced. Change would lead to success. And she was as fearless of change as she was of the men. I saw that two deep rivers ran inside Carol: compassion for the dispossessed and relentless drive. She was a Christian, but a hard-nosed one. Like Mortenson, Carol was keeping a promise to herself and to Jean Vanier to help the lonely and the marginalized. And maybe a promise to her mother and to Sir George Williams.

There was a postscript to that month's book club. Just six weeks later, in April 2011, the mainstream media were echoing Graham's hunches about Greg Mortenson. In a documentary televised on *60 Minutes*, interviewees alleged that Mortenson had exaggerated his benevolent achievements and fabricated parts of his story. Around the same time, Jon Krakauer published *Three Cups of Deceit*, which detailed Mortenson's alleged fabrications, including claiming to have built schools that others built, lying about getting lost on K2, misusing donors' funds and misrepresenting his stay with the Wazir tribesmen as capture.

Although our book club didn't know it then, this was only the beginning of two years of misery for Mortenson. Following an investigation by the attorney general of Montana, Mortenson agreed to repay one million dollars to his school-building charity, Central Asia Institute, for travel and other book-related expenses, that the charity had originally funded. Four American readers brought a lawsuit against Mortenson alleging fraud, but a judge dismissed the case about thirteen months after our book club meeting. Seven months after that, Mortenson's co-author, David Relin, committed suicide by stepping in front of a freight train. His family released a statement through his literary agent saying that Relin had suffered from depression.

We had an opportunity to regroup with the men on the issue soon after the scandal broke that spring of 2011. Frank, who had heard about the accusations, still stood with Mortenson, saying he thought the criticisms stemmed from "a bit of jealousy." "Mortenson could achieve with a thousand dollars what the government would need three million to do," he said.

Ben pointed out that Mortenson had admitted in *Three Cups of Tea* that he had "procrastinated" on his accounts. Graham, who had been critical of Mortenson during the initial book club discussion, was now prepared to cut him some slack. "Is there anyone who writes a memoir who doesn't embellish it or remember it differently from the way it happened or the way it occurred from somebody else's perspective?" he asked. Now that Mortenson found himself under attack, the men seemed to be more forgiving.

3

ARE YOU NORMAL?

A PRIL 2011'S BOOK CLUB MEETING, the first of two meetings
on books about disability, came in the midst of a late, rain-
filled spring. The Moira River, which I crossed each month on
my drive to Kingston, had risen to the top of its banks, its water
black and roiling. As I drove over the bridge, I thought of Virginia
Woolf and how she had killed herself by walking into a river in
East Sussex with stones in her pockets. The topic of suicide was
on my mind because it arose in that month's book, Ian Brown's
2009 memoir, *The Boy in the Moon: A Father's Search for His
Disabled Son*.

Closer to Kingston, the highway passed through limestone rock
cuts that were still icicle-laced, as though the rock held the cold
longer than the soil. When I arrived at the prison and opened my
car door in the parking lot, a chill wind off the lake snapped it
from my hands and blew my scarf loose. A few staffers struggled
out of their cars and joined me on the two-hundred-metre walk to
the front door of the prison. Everybody, not just me this time, was
walking with a slight forward tilt as we battled the westerly blasts
of freezing air.

By that point in the evolution of the Collins Bay Book Club,
Carol, Derek and I had all figured out our roles. Carol and Derek

would alternate leading the book club, tapping into her skills as a teacher and his as a broadcast interviewer. I would be a sort of writer-in-residence, offering comments on the authors' styles and observing from the point of view of book selection. That suited me. I was shy by nature, and still particularly shy among the men given that it was only my third meeting.

The atmosphere seemed a little off when we walked into the chapel for the book club meeting. None of the men had arrived. Something had happened at lunch. Then word came that Dread was in segregation. Dread was a private person and no one was saying what had landed him there. We sat and waited, hoping there wouldn't be a lockdown.

I reviewed a few pages of *The Boy in the Moon*. I'd just finished rereading it the previous night and images from it remained vividly in my mind. The book is about Brown's search for answers concerning his son's mysterious birth disorder, which turned out to be an extremely rare genetic condition known as cardiofaciocutaneous syndrome or CFC. Unable to speak or use the toilet, fed by a stomach tube, and given to punching himself in the head, Brown's son, Walker, needed round-the-clock care because he didn't sleep at night. He wore head protection and cylinders around his arms so that he couldn't flex his elbows to smash himself. The description of Brown's attempts to change and bathe Walker would be slapstick, if not so heartbreaking. For the first eight years of Walker's life, neither Brown nor his wife, both prominent journalists, enjoyed two nights of sleep in a row, because they alternated staying up through the night with their son. Brown documents in deft, brutally honest and often humorous prose his despair, exhaustion, guilt and deep love for his son. I absolutely loved the book for its ability to capture all the oddities of this little boy with both a tenderness that was never maudlin and an outsized curiosity. Brown takes the time to try to understand what Walker loves in any given distraction: pawing a bag full of pop-can tabs or throwing things out the car window.

Brown spends much of the book on a scientific quest to find out what is wrong with his son, then enters an acceptance phase, in which he tries to deal with the permanence of his family's challenge and to learn what Walker is teaching him. As part of that journey, he, like Carol, visits Jean Vanier and his L'Arche community, where intellectually handicapped adults live with their caregivers in a home-like setting—the kind of environment Brown wanted for Walker in the long term. Since Carol's own visit to Trosly was what sparked her idea for books clubs in prisons, this was a happy coincidence. Brown engages in a long philosophical conversation with Vanier, a bit like a consultation with a guru. Vanier celebrates the weak in society, and dials back society's obsession with strength. It was a concept that appealed to me and I hoped the men would seize upon it.

The book had won three high-profile literary prizes, and Carol and I were of one mind: this would be a huge hit with the guys, written by a man who was a guy's guy. In fact, two of Brown's previous books had been explorations of what it was to be a man.

Finally, I could hear the sound of sneakers squeaking on linoleum down the hall. The men were coming: Frank, Graham, Ben, Grow-Op and a few others. You could read from the brightness of their eyes that they were on alert. Carol and I looked at each other. Whatever was going on, we knew it was better not to ask. Better to get straight into the book.

Carol asked simply how it was for them reading *The Boy in the Moon*.

"I found the book sad," said Frank. He told us that even Alfred Lansing's *Endurance*, on explorer Ernest Shackleton's ill-fated Antarctic expedition, had more hope than this book. It was a book that the club had read before I joined. "Through all those years," he said, "Ian Brown wasn't sure what was wrong with his son and it kind of left him up in the air."

Graham, the former biker, had been hard on Mortenson, the author of last month's book, but his critique of Brown was even more cutting. He found the writer cold, and disliked the way he referred to his son as "the boy." He continued, "Where the book asks about the value of a life like Walker's because he's often in pain, the next question is about the cost of Walker's life to those around him. It seems to come back a lot to Ian Brown, and 'What am I missing out on in my career' or 'What am I missing out on in my life.'"

"Do you think that's all right or are you saying Ian Brown is self-centred?" Carol asked Graham.

"I think he's entitled to consider the cost to himself," said Graham. "But he used some terms that a lot of people would consider derogatory. I couldn't get away from the fact that the gist of the book was that he felt burdened by having Walker." Just as he had the previous month, Graham seemed to be drawing on a well-defined personal morality about what families should be.

Frank agreed. "He was angry and resenting that he had a child like this. His wife accepted it more than he did."

Several other men felt the same way. One new member named George kept making the point that Brown had upper-middle-class advantages, intelligence, a good education and a good job and that he shouldn't complain about the impact of Walker's illness on his life. George talked about family friends of his who managed with an intellectually handicapped daughter. "She's retarded and she shits herself," he said. "*Their* life ain't over. *They* don't think about killing themselves."

So finally we'd come to the suicide thing in *The Boy in the Moon*. Brown writes that by the time Walker was two years old, he seldom thought of his son without also contemplating his own death and sometimes Walker's death. He wonders about whether the years of caring for Walker would sap his affection for his wife and cause them both to fall ill. He writes frankly about imagining taking his son's life and his own.

Oddly, Brown's murder-suicide musings are slightly comic. He imagines death by hypothermia on a winter hike in the mountains. But as he plays it through in his mind, he imagines the hassle of getting through the airport and to the mountain with all Walker's gear and all his own ski equipment, and reasons that if he could do that, he could survive anything, making it unnecessary to commit suicide.

Most of the guys dumped on Brown's thoughts of death, branding him as "unstable" and "extremist." And they wanted to understand the guilt the author expressed. "There's something specific that he thinks he's done and I was thinking there's something he's holding back," said Graham, pointing to a radio interview with Brown that we played for the men before the discussion. In that clip Brown talked about the collective guilt of all parents of handicapped children because, he said, for thousands of years society has judged such defects as a sign that the parents have erred in some way. The shame trigger was hypersensitive among a number of the men in the book club. Many felt shame for compromising the lives of their loved ones and they anticipated shame in returning to their home communities and employment.

Carol and I were knocked sideways by the men's reactions. She and I were a little in awe of what Brown had managed to do as a parent, while working full-time. We had both seen how his ordeal had aged him. Brown had been an acquaintance of mine in university—a year or two ahead of me, and he now looked a decade older. But the guys were hard on him, harder than we could have predicted.

Sloe-eyed, soft-hearted Ben was an exception. Ben was less troubled by Brown's attitude toward his son and more drawn to the book's philosophical inquiries. "Basically, transformation, strength and weakness—that's what I took out of it," he said.

It was like a haiku response—so boiled-down it would be hard for an onlooker to figure out what the hell he was talking about. But from Ben's word choice, I saw that he was picking up on the passage about Jean Vanier's campaign to celebrate weakness in humankind, not strength—exactly what I'd hoped the men would discuss. It reminded me of one of my earliest lessons in love: to love people for their vulnerabilities more than for their strengths.

"I put myself in his place," said Ben. "Like what would you do?" He was trying to imagine himself as a parent in Brown's situation. "At times it was kind of touching. I found he's strong, because he's just stripped away. The way he became raw with a lot of things. It took a lot for him to do this."

And Frank too: "I felt the desperation in his book."

I hadn't seen empathy like this from prison book club members before. Here was the reaction that Carol and I had anticipated, or at least hoped for. We had often discussed the possibility that the process of stepping into the shoes of characters in books could encourage the development of empathy in the men.

With that, we had exhausted the roster of members who had actually finished the book. Now it was up to Carol, Derek and me to broaden the discussion to include the others.

Derek said that Brown was in a horrible situation but that he was absolutely honest about his feelings, and also funny. And with that we moved into laughing about one or two of the funnier anecdotes.

He read aloud the passage in which Brown described Walker howling and hitting his head in a doctor's waiting room while the other children were behaving well. We laughed and Carol said that we are all disabled in a sense, and that Brown and his son, Walker, had taught us not to be so afraid of our own silliness and imperfections.

How appropriate, then, when one of the men came up to me at the end of the meeting, described himself as having bipolar disorder and gave me three poems that he'd written for my feedback, one of which spoke about his imperfections motivating him to overcome his darker thoughts. I promised to take his poems and bring back comments.

About a week after the meeting, Carol phoned me to say that the men's reactions to *The Boy in the Moon* were still on her mind. "It's really given me pause," she said. "We were asking the men to connect with a guy who comes from the same intellectual or social milieu as we do. But if anyone has met adversity, it's these guys. The food is really meagre, they have five Counts a day, so they're regimented. They don't ever see a tree. The visits are very limited. They're humiliated. They are crowded in with people they don't necessarily want to be with. I think we need to be aware that we're taking them out of their culture, which makes their responses very interesting." The "Counts" she was referring to required inmates to return to their cells at several designated times each day to be counted by staff. I was beginning to know Carol well enough to recognize that this was no idle chat. She had decided that she had miscalculated with this book selection and that it wouldn't happen again.

Something else was niggling at her. Too many guys took a book and never reappeared at book club, or showed up at the meeting without having read the book. Watch out, I thought, she was going to start getting tough with the men. Sure enough, Carol wanted to appoint a cadre of book club "ambassadors" to recruit members and encourage current members to finish the book. Not the typical recruitment and enforcement that happened in the prison yard— recruitment and enforcement for a good cause.

"I just want to be there when it happens," I told her, curious about her bravado.

The next book group had been scheduled to meet later that month, but was postponed until May because of a break in the water main at the prison. I had driven the two hundred and sixty kilometres to be there and a plumbing problem had botched it. Despite my disappointment I managed to joke to the prison chaplain before I drove back to Toronto that a water main without water would make a great tunnel. Everyone was aware that earlier that week about five hundred prisoners, mostly Taliban, had escaped from Sarposa Prison in Kandahar through a three-hundred-metre tunnel into a nearby house.

When we reconvened in May, Carol issued a *mea culpa* that we had not anticipated the men's reactions to *The Boy in the Moon*. "I'm sure that for you, Ian Brown, who had a nanny and access to all sorts of resources, wasn't the man of courage that we saw him to be," she said to the men. "What we'd like to say to you is that we really salute you for your courage, for getting through day by day in this place, with all of its challenges, many of which we don't know. As well, many of you are making plans for your lives, and trying to keep that glimmer of hope up is a very courageous act." There were murmurs of acknowledgment, and I could tell that she had won their hearts again.

That month we were reading our second book about disability, but in the form of fiction. I had suggested *The Curious Incident of the Dog in the Night-Time* by British writer Mark Haddon, for its journey into the mind of someone with what appeared to be autism spectrum disorder. The book is narrated with subject-predicate simplicity by Christopher Boone, a fifteen-year-old boy who has difficulty interpreting facial expressions and understanding idioms of language. He has an aptitude for math and science, and lives according to a strict routine in order to avoid sensory overload. But when Christopher finds his neighbour's poodle impaled with a pitchfork, he travels outside his comfort zone to search for the killer, using the detective skills he has learned reading Sherlock Holmes mysteries. The boy's investigations unveil some adult secrets at home and in his neighbourhood, including the fact that his mother is not dead, as his father has led him to believe. In fact, just about everything in adult life appears deceptive and irrational when viewed through the absolutely factual and literal lens of a person with autism or Asperger's. And what made it worthy of the prison book club, I thought, was the book's insights into the loneliness of a person who finds himself approaching the world differently than others.

Derek, who was leading the discussion that day, kicked it off by saying that it took him a long time to like the protagonist.

Graham agreed. "The writing style drove me absolutely crazy. If I saw the word 'and' one more time, I was going to go totally insane." It was true that large parts of Christopher's narrative were told in a breathless "And I said … and he said … and I said," but it was damned believable.

Carol always sympathized with readers' frustrations. "Well, the first time I read it I really liked it," she said. "But the second time, it drove me bonkers, and perhaps it was all the 'ands.'" She went on to give the men a brief primer on autism, including that those on the autism spectrum could be very quick to anger and had enormous difficulties with social interaction.

"I liked the part where he hit the cop," said Frank, which got a hearty laugh from everyone. The scene comes early in the novel, when the police pepper Christopher with questions about why he was found holding the dead dog. The boy went into sensory overload from the interrogation and lay on the ground groaning. As a rule, he didn't like being touched, so when a policeman took hold of his arm to lift him to his feet, Christopher hit him.

It's a tribute to Haddon that, just as we're laughing at that situation, Christopher's next line in the novel tells the reader that the book will not be funny.

It was Derek who advanced the idea that we could all in some way identify with Christopher. Not that any of us is autistic, he said, but, "We're all in some way standing on the outside of the circle or the periphery of life."

"Oh yeah," said Ben, wearing a toque despite the warm May day. "Especially being in here, I guess we can all get to where he's at sometimes."

Graham picked up on Ben's point and said that just as Christopher was living in his own little world, the men in the prison live in their own little world "separate from everybody else." He said that whenever he had to leave Collins Bay for a supervised hospital or court appointment, he felt uncomfortable. "Suddenly you're in the midst of things, and then when you come back you're almost exhausted. I am anyway. I go to sleep for the day."

Carol reiterated that we are all on the margins in some way. She told the men about her visit to Jean Vanier's community in France, and about one developmentally delayed resident who approached her and asked, "Are you normal?"

Carol's story inspired Frank to describe the Exceptional Person Olympiad that the prison sponsors each summer, bringing in people with intellectual disabilities to have two days of games and sports with the inmates. "One of them gave me a hug!" he said. Several of the other men had positive things to say about those two days. One large man with a sleepy voice said, "You're in an institution. You're surrounded by hate. You're surrounded by opinions. Everybody in prison has an opinion. At the Olympiad you're with people who don't. They're very loving, very outgoing, very easy to be around."

Graham had one more gloss to add on the subject of autism in the novel. He suggested to the others that maybe autism was a metaphor for a failure of communication between all the members of the family and the chaos and suffering that ensued from that breakdown. With that comment he came closest to Mark Haddon's own declaration about the book—that it was really about everyone.

With all the empathy being expressed, Seamus, who worked as a chapel cleaner, volunteered that he'd been put in a special needs class in school, with kids who were "drooling and stuff." Seamus said he was diagnosed with ADD and was less proficient than the other students at school work.

"You look pretty calm now," kidded Graham.

"Were you a troublemaker?" Derek asked Seamus.

"No. They just put me in a special needs class my whole life," he said. His candour was touching. By then I was starting to understand how even we volunteers were outsiders. While Seamus was an outsider at school and Graham felt like an outsider when on hospital leave, as volunteers we were outsiders in the prison.

What I failed to understand when I proposed *The Curious Incident of the Dog in the Night-Time* was how uncomfortable most inmates are with the idea of other inmates who have certain neuro-developmental disorders or mental illness. "Bugs" is prison slang for the mentally ill, and bugs are generally avoided in the yard because they are perceived as unpredictable. The book club members could sympathize with the kind of extreme neurological disorder that afflicted Walker or with the kids in the Exceptional Person Olympiad, but not with mental illness.

Graham highlighted this in a brief essay on mental illness in prisons that he had written, which he shared with Carol and me in the wake of our book club discussions. "Imagine living in a world where a variety of mental illnesses were rampant and patients received little or no treatment," reads the opening line.

"Now imagine that you weren't allowed to leave this world for any reason. Imagine that violence was common and the population extremely unpredictable. Such a world exists right here in Canada and I live in it every single day."

The essay went on to describe an inmate who drinks his own urine, one who snorts coffee grounds, others who don't shower or who hear voices. He cited the suicide rate among federally incarcerated inmates in the country as 84 per 100,000, versus the rate of 11.3 for all citizens. I thought I'd check his data since it wasn't footnoted and found that he was correct: the figures aligned with those in the Annual Report of the Office of the Correctional Investigator covering 2009–2010.

Graham was quickly becoming one of the most interesting members of the book club.

Within a few days I was back at Collins Bay to accompany Carol for a meeting with four of the inmates: the men she wanted to deputize as ambassadors. The speed and urgency with which she acted to "fix" the book club was like that of a chief executive officer conscious of the need to improve next quarter's results. I concluded that there were no back burners on Carol's stove.

Her idea was that the ambassadors would pre-read books to be sure they were right for the guys, encourage others to read and recruit new members when old members left. They would shepherd the other men.

"Who have you chosen?" I asked her, when she picked me up at the Kingston train station.

"Graham, Frank, Dread and Ben," she said. No surprises there. They always finished the book. They always had something to say.

When we met with the men, they were pleased to be asked to help, but candid about the problems with the book club. Graham and Frank complained about some members not reading the book. How many times had I heard that complaint in my women's book groups when we were all young mothers juggling work and child rearing?

Carol wanted to know why some took a book but then didn't show up. Some of it was logistics, according to the guys. The men had to have a pass prepared the day before in order to attend the meeting. Since the book club meetings were held in the chapel, it was up to the chaplains to issue the passes. Then the day of, it was up to the guards to use the PA system to call pass holders to the meeting. Frank pointed out that the guards usually called out "Chapel" not "Book Club," because technically that was the inmates' destination. Whether the guards were being literal or ribbing inmates for being religious, some guys who didn't want to ruin their reps as hard-asses wouldn't respond to the call. Others just might not clue in that the call was for book club.

"Make sure the chaplain calls every block," suggested Graham.

"Also some books are harder," said Dread. "And men get distracted watching TV, working out or sleeping and don't want to show up to book club looking like a fool with the book unread."

How about the guys who showed up without their books, Carol wanted to know. Did they sell them for drugs?

"That would be some very cheap drugs," said Dread, laughing hysterically.

Carol showed them a mock-up of the certificate that would go in their files for acting as ambassadors.

"I think ours should be backdated," negotiated Dread, implying that he'd been acting as an unofficial ambassador for months.

While it was the chaplain who had made it possible for Carol to launch the book club, the meeting with the ambassadors reminded her that the book club's home in the chapel was a mixed blessing. Religion and books sometimes didn't mix. She was feeling similar unease about her partnership with Prison Fellowship Canada, which for the previous few months had carried out her book orders and shipping to the prisons, as well as extending to Carol their standard book discount. An old friend, who was her contact at Prison Fellowship, was being noncommittal about ongoing funding. Carol told me she sensed that the organization was not willing to help buy books beyond the book club's start-up period. She said that Prison Fellowship had also expressed a desire for more influence in her selection of volunteers, in keeping with its mandate. In particular, Carol told me, it wanted assurances that the book club volunteers were people of faith. Carol insisted that this was a secular book club and that she wanted volunteers whose passion was books. Impatient as always, she accelerated the process of registering Book Clubs for Inmates Inc. as a non-profit corporation, the first step in registering as a charity and tapping alternate sources of funding. Another organization was not going to call the shots.

Carol was at the wheel again that day, driving us back to Toronto. She looked exhausted and I wondered if I should offer to drive. I knew she suffered from sleep interruptions and I had heard her up at night during one sleepover at Amherst Island. She wore earplugs to bed in the spring to avoid being woken early by the birds' dawn chorus. But as we talked, I learned it was something else that had caused her to lose sleep the previous night. It was lambing season, and Carol's neighbours at Topsy Farm on the island had phoned her in the middle of the night to ask if she would help rescue newborn lambs. During one of the dampest springs on record, many lambs were hypothermic after gushing out of their mothers' wombs into fields pocked with near-freezing puddles of water. Working together with her neighbours, Carol had wrapped the lambs in towels and brought them into the farm kitchen to warm them with her body heat. Gradually they began to shiver, open their eyes and bleat, their umbilical cords lolling against their bellies. She felt maternal and literally pastoral all at once.

Now Carol had flocks inside and outside the prison. And both flocks had guards. Topsy Farm's most popular photograph of their sheep is one in which all the animals are facing the photographer. It's only when you gaze at it for several seconds that you realize that posing among the white-faced sheep, and almost identical in colouring and size, are white Pyrenees guard dogs.

4

THE N-WORD

CAROL'S EFFORTS TO MAKE the Collins Bay Book Club feel more like a book club on the outside had already moved into its next phase: inviting prominent authors to visit and answer the men's questions about the books. The first writer she targeted was Lawrence Hill, whose breakout 2007 historical novel, *The Book of Negroes*, had won a 2008 Commonwealth Writers' Prize and had become an international literary hit. The book's title refers to a real historical document, a ledger that recorded the passage of slaves transported to Nova Scotia in return for their loyalty to Britain during the American Revolutionary War. Hill brings the slave narrative to life through his protagonist: a stoic West African woman who preserves her dignity despite her deprivations—a situation with which men in prison could identify. And Lawrence Hill was particularly well positioned to have additional street cred with many of the men in the prison book club. Born of a black father and a white mother, he was a role model as a successful black man.

After Carol's first call and email inviting him to attend, Hill declined because of a busy writing schedule and the three-hour drive to the prison. She contacted him several more times and asked in a variety of pleading ways without success. Finally, as he tells it, she invited him out for coffee, where he showed up intending to say no, but found he was no match for Carol's persistence.

That was in 2010, before I joined the book group. Frank, Ben and Dread were among the members in attendance at that first meeting with the author. "It was the most intimate, detailed, focused, sustained conversation about the book that I'd had with any group, period," Hill later told me. "And that includes PhD students and graduate seminars and everything. So they were really amazing." The experience was so rewarding that he told Carol he would be happy to return.

And so on my fifth meeting of the Collins Bay Book Club, in the early summer of 2011, Lawrence Hill was back to talk to the inmates. He was wearing a blue plaid shirt and a shiny jacket that was a marked contrast to the plain-colour prison blues and whites that the book club members were wearing. One of Hill's previous books documents his journey as a light-skinned black man straddling two identities. And that day the men saw a man with a close-trimmed Afro that could pass for just very curly hair and a man whose skin tone was ambiguous.

I was captivated by the protagonist of Hill's book, Aminata Diallo, who is kidnapped, at age eleven, by slavers from her native West Africa in the 1700s and sold to a South Carolina indigo plantation. Before boarding the slave ship, she is forced to walk in a coffle to the ocean, during which time she experiences her first menstrual period. She survives the horrific conditions of the slave ship and years of plantation labour, while enduring what surely must have been the most agonizing aspect of her bondage: having her two children taken from her. Even though it was the voice of a young female narrator, it could have been the voice of some of the black inmates' female ancestors. Aminata's journey takes her to Nova Scotia after her name is entered in the ledger that comes to be known as the Book of Negroes. The actual historical ledger now sits in the National Archives at Kew in London. But Nova Scotia is not where the story ends.

The book club ambassadors had done a good job advertising the author visit and some thirty men showed up for the meeting on that hot June day. It was the largest turnout I had ever seen—double our usual numbers. Most of the new faces were black and many of the new arms were heavily tattooed. We scrambled to set up extra chairs for the attendees.

Ben kicked off the conversation by commenting, "You always cultivate this grace in all your books, I noticed." Ben had been present at Hill's 2010 prison visit, when they had first discussed the book, and since then he had read another of Hill's works, the author's debut novel, *Some Great Thing*.

The author's eyes opened wide and he smiled at Ben. He talked about imbuing his characters with admirable qualities like courage because he liked to ask himself whether he would have that courage under those circumstances. "It's the same thing with grace," said Hill. "I mean there's something to be said for people who keep their dignity, even when all hell is breaking out around them and they're enduring really horrible things and they keep their dignity and don't forget that they're just as human as everybody else." He was answering Ben's question but he appeared to be slipping in a stealth message to every one of the guys in the room: that he admired their courage and their humanity in how they were enduring prison. I felt the power of his words. And his comments affected the men too. A muscle twitched in Graham's cheek and Ben smiled his slow smile. Many of the others sat rapt.

Juan, an inmate who was vocal about his writing ambitions, wanted to talk about the writing process for such a long book. He was wearing a yellow White Sox cap, sunglasses and, hanging on his chest, a huge wooden cross. He asked his question in a staccato delivery, at high volume.

Hill told Juan that he generally started in the middle of the book and waited for something interesting to come to him. "You have to have a lot of faith," Hill said. "I'm not a religious person, personally, but I guess I have my own sort of faith—a non-religious spirituality that you have something beautiful to say, something worthwhile to say and I think every person has something worthwhile about them, something inherently dignified about them and you want to reach down and find that piece of beauty inside yourself and bring it out. And you don't necessarily even know what's down there. So writing is about pulling out secrets inside your own soul and spilling them out onto the page. It's kind of like mining. You don't know what you're going to pull up." Perhaps he had observed Juan's cross and mentioned religion as a means of finding common ground. But the subtext of his statement crept up on all of us—that even guys in prison have something beautiful inside worth mining.

"Do you decide the characters first?" asked a burly inmate with a sun and moon tattoo on his arm. His name tag read STAN.

"I think of a person in a difficult situation," Hill responded. "Story happens when a character's under pressure and we, the readers, are watching them cope. In this case I talk about a girl stolen from a village in Africa. What if this were my own daughter? I think of this novel as a road trip. She's on the move her whole life. I think about the longing she might have." The answer seemed to resonate for the men whose own lives had been stolen and whose own journeys were still uncertain. One of the guys nudged the man next to him and nodded.

Dread, who had been reading Hill's autobiography, *Black Berry, Sweet Juice*, about his childhood in a predominantly white suburb of Toronto, said, "You really opened up my mind to the experiences you had as a child. Like you're so divided—you're not really accepted by the black people and the white people saw you as a black person."

"You've said it so succinctly," said Hill. "I had to find my way in a culture that was pretty much entirely white, and the only blackness I had access to was in the United States, when we went to visit my family there. So I found my way through reading and writing and travelling. I started reading black literature and all the books that my parents had on their bookshelves. And I started travelling to Africa. And I went to live, as you know, in the States."

Carol asked Hill to read a couple of passages from *The Book of Negroes*. He read two of the most memorable passages of the book: when Aminata has just disembarked from the slave ship and is frightened by the "smoke" coming from her mouth as her breath condenses in the cold morning air; and when another slave inoculates Aminata against smallpox by implanting a lesion under the girl's skin.

Then it was time for the men to come forward to have their books signed. I was moved to see how eager they were—how precious this opportunity was for them. All toughness was gone, their respect for Lawrence Hill palpable. I was also disappointed that I hadn't heard their reactions to the novel. But I wasn't surprised. When my London book club had organized author visits by William Dalrymple and Esther Freud, the members' curiosity about the writing process dominated and we often refrained from asking tough questions about the book itself.

Sitting beside Hill, I had the opportunity to hear him talk to each man. Dread was second in line and asked for his book to be signed to his wife and daughter. Hill asked him how old his daughter was.

"Ten," Dread said. The mood between them was warm and Dread lingered, asking him about the subject of his next novel. Hill confided that it was a book about an illegal immigrant. Dread smiled broadly and left abruptly. I watched him walk away and wondered what could have affected him so much about what Hill had said.

When Ben came forward with his book, they chatted about the other novel that Ben had read, *Some Great Thing*, which draws on Hill's years as a reporter for a Winnipeg newspaper.

"Did you like the part where the guy got arrested for putting a vacuum cleaner down a mailbox?" asked Hill. "I had a lot of fun writing that."

"I liked his character," said Ben.

"I met a guy in court one time who got arrested for vacuuming letters out of a mailbox. That gave me the idea for that scene," said Hill. He'd been a reporter covering the court beat that day.

When it was his turn, Graham asked Hill to sign the book to him and thanked him for coming, in a way that communicated thanks from all the men. Carol told Hill that Graham hoped to work with youth once he was granted parole. I had a feeling that she would try to get them together "on the outs," prison slang for "on the outside."

Juan engaged Hill in a conversation in Spanish, knowing that the author had lived in Spain for a year.

As the lineup gradually shortened, I noticed that Carol had stepped out of the room and left her orange leather purse sitting open on her chair. "Nothing is ever taken," she told me when I remarked on her trust at the prison. Indeed, according to protocol, she would have left any valuables, like her wallet, keys and cellphone, in a lockbox at reception. However, the black markers for writing name tags disappeared from the name tag table by the end of the meeting that day. As we learned soon afterward, the ink was valued for tattooing. We realized that it would be better to print out name tags in advance.

An hour later, over lunch in downtown Kingston, Lawrence Hill told me there had been one question from the men this time that he had never considered before. "When Ben asked me about grace—nobody's ever put that to me," he said. "It was an utterly fascinating thing to hear my own books reflected back to me in that line.

"Those guys are likely taking a lot more from books than other people because they have more time and they have more energy and they're able to focus on it and they have more need." He said that he was particularly attuned to those who had lived on the margins due to race and that some of the books that had affected him most profoundly had come from the prison experience, which was one reason why he had felt compelled to visit the book club, despite his busy schedule.

He had also engaged with people inside before, it turned out—a few years earlier. When a secure-custody facility for juveniles in Ontario was frustrated with its inability to get a small group of young men to read, the corrections authorities called Hill and asked if he would give it a try. The kids were between the ages of fifteen and seventeen, serving long terms, and they *could* read, just wouldn't. Other interventions had failed, but Hill succeeded after getting together with the boys once a week over lunch in the prison library.

"How did you do it?" I asked.

"I gave them books individually," Hill told me. "I figured out what a kid would like after talking to him for a couple of hours." It was never a book from the prison library—too uncool. The books were gifts from him—personal recommendations. Sometimes it was a father-son memoir, sometimes a story written by a famous prisoner, sometimes one of Hill's own book proposals. "They were really interested in how I was pitching it and they were speculating about whether I'd find a publisher," he said. "It was full of drama for them." They would come back sometimes complaining that they had hated a book he'd given them. "They hated the beginning, where the character did this, the climax where the character did that, and the ending that was so unsatisfying," he recalled. In other words, they'd read the book.

Two days later, Book Clubs for Inmates held its first fundraiser on Amherst Island. Lawrence Hill was the guest of honour and my fellow volunteer Derek engaged him in an interview for the audience of local residents, who had paid twenty dollars a head to be there. It was early June, and the little island situated on the migratory flyway was at its most glorious. There were birds nesting in every low-lying notch, oriental poppies nodding their heads and old-growth lilac bushes and irises blooming in profusion. Incredibly, a robin had made its nest in the wreath on Carol's front door and each time she opened the door she had to be careful not to disturb the three blue eggs. A mourning dove sat demurely on her nest in Carol's bird feeder.

Hill talked about the title of *The Book of Negroes*. Publishers in the U.S. and some other English-speaking countries sold it under the title *Someone Knows My Name* because of concern that readers would find the word *Negroes* offensive. Hill told the people at the fundraiser that although he initially fought the idea of publishing under a different title, he came to understand why the publishers felt so strongly. "I mean if you use the term 'Negro' in Canada, most people will look at you as though you are a bit outdated and you haven't read a newspaper in fifteen years, but try using the word 'Negro' in Brooklyn, you'll get your nose broken. It's a serious, fighting word and the American publishers were concerned it would be so alienating to readers they wouldn't pick up the book. The word is now mostly a derogatory word, meaning someone who has no self-respect or self-pride as a black person, so it's a very cutting term inside black culture."

By the time Carol and I were back together again with the men in the Collins Bay Book Club three weeks later to discuss the novel *Such a Long Journey*, the whole question of *The Book of Negroes* title had taken an ugly turn. Just before Hill came to visit our book club, he had been in the Netherlands, where he had spoken to various audiences. An attendee at one of those events was now threatening to burn the book to protest the use of the word *Negroes* in the Dutch title, *Het Negerboek*. On the very morning of our book club meeting, the Dutch group, known as the Foundation to Honour and Restore Payments to Victims of Slavery in Suriname, partially carried out their threat by burning the book's cover. When asked by the media about his reaction, Hill said that the book's title was designed to focus attention on an obscure historical document and he condemned the threat of book burning as a form of intimidation against those who valued the freedom to write and read.

Carol and I were keen to ask the men how they had reacted to the title. "Let's name the elephant in the room," said Carol, to open the discussion. "It's race." There she went again—so blunt! But they looked at her approvingly. She asked them what percentage of the prison was black. Dread, who was black, estimated only 15 to 20 percent. Graham, who was white, said it was more like 40 to 50 percent. Everyone jumped in with their estimate, talking over one another.

But, Carol wanted to know, in the men's opinion, was the title insulting? "If you went past a bookstore and there were twenty books in the window and one of them was *The Book of Negroes*, what do you think?"

"The majority might take offence," said Dread.

But, Ben said, "I might want to read it." Dread rolled his eyes.

Stan said there was a new edition of *Huckleberry Finn* inserting the word *slave* to replace "the *N-word*" and that he'd seen some of the discourse in the media. "There was this one highly educated black man from Harvard or whatever and he was saying leave the word in," he said, "because it teaches kids what that word meant to people."

The conversation veered into discussions of mistreatment of other racial or ethnic groups in history, including the Irish, First Nations people and Jews. But Dread argued forcefully that slavery's duration over four hundred years had caused the disintegration of family structure among black people. "It's way way way way worse," he said. I cast my mind back to Lawrence Hill's character Aminata in the book and how the slave owners robbed her of her children.

At least one of the white inmates in the room cast his mind back as well. "It happened hundreds of years ago but the resentment gets passed on from generation to generation," said Stan. "Here's a white man," he said, referring to himself. "And I gotta look at it as someone that made it happen. It's disgusting."

"I agree with you, Stan," said Carol. "Because I felt as I read *The Book of Negroes* a sort of collective sin or guilt that it was white people such as me who did what they did."

But then Rick, the guy who'd done time in the Southeast Asian prison, brought an end to the white liberal sentiments. "Myself, I don't feel that. Whatever happened, happened. My heart breaks. What are you going to do? You can't be judged based on what somebody else has done, just because you're white. I don't feel I'm part of the collective sin."

Others simply expressed their feeling that slavery was wrong. Graham wondered aloud: "What in the world made people think that they had the right to get on a ship and go to the other side of the ocean, grab a bunch of people, enslave them and bring them back?" And Frank made the point that various African populations enslaved each other on their own continent.

I looked around the room. The fact that we were having this conversation at all was remarkable. As Graham had said in a letter to Carol two months earlier, prison was a very divided place and he was surprised by how the book club "totally knocked down" the barriers between the racial, ethnic and gang-affiliated groups in the prison.

"I'll take your comments back to Larry," said Carol. She was now on familiar terms with Lawrence Hill. "What shall I say—it was a lively discussion. I'll tell him to keep the faith."

Hill himself took an opportunity to document the Netherlands incident and his reaction to it in a lecture that he delivered some months later. Now published as a thirty-three-page book, it is titled *Dear Sir, I Intend to Burn Your Book: Anatomy of a Book Burning*.

First *Three Cups of Tea* and then *The Book of Negroes* was in the news. Reading a book that was newsworthy gave the men a sense of participating in something timely and meaningful. I made a mental note to think about that during my next round of book selections.

5

RED SKY AT MORNING, JAILERS TAKE WARNING

That summer, the intense heat in the cells at Collins Bay forced some inmates out of their bunks and onto the floor to stay cool and sleep. In the absence of air conditioning, the smell of sweat was all that circulated in the cells. But that June, something else was heating up the prison. A new federal government measure to increasingly house two inmates in cells that were designed for one sparked an inmate work strike at Collins Bay. The men refused to wax floors, cook inmate meals, clean bathrooms or show up for anger management programs. I pictured double-bunking during the heat wave, with two men trying to find enough space on the floor of a singleton cell. One man might have to lie with his head close to the toilet. But the strikers were concerned about more than that. Graham told me they were worried about their own safety. He said that doubling up the population could increase the risk of violence as the men attempted to share cells, showers, laundry facilities and telephones, while competing for spots in correctional programs. The competition for telephone time was already intense.

The strike was only twenty-four hours old on June 29, the day I had planned to meet each of the four book club ambassadors one-on-one for the first time. The correctional authorities had agreed that I could write the story of the inmates' great "adventure" in the book club and, to that end, talk to some of them at length. And I now felt comfortable enough with these four men to do so. The chaplain broke the news about the strike when he met me at security. He warned me that the men might not materialize. He explained that it would take guts for the four guys to leave their cells to meet me because anyone crossing the yard during "Work Up" (work hours) might be suspected of strikebreaking, especially since I was meeting them in the same building as CORCAN, the prison industry workshop.

The guard at reception looked at my tape recorder suspiciously—a tiny Sony digital recorder. But the chaplain assured him that the warden had approved it. All that needed to happen then was for the men to show up.

As predicted, Dread and Ben were no-shows. I didn't blame them, given the pressure. With Graham and Frank scheduled for the afternoon, I spent the rest of the morning sorting the latest book shipment and thinking back to the previous week's book group—the last one before the summer hiatus.

We had discussed Canadian author Rohinton Mistry's gorgeous debut novel, *Such a Long Journey*, about a Parsi bank clerk in Mumbai named Gustad Noble, who is unwittingly drawn into a money laundering scheme. Gustad tries to do the right thing with the stash of rupees he's asked to safeguard, a situation that Carol and I thought had the potential to trigger interesting debate because of the ethical dilemma it posed. And we hoped the men would enjoy the chance to laugh a little at the book's comic episodes and to escape in their minds to the bedlam of 1970s politics in India. We assumed that books that enabled armchair travelling beyond the prison walls would be popular in prison.

Twelve guys showed up for the meeting that week. I could see that the Lawrence Hill Effect had evaporated. No surprise really. Back in London at my "Literary Ladies" Hampstead book club, attendance always surged when we had author visits. I looked around the room. The four ambassadors were there: Graham and

Frank, Dread and Ben. Three guys were sitting just inside the door. "The Muslim guys," explained Graham, indicating three black men. "They're all buddies." One of the three, Winston, had arrestingly intense eyes. Elsewhere in the room were Rick, Juan the writer and Marley, with his pink-mirrored sunglasses. I could never discern what Marley was thinking behind those lenses.

As I was greeting everyone, an inmate with a Marine-style "high and tight" haircut and military posture walked in. I had seen him at *The Book of Negroes* book club meeting and had overheard Lawrence Hill urging him to read John Steinbeck. "Hi," he said with a broad smile, shaking our hands in a manner that suggested he was hungry for contact with the outside world. "I'm Gaston." He chose a chair between two other burly white inmates: Graham and Stan.

When *Such a Long Journey* was first published in 1991, it made the Booker Prize short list. It also won Canada's Governor General's Award for fiction that year, beating out a book by veteran novelist Margaret Atwood. Quite a warm reception for a first-time novelist. However, the jury of prison public opinion was still deliberating.

The session started off well with an animated discussion about Gustad, whose sedate life goes off the rails in other ways. His high-achieving son, Sohrab, rejects his father's plan for him to attend the prestigious Indian Institute of Technology, his daughter falls ill and his wife yields to superstition. Then Gustad finds himself agreeing to store a package for an old friend who now works for Indira Gandhi's spy agency. His strong moral principles, derived in part from his sense of loyalty and his Zoroastrian faith, fail to give him insight into his actions. Meanwhile, chaos mounts around him in his interactions with the quirky characters in the novel.

"Gustad's a complicated character," said Carol. "Maybe you liked him, maybe you didn't. Maybe you thought a lot of things about him were kind of heroic." I confessed that I didn't like Gustad much at the beginning because of the way he stifled his son's artistic ambitions. We opened it up to the men.

"At first I didn't like him," said Ben. "But when I thought back, he was a religious guy and so I understand why he was such an honest person, patient, obedient and ambitious for his kids too."

Rick admired the protagonist for not running off with the money. So did Frank: "I felt he was an honourable guy. If you're doing a deal with him, you know he'll hold up his end."

Gaston, who I later learned had robbed a string of banks, was amazed that Gustad was never tempted to steal the piles of money accumulating in his house. "You know sometimes, thinking a little bit criminally, thinking what I would do, I would have taken some of it," he said. And Gustad would have been justified in skimming some, in Gaston's view—he argued that better the money go to a guy making an honest buck and caring for a sick daughter than to thieves. "He's gonna give his money to the money launderers and obviously they're going to steal it, when he could take it and he's a guy who obviously works for a living."

As a man who had stolen his share of fresh banknotes when he was "thinking criminally," Gaston must have paused at the passage about the smell of rupees—in which Gustad says that five-rupee banknotes smell different from ten-rupee notes, and the smell of hundred-rupee paper is the best.

"He should have kept the money, then?" Carol asked Gaston.

"Yeah and paid the painter and got his wall built," said Gaston.

I had doubts about the morality of Gustad keeping the money, but Gaston's mention of the painter demonstrated the kind of attentive reading that Lawrence Hill had talked about earlier in the month. Gaston had clearly got to the end of the book, and recognized that the pavement artist had a certain significance. To me, the painter seemed to be Mistry's symbol of the impermanence of life in India. At Gustad's request he paints a riotously colourful mural of prophets and deities from many religions on the community's boundary wall to discourage passersby from using it as a latrine, yet is unconcerned when wreckers demolish the whole thing.

Dread liked Gustad for different reasons altogether. "He worked and helped his parents pay for his own schooling. And I liked the way he sacrificed himself when a taxi was going to hit Sohrab and he put himself in the way to protect. He's an okay guy."

Graham was the only one who had nothing positive to say about Gustad, observing that he was "plodding and kind of dumb."

Many of the other readers in the book club just hadn't been able to get traction in the novel because they had difficulty with the descriptive passages. I could connect with the men's frustration to some degree because I'd had some difficulty with the untranslated Hindi and other words, which occasionally made me feel like an outsider. But for the men, it was more basic. It came down to too much scenery and not enough plot.

"He spent twenty or fifty pages on the chicken," Graham complained.

An exaggeration, sure, but for Carol, hearing a comment like that was like telling a Hells Angel that he should consider trading in his Harley for a station wagon. She let loose a passionate plea for description as a sensual experience that yanks the reader into another world. The former English teacher in her had seen an opportunity to light a fire and she was going for it. She read aloud to the men Mistry's description of the teeming Crawford Market in the second chapter. As she read, we were immersed in the market's dirt and odours, its floor slippery with animal viscera, the air swarming with flies and the butchers covered in sweat and bloodstains. Carol used her most dramatic voice and hand gestures to make it come alive.

"Do you ever want to buy any meat there, with those flies?" she asked the men. "It's disgusting. Can't you just smell it? Try to enjoy it for this incredible artistry, because it's extraordinarily evocative."

"It's visual," allowed one man.

"Yeah, almost 3-D," said Dread.

Ben got it too, marvelling at how Mistry manipulated the language.

"It's a world that from our sensibility is chaotic, crazy," said Carol.

But Stan pushed back. "I just found it too self-indulgent, like he was trying to show off."

Vivid description was okay once in a while, said Winston, speaking for the first time at the book club, but he thought it happened too often in the novel. "You kind of lose the importance of certain events if you over-explain every event," he said. It was a valid point generally, though I hadn't felt that in this book.

And it depends *what* you're describing. Graham would have been happier with fewer pages on Gustad's chicken, and also less graphic description in the scene where Tehmul, an intellectually disabled man in the neighbourhood, has been rejected by the prostitutes and is found masturbating over a doll that belongs to Gustad's daughter. The scene runs for two quite specific pages, ending with a description of the semen on the doll's body and Tehmul's erection.

"Why was that necessary?" asked Graham. "That was so graphic. He could have done the same by saying the doll was naked." A few of the men shifted in their chairs but no one added further comment.

"Because even that is so foreign to our sanitized culture here in Canada," said Carol.

Frank, who had read two other novels set in India—Mistry's *A Fine Balance* and Aravind Adiga's *The White Tiger*—said he admired how Mistry used these odd and sometimes comic secondary characters. "This writer's got a real knack for bringing in characters and threading them through the whole story," said Frank. "Even the prostitute—he had a role for her down the road."

I'd been given a copy of *A Fine Balance* years earlier by one of my brothers and had never gotten around to reading its nearly eight hundred pages. But if Frank had read it, I decided it would be my summer reading.

As the men left the meeting I thought about the prison in England that might still be holding the man who had attacked me and whether the summer heat was ever unbearable in the cells there. England was rarely as hot and humid as Southern Ontario in the summer, but any room without circulation can be stifling. I had often done the math to figure out when his eight-and-a-half-year sentence would expire. That summer I realized his time in custody was up, if he hadn't already been released on parole.

I packed up and labelled the last batch of books and looked at my watch. It was late morning, still hours before the afternoon Work Up shift when Graham and Frank might appear. I wouldn't be allowed in the prison cafeteria, of course, so I drove to the centre of the city for lunch at Chez Piggy. After giving the waiter my order, I reached into my plaid satchel and pulled out a letter that Carol had given me. It was a letter Graham had written, with her encouragement, to apply for a volunteer position with at-risk youth because he had hopes of being paroled in the coming year. He was happy for me to see the letter too so I could understand him better. In it, he mapped out many of the devastating events of his life, some of which had led him into crime. They were, after all, his calling card when looking for a position of that type. He argued that he could relate to young people with similarly tough life stories because he'd been there. The letter also said that two of his relatives had been convicted of murder and a number of other family members had criminal records.

"My father was a chronic alcoholic who I personally cared for throughout my younger years," the letter said. "I would often have to put him to bed, take burning cigarettes out of his hands after he passed out, and go to bars to pick him up because he was too drunk to walk home."

It must have been a frightening feeling of insecurity. For me, a sensitive person who had grown up in a secure, stable nest with loving parents, I know I couldn't have survived those circumstances.

As the letter went on, he explained that much of the criminal activity he had witnessed at a young age, including drug dealing, was the same type of criminal activity he would engage in as an adult. It started with thefts, break and enters and small-time drug dealing, and gradually escalated to tobacco smuggling, drug trafficking and extortion. In due course, he joined a street gang and then the Hells Angels. It was like hearing someone describe the progression of a drug addiction, starting with marijuana and building to heroin in search of ever more exhilarating highs. But he claimed he had never become addicted to drugs. And maybe that's what saved him. "These experiences have taught me how important families are in helping at-risk youth," the letter argued. I refolded the paper, put it in my satchel and attacked my salad.

I returned to the prison after lunch, hoping that Graham and Frank might appear. Just as I was about to give up, I heard a heavy footfall in the corridor and there he was: Graham had braved the strike to come and meet me. Frank was close behind him, and would have to wait in the chapel while Graham and I talked.

The chaplain showed Graham and me into the chapel storage room, which was adjacent to the chapel where the book club met. There we could close the door and converse freely, without being interrupted by the hymn-singing next door. Here was a new challenge for me. I could see no security cameras in the room, and the guards sat in a guard station some twenty-five metres down the outside corridor where they could neither see me nor hear if I called for help. I was a little apprehensive. I felt certain that Graham wouldn't harm me, but it took some getting used to—my first time alone in a room with an inmate.

Graham sat on a garish orange stuffed chair that looked scratchy, the only soft furniture I'd seen in the prison. I set up a metal folding chair and placed the tape recorder on a stack of Bibles that I had borrowed from the room's bookshelf and arranged on a low coffee table. Someone had tried to make the table more cheery by covering it with a red chiffon tablecloth. Two four-foot-high plastic religious statues stood watching us: Jesus and Mary, with identifying notes taped to their chests: *Chapel Jesus* and *Chapel Mary*, presumably so they could be returned to their rightful place if they went missing. Chapel Jesus had one hand broken off. Chapel Mary had a gentle face and jewels at the neckline of her garment. The rest of the room was filled with guitars, music stands, keyboards and sets of Bibles and other religious books.

Graham was angry about the double-bunking plan and wanted to talk about it up front. "There's already fights over the number of phones. There's problems over seating in the cafeteria, over there being enough supplies in the canteen, program spaces, school spaces. They're talking about adding another twenty, twenty-five bunks for every unit. That's an increase of 25 percent in your population." He talked about the risks of sharing space with another inmate who might bring in contraband or might have enemies in the prison. I couldn't imagine even being able to fall asleep in that situation.

I commented on his nerve in crossing the yard to see me. He seemed genuinely surprised. He'd been through worse, he said. "You've read my biography, right?" he said to me as I sat down with him for our chat. I nodded. "I'm still in one piece," he said.

I told him I had read his letter and expressed my sympathy for what he had gone through as a child. "There are others who went through similar things," he said, "and they made better decisions than me." His answer struck me as noble. I was too reticent to take him up on his implicit invitation to speak frankly about the childhood he'd described in his volunteer application. Not yet. I wanted to get to know him better first.

I asked him to cast his mind back to his exposure to books growing up. He couldn't recall whether his parents had read to him. How empty that feeling must have been. I remember many happy evenings as a child cuddled next to my mother as she read storybooks in both French and English: the Babar books by Jean de Brunhoff, the Madeline books by Ludwig Bemelmans, the Beatrix Potter series, *The Hobbit* and others. But Graham did have memories of participating in reading drives in public school. He wasn't an avid reader, preferring baseball, soccer and video games. Then in high school, the books that left an impression were *Animal Farm*, *The Catcher in the Rye* and *To Kill a Mockingbird*.

As an adult in prison, his reading taste ran to non-fiction. He read history and biography for pleasure, when he wasn't studying legal materials. And he'd formed a good relationship with Clive, the prison librarian, who had given him a book to read by the French philosopher and social theorist Michel Foucault, *Discipline and Punish: The Birth of the Prison*. The book's discussion of the design similarities between schools, hospitals and prisons intrigued him. But now the book club had sparked an appetite for fiction. He said he had a copy of *Lord of the Flies* next to his bed.

A few beads of sweat had appeared on Graham's forehead. It was only twenty-four degrees Celsius outside, but inside the room the heat seemed to bounce off the walls and intensify, like a convection oven. The open window and the fan made no difference to the oppressive Mumbai-like conditions, like those in *Such a Long Journey*. As always, I kept my wool jacket firmly buttoned up, and so I was feeling it too—a runnel down my spine.

"I'm wondering, have you ever looked on the internet for Frank and me?" he asked, wiping his brow. I think he was wondering if I really knew what he was capable of. I told him I'd started to do that one evening, but hadn't found much. Later I did spend more time researching him and discovered he had been a high-profile crime figure from Western Canada who'd been caught in a police sting. A man he'd been extorting turned out to be a police agent wearing a wire.

"I understand that you were involved in drugs and the Hells Angels ... and extortion."

"I was a member of the Hells Angels. Convicted of extortion, yes. A whole array of charges."

"Were those fair convictions?"

"Oh yeah. I was guilty as sin. As guilty as they come."

I gave him credit for his honesty. It wasn't boasting. He seemed to me like a man who was owning up and putting it behind him. He laughed hard at himself, making me laugh too. But when I assumed that this was his first time in prison, he corrected me. "In the past decade I think I've only been out for eighteen months."

He said he was a little in awe of the bravery that Carol and I exhibited. "It makes me laugh," he said. "Some of the men in the book club are convicted murderers, some are dangerous offenders, and here is Carol controlling the group. I wouldn't be able to do it. They know it takes courage for you guys to come in here just cold from the street to start a book club. Everybody may not be able to put it as eloquently as me and Frankie, but they appreciate it."

Not only that, he said that the book club members would talk about their progress in reading the books when they ran into one another around the prison. "I hear guys walking the track at night and talking about the book," he said. "If I see a guy from the book club in the weight pit, I'll talk to him about it and say, 'Hey, what did you think?'"

It was even bridging prison ghettos according to Graham. "Prison is a very divided place," he said. "You've got Muslim Group, Celtic Group, Native Group, Hispanic Group, BIFA Group ... that's Black Inmates Friends Association." Inmates tended to stick with their clan and avoided talking to others. He said book club helped break the ice.

I asked him how the book club compared to the other correctional programs in the prison. I knew that inmates who had not completed grade twelve were required to attend the prison school and that other correctional programs focused on changing behaviours. "The correctional programs are useful in helping people identify their triggers and there are statistics on that that suggest they do lower recidivism rates," he said. He spoke like a criminologist, not a criminal. "But a lot of people going in are hostile because they don't want to be in those programs. And there's no immunity there or even in a psychologist appointment if you say something that links you to a crime. But the book club is a voluntary thing. And I think it teaches people to open up and communicate with others."

"Like a sanctuary?"

"It's a relief."

Then he put on his ambassador's hat and suggested we should consider moving future meetings out of the chapel. "Prison is a place where people want to appear as tough guys and there's guys who won't go to the chapel for anything." He knew because he'd been one of those guys and had held off for a year before joining because of the potential taint.

Before I said goodbye to Graham I gave him a hardcover journal that I'd bought at an office supply store in which to write further thoughts to share with me on the books we were reading. The journal had cleared the X-ray machine and been checked and approved by the chaplain. I had chosen one with a plain navy cover, guessing that the other diaries on offer, which had flowers, maps or glitter on the cover, wouldn't survive in a men's cellblock. He accepted it and we shook hands, my hand dwarfed by his.

When Frank took Graham's place in the orange chair, he told me some of his life story. The child of Italian immigrants, he was three years old when his parents moved to Canada, bringing Frank, a brother and sister and two half-brothers. He had always liked reading, particularly the Classics Illustrated comic versions of *The Iliad* and *Mutiny on the Bounty*. But school was a problem because he hated sitting in class. "I didn't want to sit still and my mother used to make me wear those wool long johns and I'd be scratching all day," he said. "I guess she didn't realize I was actually feeling tortured."

By grade seven or eight he started skipping school and he said his parents placed a greater emphasis on work than school. He persevered, though, and completed high school. At sixteen he was convicted of assault in an incident that he claims was not his fault and spent ten days in an adult jail. After starting university, he quit when he failed to get into the pharmacy program. There was a theft charge when he was working for a trucking company in his twenties, then a drug charge in his thirties, a cocaine addiction that took over for a while, a marriage that began and ended. He had spent some years boxing, like a character in a Harold Robbins novel that he'd read and loved, *A Stone for Danny Fisher*. Now he was in his sixties.

"Why did you like *A Stone for Danny Fisher*?" I asked.

"I always went with the underdog, with the person that was hopeless," he said, smiling in a way that made the dimple in his left cheek appear. "This book was about a Jewish boxer in New York City. His parents died young. They had a hard life. Then he ended up working for the Mob."

We talked some more and then it was time for Count and he had to go. Frank hadn't told me anything about his current sentence, but I learned later that he was serving time following a gun incident in a restaurant in Toronto's Little Italy. He gladly accepted a journal and agreed to note observations about the books and the changing seasons. I was stunned that both men had been so open about their history. I realized that I still had things to ask them about *Such a Long Journey*. I didn't know it then, but that would be my last day to see Graham and Frank at Collins Bay.

I made another stab at getting together with Ben and Dread three weeks later, hoping that the inmate work strike was over. I left Toronto at 5:45 on the morning of July 19, in the middle of a forty-degree-Celsius heat wave, to travel to Kingston. It had been days without rain or relief from the heat. Before me, above the highway, the sun rose as a pale red orb in a red-tinted sky. Within five minutes it was an orange fireball, then yellow and blinding.

When I pulled up to the prison more than two hours later, my air conditioning blasting, paramedics were loading a stretcher into an ambulance. The staff at reception asked me to stand aside. I could smell their fear. Perspiring corrections officers, some with their stab-proof vests partly askew, stood with spray cans, presumably pepper spray, behind their backs, and batons at the ready. I wondered if they were concealing the spray canisters so that the inmates wouldn't try to grab them. A line of hulking men with thick tattooed necks and smashed-in noses—men with a brutish appearance I had never seen among members of the book group—filed past the guards from the west wing of the main building. Those were guys from the "pill parade" someone told me, men receiving methadone and insulin from the clinic. And then I realized that the person on the stretcher was a guard. "The whacker," a staffer told me, was a lifer who had struck the guard from behind. He had used a wooden cribbage board, then stabbed the guard in the neck with a pencil. According to another inmate whom I spoke to much later, it was not a premeditated attack. He claimed a relatively new guard had ill-advisedly walked into an inmate's cell without backup. He'd seized the inmate's prized cooking pot—a sort of 1970s-style slow cooker that the authorities were attempting to eliminate throughout the prison. But the inmate was a Muslim and was attached to his pot for preparing halal dishes. And it had all happened on Unit 4, where Dread and Ben had their cells. I felt sorry for everyone. I would not be allowed to enter the prison that day and I had no option but to return to Toronto.

As I drove west along the highway, past the roadside drifts of nodding blue chicory and blousy Queen Anne's lace, a variation on the old mariners' saying occurred to me: "Red sky at morning, jailers take warning."

6

SUMMER READING

I LATER GOT THREE DIFFERENT PERSPECTIVES on what happened that day in July when the inmate on Unit 4 attacked the guard. Ben recalled that it was early in the morning, and he'd just stepped out of the shower. Hearing screaming, he looked down from his upper-level range to see a commotion and a melee of guards. "I thought, wow, this is it," he said. As for Winston, he just smiled slyly at me and said, "Yeah, the guard slipped. Got attacked by a floor. The floors are violent around here." Winston was serving life for second-degree murder. Dread just changed the subject. What happens in Unit 4 stays in Unit 4. It was only much later that Graham filled me in on how even pepper spray didn't quell the attacker. It took a female guard who knew the inmate to talk him down so that he would release the fallen guard.

What they did bend my ear about, though, was the lockdown that followed. "During the hottest week known to man," said Winston. "They didn't give us no showers. We were trapped in our cells for eight days. I thought, like, I was going to have a heart attack."

A rare "heat dome" over Southern Ontario had made it suffocatingly hot and humid during those weeks in July, feeling in some cities like fifty degrees Celsius, given the humidity. It was so hot, Ben told me, that he couldn't lie down on his bed or sit on his chair—the skin contact was too uncomfortable. "It was brutal you know, Miss," he said, sucking his teeth. "It was just sticky and gross and you're sweating. You couldn't even keep your clothes on. And I have no fan and no breeze and nothing cold to drink. My cases of water are at room temperature." Worse, his window was a few metres from the cafeteria garbage bins, which produced a high stench every two days when the garbage trucks emptied them. One way to get through the heat, said Ben, was knowing that the guy who attacked the guard had it worse in solitary confinement. "The guy who beat up the guard—he's having a rougher time than me, so I have to just bear with this and push on," he told me. "That's where I get lost in my books. I just decide, a hundred pages a day and I'll be all right."

August was usually holiday month for the Collins Bay Book Club, but Carol had scheduled a get-together to give the men a chance to talk about their summer reading. At the beginning of the summer, Carol had donated to the prison library some three hundred used books that she'd rounded up from our Toronto book club members and other friends—books intended to be good recreational reading for the hot months. Like any other book club, this was a chance for the members to recommend good books to each other.

I was uncertain how the book club would look in late summer. Graham and Frank had already been transferred to Beaver Creek, a minimum-security prison north of Toronto. With those two important contributors gone, I wondered whether our discussions could possibly be the same. Funny how in five short months I'd grown attached to these guys. I had no idea then how circumstances would bring us back together.

The first group of book club members arrived from their cells with sweat beading on their faces and their arms covered in a sheen of perspiration. Now that they had shed their cool-weather long-sleeved waffle-weave shirts in favour of short-sleeved T-shirts, I could see that some arms were alive with tattooed images of coiling snakes, yowling skulls, spiderwebs and Gothic crosses—some faded and some seemingly fresh. A few of the men squeezed into the chaplain's offices for relief from the heat before the meeting. The offices were air-conditioned, while the cells and other common spaces like the chapel were not.

When we had all moved to the circle of chairs in the chapel, Carol asked who wanted to start off the meeting with a book recommendation. Ben stepped up first, while some of the others fanned their faces.

"I was reading *Six Suspects* by Vikas Swarup," he said. "He's the author of *Slumdog Millionaire*, eh? It's about a murder that takes place and six suspects that they're trying to investigate and it happens in India. Basically showing that the political system is a bit corrupted from high officials to the slums. It's hard to get by over there. It's a really good story."

Carol turned to Gaston and asked him whether he had a summer read to recommend.

Gaston said he'd read *Of Mice and Men* over the summer because he knew the book club was scheduled to read another Steinbeck novel in the fall, *The Grapes of Wrath*. I remembered that Lawrence Hill had also recommended Steinbeck to Gaston when he signed his book. "It's a good short book, easy to read," he said. "This story is back in Southern times in the 1940s or '50s. If you're easily offended by the racism in those times, I wouldn't recommend reading it, because of the slang they use, but it's an interesting story." He had also read Jonathan Swift's *Gulliver's Travels* that summer. "It's the book that Aminata was reading in *The Book of Negroes*. I just wanted to see what she was reading. It's almost like a fairy tale with giants and midgets." I loved how his curiosity guided his book selections. It was how I often chose my own reading material.

"*Gulliver's Travels* is a hard read," said Carol.

"Yeah, I had to stop figuring out the purpose of it," he admitted. "I was overthinking it."

Dread, who was wearing his wool tam over his dreads despite the heat, gave Stieg Larsson's bestselling mystery novel *The Girl with the Dragon Tattoo* a rave review. "It's extremely entertaining," he said. "The entire story is extremely twisted and well thought out."

"Lisbeth's a wonderful character," said Derek, referring to the girl of the book's title.

And Winston recommended both of the books he had read: *Blink* by Malcolm Gladwell, and the novel *The Cellist of Sarajevo* by Steven Galloway. "I liked *The Cellist*," he said. "It had four or five perspectives on the war in Sarajevo and the way the author wrote it was a little different from anything I'd ever read before, following different people simultaneously." The name on Winston's name tag had changed from the previous month, when he'd used his middle name, Dorian. I was getting used to that in the prison. Some men identified by their last name and prison number, which was standard prison protocol. Others used first names, middle names, aliases, prison nicknames or other monikers. The most accurate identifier was their tattoos.

Stan said he'd read Bret Easton Ellis's *Less Than Zero*, and ranked it as "more twisted than the movie."

No one had come to the meeting expecting to pitch books to their peers, and none of them had been compelled to select books from the donated summer reading material. They could have slacked off and watched TV all summer or fallen back on pulpier books. But it seemed that the hunger for good reading material was growing.

At the end of the meeting, several of the men streamed by to shake hands with me and say goodbye until next month. As I said goodbye to Dread, I extended my hand for what I assumed would be a conventional handshake, but he deked his hand sideways and gave me an elaborate "brother handshake" instead. He smiled broadly as he did so, making me feel I had entered some inner circle of acceptance. Before he left, we made plans to talk at the prison the following day.

On the ferry ride back to Amherst Island after the book club discussion, Carol, Derek and I found seats together on the upper deck, where a warm, dry wind was blowing. Carol applied some lipstick without looking in a mirror, a skill that I watched with admiration. She was wearing a scarf to protect her hair from the sun, "so it doesn't turn brassy," she informed me. I pulled at a strand of my own hair and saw that the colour had indeed bleached out over the summer. It wasn't something that mattered to me much, though. All I cared about at that moment, after that day's session in the stale air of the prison, was spending a moment with my head thrown back, eyes closed, enjoying the breeze on my face and being on the water, feeling gratitude that I was free to step outside the prison walls.

Carol opened her purse a few minutes later and pulled out a letter that had been mailed to her via the Collins Bay chaplain. It was from Graham writing from Beaver Creek, where he and Frank were now serving the next stage of their sentence. She read the letter aloud to us. Graham wrote that there was no book group at the prison and could Carol please help him start one. She looked up, her eyes shining. I whooped for joy. Derek and I high-fived. Here were men who were becoming hooked, not on drugs, but on books. It was the first concrete triumph for Carol's project.

Derek waved goodbye to us as he drove his car off the ferry and turned east to his island house, while Carol and I drove our cars off the ramp and turned west to her house. Once settled at her place, she proposed a swim. We grabbed towels and bathing suits and walked across the sheep pasture to the island's westernmost tip. Rams with enormous ankle-grazing testicles led the way along the sheep path. That night I celebrated Carol's birthday with her, giving her a Guinness ginger bundt cake and one of my favourite novels: *The Summer Book* by Tove Jansson, a series of funny vignettes about an inquisitive six-year-old girl and her crusty grandmother and their family summers on a remote island in the Finnish archipelago. It was a perfect book for summer and I had given it to some of my most cherished friends.

Carol talked about the frantic feeling that she sensed was building in the men because of the difficulties of prison life. One inmate for whom she had found legal representation had been caught with pineapple juice, she told me, which meant that he was suspected of fermenting it in a plastic bag to produce hooch. She seemed to be frustrated that just as she was helping him finally get a fair shake, he was busy screwing it up.

The island fauna, too, were under stress following the unusually wet spring and the summer heat. As I fell asleep I heard coyotes howling and a lone lamb baa-ing. One animal penned in, the others desperate to get at it. The next morning, on my drive to the ferry, I passed, quite close, two young foxes with white-tipped tails, black stockings and amber eyes, lounging by a stream bed. They should have run off. But they just sat there staring at me, perhaps dazed by the already oppressive morning heat.

As the ferry pulled away from Amherst Island, I looked back at the nodding shoreline willows and thought about the island's absurdly abundant and bold animal life, reflecting on why it was so important to me. My parents had raised my three brothers and me to be keen observers of the natural world, believing that a close connection to nature would help us put the human experience into perspective. They imbued us with a sense of wonder and curiosity, teaching us where and when to look for marsh marigolds, gentians, Dutchman's breeches and lady's slipper in the wild and how to identify birds by their song alone.

What was it about nature that I now found so pleasantly distracting and reassuring as I interacted with men in prison? Its umbilical cord back to my safe childhood, I suppose, and its predictability. Each spring, blossoms unfurled in the same order: snowdrops and crocuses first, followed by carpets of indigo-coloured scilla and on and on through forsythia and magnolia. I was awed each year when plants emerged from the ground knowing how to assemble themselves into their predetermined shapes, each so distinct from the next. The progression of bird migrations was equally reliable, as was the birdsong that tinted the air as purple finches and others passed through.

But even non-naturalists couldn't help but encounter wildlife on the low-lying twenty-kilometre speck of land that was Amherst

Island. Animals had taken over there, thanks in part to its position on an avian migration route. The lounging foxes were just the latest. And I'd even seen my first whippoorwill—a rarely viewed, seemingly neckless bird sitting nonchalantly on the edge of the gravel road one evening soon after sunset, its large doe eyes gleaming red in my car headlights. I was so grateful to Carol for sharing her island paradise with me and I resolved to share my enthusiasm for nature with the men whenever possible.

The drive from the ferry to the prison was quick that day, just fifteen minutes. After all the failed attempts in June and July, I was finally going to sit down with Ben for my first one-on-one to get to know him better. We found seats in the chapel storage room. A fan whirred in the far corner to help move the air and the window was open in an attempt to capture a breeze. The air remained stubbornly close, though. Through the windows, we could hear the sharp chirp of sparrows over a lower chorus of crickets, then suddenly a loud burst of men shouting. I jumped. Ben looked unfazed.

"What's happening?" I asked.

"Those are the guys in segregation. Calling from their windows."

"Who are they calling to?"

"Other guys are walking by right now, probably going to work at CORCAN and they'll shout to anyone they know is in the hole."

So *that* was segregation, a.k.a the hole: solitary confinement. The seg cells were housed in one of the old wings branching off from The Strip. Inmates wind up there either by requesting it for their own protection, or when the warden deems they're jeopardizing the security of the penitentiary or the safety of others. In Canada's federal prisons at that time, fewer than 20 percent of those in solitary were voluntary admissions. While there, they spent twenty-three hours a day in their cells, with one hour out for exercise. Some men from our book club ended up there from time to time.

We walked to the storage room window and listened to the exchange for a minute. "You fucker" was all I could hear clearly. It died out quickly. The passing inmates had to report to their prison jobs. Ben and I settled back into our chairs.

He spent some time giving me a few glimpses into his early life. He'd been born in Canada, but went back to Jamaica with his mother for his early schooling. "Education is like number one there," he told me. "You're nobody if you don't have an education. They're so competitive there: spelling bees, math bees. We used to go around in school and sing our times tables." His aunt was the principal of the school so there was no slacking off. He remembers having access to books in the house: geography books, dictionaries and *Ebony* magazine.

When he returned to Canada for grade seven, the school authorities placed him in grade six, not recognizing the test he had passed in Jamaica enabling him to skip a grade. "It was discouraging, Miss. And what I was learning in Canada wasn't of any substance. They're teaching you home ec. or some ridiculous stuff—life skills that are not intellectually stimulating. Or they have the whole class playing recorders. I got distracted."

In high school, he read books only if required for an assignment, finding it increasingly difficult to concentrate. His friends in grade nine started smoking weed and experimenting with LSD. "I could get a little bit of weed here and there and kids started buying it off us at lunchtime. You see the money coming in. It's pulling. I got to grade ten and dropped out due to circumstances."

I asked him which of the books we'd read in the book club had been his favourite. "I don't know if I have a favourite," he said. "Each time I do a reading, it opens a window in me. Each book is a humbling situation and allows me to be more clear and detailed in my life. All the books that I've read have contributed to who I am today and how I look at life." His answer was so complex and fascinating that my question sounded simplistic by comparison. As I had for Graham and Frank, I gave him a journal to track his reflections on books and prison. He was pleased to be asked. We shook hands and said goodbye. He made his first journal entry later that day.

Dread, who'd been waiting in the chapel while I talked with Ben, walked into the room with a gait so loose-limbed I thought his thigh bones might detach from his hips. Prison hadn't etched worry lines in his face, and Canada had barely dented his strong Jamaican accent, even though he had left his home country at the age of eleven. Too impatient to read in Jamaica, he spent his youth there riding his bike, hunting doves with a slingshot, fishing for perch and snapper and watching TV. As an adult now stuck in the confines of a prison, he expressed that kinetic energy in competitive chess games with other inmates and an irrepressible flow of ideas for business schemes. It seemed natural to ask him, therefore, if he had had a job before coming to prison.

"Yeah."

"What did you do?"

"I sold drugs," he said, breaking into a long wheezing laugh that turned *drugs* into a five-syllable word.

"Stupid question."

"No, but I had legitimate jobs too. I'd buy homes, renovate them and put them back out. But drugs was the majority thing."

He describe at length how he "cooked" cocaine, to stretch it and make a greater profit, which led him to describing his affinity for cooking "legitimate" food. Despite being on Unit 4, which didn't have a full kitchen, he managed to fry chicken on a piece of foil above toaster slots.

Dread was one book club member who had had some experience with a book club before coming into prison. His "girl," the mother of his two children, had a book club with her female friends and he would prepare food and drinks when the meetings were held at his house. Even though he missed his children acutely, the prison book club gave him "another little family, another little escape," he told me. He said he had internalized Carol's pitch on the power of Rohinton Mistry's writing style and it had changed his perception of books. He equated it to acquiring a taste for wine and becoming a wine connoisseur. "A little light went off inside me. You start looking for the literary genius, the oak, the flavours, not the excitement." He admitted that he was tempted to pounce on some of the "stupid questions" that other members of the book club asked from time to time, but that he was learning from us how to welcome others' comments politely.

When it was time to say goodbye, I gave him a journal too.

For months I had been curious about the prison library and its role in the book club members' lives. It resided in another building in the prison, and volunteers like me couldn't just walk there alone. Clive, the prison librarian, had to come and get me. In the dog days of that hot summer he agreed to give me a tour of the library at a time when the inmates would not be there.

Blond and soft-voiced, Clive had worked in bookstores around town while pursuing courses in filmmaking. We hit it off immediately and I recommended that he read Avi Steinberg's hilarious memoir, *Running the Books: The Adventures of an Accidental Prison Librarian*, which was on my bedside table. As we walked through the grounds, Clive told me the harrowing story of his first days on the job three years earlier. Back then, the library had occupied a deteriorating wing off The Strip. The carpet had mould and the heaters were falling apart. His mother, who had been the previous librarian, had moved over to a teaching role in the prison and there was no one in charge for a time. Given the gap in supervision, one or two inmate contingents had moved into the stacks, controlling parts of it as their territory, according to Clive. I pictured one gang in Fiction, and the other in Non-Fiction.

"And that's good, I guess, that the inmates see books as prime territory?"

"Well, it was bad, because if you wanted to go into the library you had to pay."

"Oh."

On Clive's first day on the job, the prison was in lockdown and guards were searching the old library. "When I opened the door there were about a dozen officers tearing the library apart—taking books out, examining them and then kind of haphazardly putting them back on the shelf. It was an unbelievable mess." As he was talking to one of the guards, he spotted another officer picking up a large hardcover book. "Out of the spine of the book slides this huge shank and it just missed his foot and hit the floor. It just went *thunk* and fell over." By the end of the search, the officers had also unearthed stills to manufacture alcohol from juice. Clive couldn't show me the old library premises. The whole wing was shut down. Its orange-painted "fishbowl," the windowed guard post at the entry to the wing, sat empty and the books had been moved to a new building.

Our walk to the new library took us outside the main building, past the more recently built hub-and-spoke cellblocks, Units 7, 8 and 9, and around the back of the cafeteria. The inmates were all in their cells, but I could imagine dozens of eyes watching me silently from the windows. Clive pointed out the grassy area where aboriginal inmates constructed temporary sweat lodges for traditional ceremonies.

The library was part of the relatively new programs building, and was air-conditioned. It had the look of a gymnasium, some seven metres high, with a row of windows beneath the roofline. A small law library occupied a glass-walled locked room at the back, with case law going back to 1890, and library users could request access. It was there that guys who were going to be deported went to consult the Immigration and Refugee Protection Act for example. And it was there that Clive had made temporary space for the book club's summer reads. For two months the books donated by Carol's friends had been available only to the men in the book club. That specialized access was irresistible to inmates, because it conferred a certain status and identity. Once the summer was over, Clive would move the remaining books to the open shelves.

During its normal opening hours, three days a week, the library was relatively quiet and inmates needed passes to be there. At those times, Clive was able to help men carry out research for their courses or their cases. But two evenings a week, when the entire inmate population was in the programs building for recreation,

Clive unlocked the door and inmates flooded in, sometimes forty at a time.

He let them know that he ran a pretty tight ship. No contraband in his library. No weapons, no alcohol and no "kites," the secretive notes about drug debts or other matters that inmates leave for other inmates in hiding places in the prison.

Clive soon learned which rules were worth enforcing and which weren't. After three years of battles, he had recently given up on the question of magazines. Magazines were not supposed to leave the library, so that all the inmates could have access to the latest issues. But whether he housed them in binders on a high rack or kept them locked in his storage cupboard, they disappeared, either to be read or, possibly, taped to their bodies under their clothes as body armor. "One guy would distract me and the other guy would grab it," he said. He finally told the men: "Here they are. Do whatever you want with them, and don't complain to me if I don't have the new issue of *Men's Health*."

While he operated with a three-book borrowing limit, it was a limit in name only. Nor did he go to the units to hunt down overdue books. Prison librarians could always count on plenty of book returns each time there was a lockdown and cell sweep. Clive had also grown to accept that when books came back from solitary confinement, the covers might have been shredded by men rolling up strips of paper to use as filters for smoking tobacco or other substances.

I was curious about the reading tastes of the inmates in a medium-security prison. According to Clive, the most popular book among the general inmate population at Collins Bay was *The 48 Laws of Power*, the 1998 bestseller by American author Robert Greene, with its tips on how to influence and manipulate people. In fiction, the hottest books were novels by James Patterson, Tom Clancy, Sidney Sheldon and Wilbur Smith. And Jackie Collins.

"Jackie Collins?"

"Yes, surprisingly, some romance. I have a whole shelf of Danielle Steel." My assumption was that the men were reading along with their wives and girlfriends, or trying to nurture their sensitive side. But according to Clive, one of the inmates told him that it was the sex passages that appealed.

"What I really want to know is whether our Collins Bay Book Club is having a trickle-down effect on other readers in the prison," I said.

"Sure," he said. Some of the books that Carol was giving to our book club members to keep each month were eventually finding their way to the library, usually when those inmates were transferred to a new prison. Rather than just gathering dust on the library shelves, the book club books remained in active circulation, according to Clive. "It must be a word-of-mouth thing—somebody they know said it's a good book. And the fact that there's multiple copies of the books." Indeed, when we walked over to the circulation desk, it had two copies of Dave Eggers's *Zeitoun*, and several copies of Frank McCourt's *Angela's Ashes*, Joseph Boyden's *Three Day Road* and Mark Haddon's *The Curious Incident of the Dog in the Night-Time*, all stacked and waiting for sorting. Except for the book club books, it was rare for the Collins Bay prison library to have more than one copy of any given book.

If the book club was having a trickle-down effect, then which of the recirculated book club books, I wanted to know, were the most requested by other inmates? Clive had no hesitation before answering: "Books by Lawrence Hill or *Dreams from My Father* by Barack Obama. The Obama book was huge and is still read widely." I suggested he consider setting up a shelf of Collins Bay Book Club recommended books.

It was our second confirmation that month: the book club was stirring something in the men. How far would that go?

He walked me out of the library, pointing out proudly his shelves of foreign-language titles, including Korean, Spanish, Chinese and Russian, and talking about his hopes to reorganize his collection in categories like a bookstore. The library's existing Dewey system for classifying books didn't make much sense in a prison environment, he said. I had to agree.

Finally it was time for my summer reading vacation. My husband and I drove north for a cottage getaway. I took my copy of *A Fine Balance*, thinking of Frank, but I opted instead to start Hemingway's slim volume *A Moveable Feast: The Restored Edition*, about his writing and drinking life in Paris. I loved Hemingway's description of all the books he had bought from Sylvia Beach at her Shakespeare & Company bookstore and how they changed him— books by Turgenev, Gogol, Chekhov and Dostoevsky. Meanwhile my husband read *All the Pretty Horses* by Cormac McCarthy, which he loved, and when he finished it, I read it too. I decided to put it on the book selection list. The summer heat had eased. As I sat on the dock, a kingfisher scolded at the shore and I thought about how fortunate I was to be sharing books with inmates.

7

THE BOOK CLUB ALIBI

THE SOUND OF BIRDS woke Ben one late-summer morning in his cell, he noted in one of his first journal entries for me. But it was the prospect of calling his "common-law" that got him out of bed that day. The scrawl in blue pen read: "Knowing that someone is actually there waiting to hear from me. I love her deeply." He wrote about how empowering it was to have Carol and me also caring about his direction in life. These musings gave way to more anxious thoughts, as the prison went into lockdown following some guards' sighting of metal pieces being smuggled in to make weapons. "You do see a lot of homemade weapons—shanks—that could kill or do real damage to a person. There's been a lot of tensions on this block lately. I avoid it at all costs. You could end up doing life if you react to everything."

I was grateful that Ben could escape in his reading to the gentle and humorous novel up for discussion that month: *The Guernsey Literary and Potato Peel Pie Society* by Mary Ann Shaffer and Annie Barrows. I had recommended it chiefly because it was set during the World War II German occupation of Guernsey—a relatively obscure episode in the war when the English Channel island became a virtual prison. Although the residents managed to evacuate some four thousand of their children before the Germans invaded, food and other resources were in short supply for the islanders who remained. But I also wanted the men to read the novel because it dealt with how a book club helped the characters survive the occupation.

In the story, when a German patrol apprehends a group of island residents out past curfew, the islanders invent an alibi. They explain that they were simply attending a meeting of the Guernsey Literary and Potato Peel Pie Society. In order to give credibility to their alibi, the individuals start reading, even though some of them are farmers and fishermen who have rarely picked up a book in their lives. For anyone who has found community through talking about literature, the situation is instantly recognizable. The book topped the *New York Times* bestseller list at one point and, when I last looked, had one of the highest Goodreads average ratings at 4.1. That beat the Goodreads rating for *One Hundred Years of Solitude*, *The Catcher in the Rye*, Jane Austen's *Emma*, and *The Girl with the Dragon Tattoo*.

Carol was a little worried about my book choice, given that literary female readers were considered its primary audience. An epistolary novel that opens in 1946, the story revolves around Juliet, a thirty-two-year-old London-based newspaper columnist who receives a letter from a stranger named Dawsey, writing from Guernsey soon after the war has ended. Dawsey explains that he found her name inside a book by Charles Lamb called *Selected Essays of Elia*, and he asks for the name of a London bookstore where he could find more books by the same author. He also mentions the island's book society. Juliet's curiosity is piqued and she begins a correspondence with Dawsey and other islanders to find out more about the book club. In no time, she is caught up in the lives of the residents and travels there, ostensibly to include Guernsey's book society in an article that she is writing for *The Times* on the philosophical value of reading. As she tells Dawsey in a letter, all she'd come up with so far was the idea that books helped prevent people from going crazy.

It was perfect for the men, I assured Carol. After all, reading was keeping them from going crazy.

Gaston arrived early for the meeting and walked purposefully toward Carol and me. I couldn't help thinking that the way he shaved the sides of his head for a "high and tight" brush cut made him look more like a cop than an inmate. "I have an interesting proposition," he said to us. "I'm coming up on exactly one year to my statutory release. I'm thinking what could I do to challenge myself for one full year that would form as a habit to make me a better person when I get out."

Carol and I looked at each other. "Do you want to read the classics?" she asked him. What was she thinking? I wondered. Wasn't he already tackling a significant amount of reading?

"There we go," he said, then hesitated, the two vertical creases deepening between his sandy eyebrows. "But I want something that will be beneficial, not a waste of time." He explained that he'd already done some college courses on business and counselling and that he expected to return to landscaping when he got out.

"It's not a trade enhancement, Gaston," I said gently. "It's a life enhancement. And if you could commit to writing a journal about your reading every day for me, it would reinforce the habit."

"What would you do, Carol?" he asked.

"I would read the 'great books' and I'd get Dennis Duffy, a former English professor of Ann's and mine to draw up your reading list." And that was that. Carol was a firm believer in the value of reading.

Gaston then introduced a new member he'd recruited, Peter, a slight man in his mid-thirties, who seemed to be conscious of not horning in on Gaston's camaraderie with Carol and me. The other members began streaming in, and it was time to start. Carol gave them all leather bookmarks that she'd purchased on her summer vacation in Tuscany. Ben chose one that had gold decorations and a fringe.

The men's enthusiasm for the book spilled over in the early minutes of the book discussion when Carol and I asked them to talk about how they felt about the main characters. Every member had plot and character details at his fingertips and they all laughed in recognition at one another's recollections of high points in the novel. Ben thought Juliet was gutsy. He liked the fact that she decamped from her bombed-out apartment in London to travel to Guernsey on the basis of a few letters from Dawsey and other islanders. Gaston, the bank robber, liked that she turned down a rich American suitor. "He said I'll give you everything, riches and all, and she still said no," Gaston recalled.

But Dread singled out another character for the men to consider: Elizabeth, the woman whose quick-wittedness saved the group of islanders out past curfew. When German soldiers trained their guns on them, it was Elizabeth who coolly concocted the literary society alibi to conceal the truth that they'd just finished dining on a roast pig, a rare smuggled treat at a time when food supplies were low.

A new member with a name tag that read JAVIER agreed with Dread. He spoke in a voice that was even deeper and richer than Derek's, and was handsome, with a small pirate earring gleaming against his jawline. Javier found Elizabeth outspoken and brave to stare down the barrel of the gun and invent a story. But Peter wasn't so sure. He had noticed that the soldier holding the pistol was also grinning suggestively at her. Peter's suspicion was that the soldiers were aware of her covert affair with a kindly German soldier among their ranks. "It just seemed kind of lenient," said Peter. I flipped to the page. The novelists hadn't insinuated that the German's reaction was anything more than a delighted smile, certainly not leering. But it was interesting that Peter read the situation that way.

"The whole climax was built up around Elizabeth, hoping that she would still be alive," Dread went on. "And when she died, it was so devastating."

As the character discussions moved on to Juliet's various suitors, it was clear that the men were comfortable with discussing love interests. First, they assessed Juliet's London-based book editor, Sidney. "Sidney had a crush on Juliet," volunteered Javier.

Someone in the corner disagreed: "Sidney's a homo."

"Are you saying he's a gay man?" asked Carol, gently trying to steer the group away from homophobic slurs.

"But it doesn't actually say that," said Gaston. "It's after that you find out that's his preference."

"Right," said Carol. "Did you imagine Juliet as beautiful and charming?"

"Yeah, I imagined that," said Javier.

"And she ended up with … ," said Carol.

"Dawsey!" everyone said simultaneously, keen to fill in the blank.

Dawsey is a character of few words in the novel and, as Gaston said, was "never going to put it together" to reach out to Juliet, but his kindness was magnetic to her.

Now that I knew that Jackie Collins and Danielle Steel were popular in men's prisons, it was less surprising to find that the men appreciated romance in literature. I sensed that it was a reassuring reminder of the world that waited for them outside prison, when they could fully resume lives with their partners.

We asked the men how they felt about reading a novel that unfolds as a series of letters between Juliet, the island inhabitants and others. I expressed how some of the early letters between Juliet, Sidney and Juliet's friend Sophie seemed a bit precious and self-conscious to me. But Peter said it was "like being an invited eavesdropper. It made me feel like I was part of it. You get to be trusted with information people are willing to share only with people that are close." And Javier said that he'd enjoyed another epistolary novel about an inmate who wrote letters home that tracked his transition and his moods. I recalled that one of the earliest epistolary novels in the English language was written by an inmate in Fleet Prison in the 1640s, James Howell.

The chaplain, who had also read that month's book, said to the group that reading a book told through letters was like opening the mail. He was talking about that moment of anticipation before you open the seal of a personal letter. I realized that letters, after all, were a lifeline for people in prison. Under the rules at Collins

Bay, however, by the time an inmate receives a letter, the seal is already broken. All letters in and out of federal prisons are opened and their contents inspected. If a security issue is suspected, the authorities also have the right to read the letters.

What strained credulity, according to Gaston, was that the British postal service delivered letters at the speed of email or a courier. Carol, who spent some of her childhood in England during the postwar period, explained that the Royal Mail prided itself on frequency and speed. "I still remember that people would wait for the afternoon post and a letter mailed in the morning in Scotland would arrive in the afternoon in London," she said. "The postal service in those days was absolutely phenomenal." By the time I was living in England, we received just one delivery a day, but the postman still delivered on Saturdays.

But wasn't the whole letter thing a bit forced at times, Carol wanted to know. The men didn't think so. "I liked the way the author did it to bring out the personalities of each character through their writing," said Winston.

If ever there was a bookish novel, this was it. Juliet lost her book collection when her flat was bombed, she was in a book club in London that was encouraging her to write her novel and now she was wrapped up in Guernsey's literary society in order to write an article about the value of reading. The men appreciated all of it. But most of all they liked how the book club evolved. "It started up kind of as a con," said Javier. "But then it turned out the members found books that related to themselves." Given the scarcity of books on the island, each member of the Guernsey Literary Society read a different book for their meetings, rather than all preparing to discuss the same book—kind of like the previous month's book club at Collins Bay when the men talked about their summer reads. And some of the Guernsey members were inexperienced readers, like some of our prison book club members, tackling difficult books like *The Letters of Seneca: Translated from Latin in One Volume, with Appendix*, yet managing to extract something of value. In that case, the Stoic philosopher's advice on behaviour kept that character from drink. The book society was one way the islanders skirted the occupiers' restrictions and curfews. The parallels were obvious to the men, for whom the Collins Bay Book Club was a way of temporarily leaving behind the boredom and deprivations of prison. They were warming to their new identity as members of a book club, which they saw reflected in the story.

"If I told you that I thought the theme of this book was actually kindness in dire circumstances, what might your response be?" asked Carol. I thought about Elizabeth, hiding an escaped slave labourer, then paying dearly for it by being sent to a concentration camp herself.

Dread talked about the islanders sharing the roast pig when food and firewood were scarce, or making soap for people who hadn't had soap for weeks. "They use each other and lean on each other for strength," he observed.

It reminded Javier of his childhood in a poverty-stricken community in Montego Bay. "We didn't have bathrooms," he told the others. "Five in one bed. Kerosene for lights. Through struggle, people get closer. Those are the happiest memories."

But Winston expressed doubt that such mutual support was possible for most of them present, given the neighbourhoods they were from. "Us in this room, we come from big cities, and don't really have that sense of community. A lot of us never had positive social groups. You hang around with the wrong crowd. I never had an opportunity to sit down and bounce thoughts off each other or have the stories that we're reading." No one else stood up for a city neighbourhood where they had found community.

At the coffee break, I was chatting with Gaston and Peter when Carol joined us. "How would you like to be one of our book club ambassadors?" she asked Gaston. She had seen something in him that day that told her he had the potential to fill the shoes of Graham and Frank. And he had shown his ability to recruit by convincing Peter to join.

"Okay," he said.

"Just be sure any new members (a) can come, and (b) can read."

He nodded. And she whispered, "I'll get you some extra books, the classics."

It was a deal. She would help him be a "better person" by his statutory release date if he would help her build a better book club membership.

After the meeting, I sat down with Gaston for our pre-arranged one-on-one. He wanted me to know his story up front, assuming that I might be too shy to ask. Until shortly before he was arrested, he was a recovered crack cocaine addict with a previous conviction. He had gone several years clean and sober—long enough to make a life for himself. At forty, he had a wife and three children and a house and was juggling a freelance landscaping job in addition to his day job tending seniors' properties for a social service agency. He had some recovered addicts on his crew, but then they stopped recovering. On some days after work they would ask him to drop them off at a drug house. Then one day, he followed them in. "In I walked," he said. "And eight days later, I came out of that house, after spending about seventeen thousand dollars on drugs." As Winston had said back in the book club meeting, hanging out with the wrong crowd could lead to trouble.

Gaston's wife had no idea where he'd been. His employers fired him, not just because of his eight-day absence, but because they discovered he'd lied about not having a criminal record when he originally got the job. A mentor and benefactor who'd handed him several lucrative corporate landscaping contracts also pulled his business. And during the drug bender, Gaston had sold his nine-thousand-dollar truck for a thousand dollars to buy more drugs—meaning he had no equipment to stay in business anyway. "When I left that drug house, I had nothing. I lost pretty well everything—everything that I'd worked for."

Although within six months he'd managed to get a job as a machinist and downsize his family to a condo, he obsessed about the lost money, especially when his wife was home on maternity leave with a new baby—their fourth child. "I'm thinking, I've got to be further ahead, so I talked to a few of my shady friends about how to make some money. And to make a long story short, I was robbing banks."

He claimed that robbing banks tapped into a deep resentment that he'd nursed ever since a merger in the 1990s cost his mother her long-time bank job. "I remember her being devastated," he said. "All the senior staff were fired on the spot and escorted out of the bank like criminals. She became a miserable, angry woman." Gaston was a teenager at the time. "So I bore a big grudge against the banks. I thought they ripped everybody off." At the same time, he was fascinated with his mother's tales of robberies at her branch, which targeted the bank vaults, not the tellers' cash drawers. His voice had a strained edge and I could tell he was still angry. "I think I formed an actual hatred toward banks," he said, turning to look out the window and not have to meet my eyes.

"You rob the first bank and it's addictive like a drug, pretty close to the same as a cocaine rush. The adrenalin is a high in itself beyond anything I've ever done. You run out of the bank, you've got handfuls of money, you're into a vehicle and speeding off. 'Go, go, go!' I did thirteen banks in one month." Often he was high as well, he told me.

He didn't attempt the vault heists that his mother had witnessed as a bank employee. He lined up like all the other customers, sometimes with a goatee, painter's cap or other disguise, and passed a note to a teller instructing her to hand over her cash, insisting on no bundles with exploding dye packs. Then he would leave quietly without causing a fuss. "It was a terrible thing to do," he said to me, his blue eyes looking straight at me. "It could have terrified people."

The gig was up when he walked into the drug house one day with a robbery note in his pocket and a gut instinct that something was wrong. He took the note and placed it on top of a cupboard to get rid of it—just before police stormed the house and arrested him. "I was relieved, to be honest with you," he said. "I was glad it was over." The police were ready to charge him with six or seven robberies, he told me, but he copped to thirteen and pleaded guilty, which reduced his sentence to six years less time served, crediting three days for every one day of dead time waiting for trial.

He wanted to assure me that telling me the story wasn't about boasting. "What I did was horribly wrong. And I embarrassed my family. We were members of the Salvation Army church. We went to Bible Study on Monday nights." He couldn't meet my eyes.

The pitch of his voice suddenly deepened, and he sighed, as though exhausted. For a moment he stopped talking and through the open window we could both hear the seagulls calling and bursts of shouting from seg. Why was it that the only word I could ever pick up as the guys in the hole called to their buddies was *fucker*? In the chapel next door, other guys were singing "Amazing Grace."

I asked him if his wife had forgiven him, whether she was in solidarity with him.

"She forgives me, I think. The fortunate thing is I had a lot of years of sobriety. In ten years, I think back and there's never been an argument between us. She stood by me but this will be it. She said if it ever happens again, she couldn't do it again." He clasped his hands together and his voice broke, as though he was afraid of ever crossing that line.

I asked if he really thought he wanted to do the "great books" challenge and journal about it. His schedule was already packed. He worked full-time at CORCAN during the day, so only evenings and weekends were free. But he said that he had a schedule that he followed rigorously and he'd written a journal during his previous jail term about books he was reading. He was up for it. His "sign from God" that he was on the right path with reading the classics was the mention of Jonathan Swift, an author of classics, in *The Guernsey Literary and Potato Peel Pie Society*. I promised to bring him a journal next time.

I thought about how Gaston had read *Gulliver's Travels* because it had been significant for Aminata in *The Book of Negroes*. Surely if Gaston, who came into prison with a grade nine education, could do that, I could sit down with Charles Lamb's *Selected Essays of Elia*, the book that launches the story in *The Guernsey Literary and Potato Peel Pie Society*. I'd never read Lamb, but was vaguely aware of him being a contemporary of Keats. I made a note to find the essays at my local library.

And then, as though he'd just got another rush of adrenalin, Gaston launched into a description of how the book club had changed him. "You get a chance to relive the book, but through everyone else's eyes. What makes this book club so interesting is people bring alive the points that you don't even notice. I was thinking about the history and the love story in the Guernsey book. I never thought about the kindness." He described how, even though this was only his third meeting, he was already breaking his "mind your own business in prison" rule and chatting with some of the black book club members in the yard about how far they were in that month's book and what the main character was doing. And to my delight he mentioned that Carol's passionate defence of descriptive narrative in *Such a Long Journey* had stayed with him. "I don't just look for flashy bang and cool story, anymore, but I'm looking at what the writer might be thinking, or the words he's using, or the way he's phrasing it. It doesn't have to be the kind of books I used to read: Sidney Sheldon and fantasies, fairy tales and all these crazy lives. But real life."

I watched him walk down the hall and turn left toward the CORCAN workshop. Then I packed up my satchel and left.

On the drive home, I thought about the lessons of *The Guernsey Literary and Potato Peel Pie Society*. The authors seemed to be saying that anyone, in any circumstances, with some literacy, could find community, shelter, kindness and belonging through reading and discussing books. I reflected on the two book clubs in Hampstead to which I had belonged during my time in England. When I first arrived in London, I knew almost no one, and was caught up in unpacking boxes, settling my daughter into her new school and learning how to drive on the left. But Carol Clark, a warm and generous American woman who was the wife of my husband's boss, reached out to me and invited me to join her book club, Literary Ladies. It was ridiculously large, with about forty members, so it could meet only at the houses of those members who had more spacious living rooms. An American expat named Sue Rees ran it, and as I recall, at that time she charged members two pounds per meeting to cover her administrative costs. Each month, she began the meeting by providing a profile of the author, reading from her notebook with its tiny perfect lettering. Who her sources were, she never revealed, but she treated us to biographical details that I could find nowhere else.

Her rule at that time was British authors only, because who knew how long each of us expats might remain in London. Every spring, she organized a bus trip to study an author or group of authors in depth, with individual members researching interesting aspects of the author's life or milieu. One year, we chartered a bus to Belgium and northern France to trace the lives of World War I poets like Wilfred Owen and Siegfried Sassoon. I'll never forget many of us tearing up as one member read aloud Rudyard Kipling's 1916 poem "My Boy Jack," about his son who went missing at the Battle of Loos. That achingly sad opening line, "Have you news of my boy Jack?" Other years we explored the Shropshire pottery towns of Arnold Bennett novels and the knitting mills of Cheshire, which was Elizabeth Gaskell country.

My other London book club was, in contrast, small. Just five or six members, including my dear university friend Jane Crispin, who I discovered—thanks again to Carol Clark—was living just two blocks away. Jane not only invited me to join her group, but, together with another member, bought me a copy of that month's book, Wallace Stegner's *Crossing to Safety*, and dropped it off at our house because the next meeting was only a few days away. In Jane's group, we read without restrictions and I loved the intimacy of our gatherings.

Living in Hampstead meant being reminded of some of my favourite authors at almost every turning in the road, with Blue

Plaques marking the buildings in which they once lived. It had long been a literary and artistic community within London. Keats, whose poem "La Belle Dame Sans Merci" my husband had once recited to me at the beginning of our relationship in university, had lived at the bottom of East Heath Road on what is now Keats Grove. Daphne du Maurier, whom I read avidly in my teens, had resided at Cannon Hall, the former courthouse at the end of our lane. A childhood favourite of mine, Eleanor Farjeon, whose *The Little Bookroom* is a collection of literary fairy tales that I read to this day, had spent many years not far away, at 20 Perrin's Walk. I still have that book, though the dust jacket with its charming illustration by Edward Ardizzone is long gone. The novelist David Cornwell (John le Carré) had a house nearby and signed my husband's entire collection of le Carré spy novels. I thought I had landed in a writer's paradise.

As I pulled into the driveway of our Toronto house, my thoughts of Hampstead fell away. I was home.

The morning after the Guernsey book club meeting, I hurried over to the library. I found that there were no copies of the *Selected Essays of Elia* described in the novel and only two circulating copies of Lamb's *Essays of Elia* in the entire Toronto Public Library system, which indicated just how obscure it was. A nearby branch had one of them: a nice 2009 trade paperback edition by Hesperus Classics with a foreword that described how it was originally published in 1823. I discovered that Lamb was a noted British critic and essayist in the late-eighteenth and early-nineteenth centuries and a popularizer of classic works of literature. He had spent time in Hampstead with Keats. And like some of the Romantic poets in his circle, his subject matter was often a nostalgia for old England. According to the foreword, *Essays of Elia* became a popular staple in British households for the next hundred years.

I opened the cover, eager to indulge my own nostalgia for London, hoping he might have something to say about Hampstead, and eager to continue to revisit my own memories of happy times there with friends among the English and expat communities. I was taken immediately by Lamb's opening essay describing South Sea House, which still stands near the corner of Threadneedle Street and Bishopsgate, and his word portraits of miserly bachelor clerks who worked there for the South Sea Company. Lamb himself was a former employee of the company, which was notorious for the eighteenth-century stock speculation and collapse known as the South Sea Bubble. His writing was authoritative and playful, making me laugh at his description of a South Sea clerk with "frizzed-out" hair who was "melancholy as a gib cat over his counter all the forenoon." I could conjure the image.

It had been years since I'd read literature of that vintage, with verbal flourishes and antiquated references that I didn't understand. Like Gaston, who had decided he was "overthinking" *Gulliver's Travels*, I just let *Essays of Elia* flow over me. Without Gaston, I would never have discovered Lamb.

8

FRANK AND GRAHAM'S BOOK CLUB

B ARELY A WEEK after Carol opened Graham's letter during the ferry
ride to Amherst Island, she and I met with Graham and Frank to
discuss the launch of their very own book club. I knew that Beaver
Creek Institution would look different from Collins Bay because
inmates called it "camp" and described it as the most comfortable
minimum-security facility in Ontario. But I was unprepared for how
different. Located two hours north of Toronto, in a summer-cottage
area of dark lakes and pine forests, Beaver Creek was just a cluster
of buildings on a country campus without a perimeter wall or
barbed wire. Instead of occupying cells, the men lived in two-storey
bunkhouses with their own cooking facilities. The inmates could
just walk away, and some did, though the consequences were a
return to a higher-security prison. Families could bring in food when
they visited. And some inmate work details involved off-site work,
including harvesting cranberries in a nearby bog. Even the name
Beaver Creek suggested a family campground, not a correctional
facility. Carol later regretted that we hadn't brought a picnic for the
men and a gift of olive oil for Frank.

We were ushered into the prison's administrative boardroom
and within a few minutes, Graham and Frank appeared in the
doorway smiling broadly. I had a sense they were going to hug us,

which I knew was against regulations. Sure enough, they wrapped their arms around us. My first hugs from inmates. Accepting an embrace from Graham's six-feet-four frame was awkward for me at five feet five. My head sort of ended up on his chest. "I've been looking so forward to seeing you guys," he said. They were both so excited that they talked over each other. Carol told Graham that he looked tanned and slimmer than he had at Collins Bay. "Frankie takes most of my food, right," he teased. "And I trained really hard. Frankie has me on a rigid schedule."

We only had an hour to hammer out a plan for the book club before Count. Already the pair had recruited nine other interested guys, many of whom were quite sophisticated readers, they told us. The prison warden himself had been wonderfully supportive of the idea. But there was a problem. Donna, their liaison person in the administration, was so keen on the book club that she wanted to join it and had independently been pitching it to some of the inmates. "What I don't want to do is scare away some guys who are gonna say that it's the warden's pet project," Graham said.

At that point we invited Donna to join the meeting. With Carol backing them up, Graham and Frank politely explained to Donna that, for the idea to work, it had to be seen as an inmate-run book club, that only Graham and Frank should undertake recruitment, and that, while Donna was welcome to join the book club, she might have to withdraw if the members grew uncomfortable. Donna was surprisingly amenable to their recommendations and offered them the boardroom in the programs building for their monthly meetings. That was a bonus, because meeting in the chapel was always a harder sell among inmates who were averse to religion. Then Graham turned to Carol and said that instead of her plan to have Frank and him choose the books that day, he'd rather convene a meeting of the members and let them decide. Like Donna, Carol conceded, which surprised me even more. Everyone saw the value of what Frank and Graham were trying to accomplish.

But the pair had to choose the club's first book that day, because the inaugural book club meeting was just six weeks away. "For the first book," suggested Graham, "something medium-sized and catchy that these guys will all relate to." Carol had just pitched them on nearly a dozen books from my selection committee's lists.

"How about *The Cellist of Sarajevo*?" she asked. It was a novel that Frank had read with the Collins Bay Book Club before Graham joined.

"That was a good book," said Frank. "I wouldn't mind repeating it." Graham agreed.

We said goodbye in a flurry of good wishes and they were gone in a sudden repeat of the hugs. When the men were out of sight, Donna pointed out that hugging wasn't okay between volunteers and inmates. We told her we were aware, and that it wouldn't happen again. They just seemed so overjoyed to see us.

Six weeks later, it was introductions time at the inaugural meeting of Graham and Frank's Beaver Creek Book Club, with Carol and me in attendance. We were sitting in plush boardroom chairs around a long table in the building that housed the prison library and programs classrooms—much cushier than the circle of metal chairs at Collins Bay. I sensed immediately that this was a different crowd from the book club at Collins Bay: fewer visible tattoos, more white-collar criminals and, ironically, more lifers. While I'd heard from Carol that one of the members had killed his parents and siblings when he was a teenager, I had no idea which fellow it was, or whether the men would reveal their crimes as they went around the table.

"I've always wanted to join a book club but never ran with that kind of crowd," said a dark-haired man in his early thirties whose name tag read DALLAS. Snorts of laughter followed from around the room.

"Well, you're runnin' with a book club crowd now," said a gravel-edged voice from across the table—a middle-aged guy named Earl.

One man admitted he'd quit school at age twelve and said his favourite book was *Don Quixote*, which he'd read at age seventeen.

An inmate with a T-shirt that read *Rock 'n Roll* identified himself as Bookman, the prison librarian. The prison librarian was an *inmate*? Bookman said he couldn't sleep when he first came to jail and reading had helped him doze off. He declared his number one book to be "from the nineteenth century, by Victor Hugo, *Les Misérables*."

As the remaining eight men introduced themselves, I took particular note of Doc, a ginger-haired man with freckled skin and wire-rimmed glasses, who looked like he had just popped in from his country club in his V-neck pullover, and Tom, a reader of fantasy and sci-fi, who had shoulder-length hair and unusually long nails. Tom copped to making money in high school by "writing original stories for people in creative writing classes." I figured he'd done something worse than that to land in a federal prison.

Graham and Frank knew everyone already, but they introduced themselves all the same. I wanted to see what they would say to other inmates about themselves. Frank told the others he had been in and out of jail since 1965. I noticed for the first time how much balder he seemed than a few months ago. "I got through by doing a lot of reading," he said. "But if you have no one to share it with, it fades." So true.

"Frankie is the reason I originally came to the book club at Collins Bay," said Graham, easily the biggest guy in the room, with the most booming voice. "I fought and argued with him that I wasn't going because they were holding the meetings in the chapel and I thought they were trying to convert me. But Frankie joked that that didn't happen until at least the second meeting."

When it was my turn, I explained that I couldn't miss seeing Graham and Frank start their own book club at Beaver Creek and asked the members if they would let me sit in for a few months. No one objected. Perhaps that was because Graham and Frank had sat me between them in a proprietorial way. If anyone had said no to me, they would have had to answer to Graham.

It seemed to me that the greatest risk to Graham and Frank's book club was the presence of prison staff at the meeting. Unlike at Collins Bay, where Carol's book club volunteers came from outside the prison, the volunteer facilitators at Beaver Creek were two off-duty Beaver Creek employees. Phoebe, the lead facilitator, was considered cool and not part of the penal mainstream because she was the popular young English teacher. But her co-facilitator worked in the department that administered the prison's correctional programs: a serious-minded and sensitive woman named Meg. Typically the presence of someone from the corrections team makes inmates clam up because staffers usually file reports on inmate behaviour. Also at the table was Donna, the prison official who was instrumental in helping Frank and Graham start the group, but who was a stickler for rules, as I knew from my meeting with her the previous month. Wiry and dark-haired, Donna seemed tense and hyper-alert, a human radar for lies and wrongdoing. Whenever her eyes settled on me, I felt she was reading my conscience, causing me to wonder if I had done something wrong. Donna and Graham had had a frank conversation prior to the meeting and they agreed that if any of the book club members objected to her presence, she would bow out. As it turned out none of the men balked. They seemed prepared to give the "volunteers" a chance.

Given the many solid readers in attendance, Carol abbreviated her usual speech about how the book club worked. There was no briefing about civil discourse or polite listening, no warnings about showing up to future meetings without the book. "Half of the enjoyment is this private thing that you do: reading," she said in a warm confessional tone. "The other half is coming together and discussing it. It enriches your whole understanding. Books become your friends.

"You're not going to like all of the books," she told them. Confronting this truth up front is critical for any book group, even my women's book clubs. "But I've been in book clubs for years and years and I try really hard to get to the end of books I don't like because I'm part of the discussion and I'm part of something that happens communally. And very often when I get to the end I say, 'You know, that book had a lot to tell me.'" Then she offered the carrot: "If you are a good attendee there's a certificate that goes in your file." Several of the men smiled.

Every inmate at the table had his copy of that month's book: Steven Galloway's novel *The Cellist of Sarajevo*. Set in the 1992–1996 siege of the capital city of Bosnia and Herzegovina, the novel draws on the true story of Sarajevo cellist Vedran Smailović, whose response to a brutal mortar shelling that killed twenty-two citizens lining up for bread was to risk his life playing Albinoni's moving lament, Adagio in G Minor, every day for twenty-two days in the city's ruins, one day in honour of each of the victims. In life and in the novel, the musician was a symbol of hope, humanity and courage. Galloway's story imagines a protagonist who is a female counter-sniper, code-named Arrow, hired to protect the cellist from Bosnian Serb snipers. The other two main characters are civilians struggling to survive in the besieged city: Kenan, head of a young family, and Dragan, a middle-aged baker. The action veers between claustrophobic scenes of citizens inching through the city as they dodge snipers' bullets, and detailed passages of sniper tradecraft as Arrow sets her trap. The themes for discussion are rich: identity, courage and morality, and the power of the arts to bridge hostility and hatred. It was, as one reviewer described it, "catnip" for book clubs. For those reasons, it was the book Carol often chose for a new prison book club's first meeting.

To set the scene, Carol distributed images of Smailović playing his cello in the ruined city and of citizens crouching in fear. Then she played a recording of Albinoni's cello piece. The expression of grief in the music never failed to produce a hole in the centre of my chest, an unwept sob. The members fell silent to listen. For the first time, I detected a waltz rhythm in the pacing, like some wailing funeral dance. The strains seemed to evoke deep feelings among the inmates as well. Several men listened with their eyes closed, including Doc, who swung his finger as if conducting with a baton.

As the music came to a close, Carol said, with emotion constricting her voice: "He must have played his heart out—just played his heart out."

Tom opened the discussion about the cellist with a spot-on insight. "The cellist is a secondary character," he said. "Other than the one chapter specifically about him, we don't get his point of view." I'd never considered that until he mentioned it. Why *does* Galloway drop the cellist's point of view after the first chapter? Tom made the point that the cellist played the adagio partly to erase the war in his own mind. As he said this, I looked again at his fingers and realized that only the nails of his thumbs and first fingers were pointy. They were long enough to be weapons and inmates have been known to file their nails for that purpose. Tom was a lot to take in—an intellect with a hint of the macabre.

"I think the cellist responded to a major act of inhumanity by trying to bring humanity back for other people," said Dallas.

"Yes," said Carol and I simultaneously.

The theme of humanity caught on. We talked about another character who seemed already dead—a sour, ungrateful elderly woman who'd lost sight of what Sarajevo had once been.

"She's the focal point for other people analyzing their own humanity," said Tom.

But no one was willing to agree with Carol that Dragan had evolved from looking after his own skin to helping others as he crossed sniper-patrolled streets to get to work at the bakery. When the book club members looked doubtful, Carol reminded them that Dragan had risked his life to drag a corpse from the road before a cameraman could film it. I flipped to the page in my book to jog my memory and found that he was inspired by the selflessness of a female friend who was hit by sniper fire while trying to bring medicine to her mother. Carol made the case that Dragan was trying to keep alive his memory of Sarajevo before the war, as a place of kindness.

"I have to ultimately disagree with that so strongly," replied Tom. "I don't believe Dragan made a *choice* to become a *brave* person. He was numb." Nor did he agree with her argument that the characters viewed Sarajevo as a kinder place before the war. He dug in his heels, which prevented Carol from proceeding in her usual vein: inviting the men to see the value of helping others in their own lives.

"Anyone else on this point?" she said, searching faces.

Finally Richard, a middle-aged inmate with thick-lensed black plastic glasses and a madras plaid shirt, who'd earlier said that reading had kept him sane during his many years in prison, introduced a new angle on the humanity question. He asked if anyone had seen the documentary on PBS the previous night about the atrocities committed against women during the siege and about the war crimes tribunals. "I wanted to shout out to the book club members!" he said. "I thought it was interesting the way Galloway's novel totally avoided the conflict between Muslims and Christians in the region. The documentary showed how they began as neighbours and friends, even intermarrying. But within weeks they were mortal enemies." I studied Richard's face, intrigued that he was watching PBS on his TV, because I understood that at Collins Bay, reality TV and movie channels were preferred viewing.

Dallas suggested to Richard that the novelist couldn't have "painted" religion into the novel because it would have made the story "too political." "He's avoiding that and painting it in human terms," he said. Several of the guys around the table nodded and indicated to Graham that they'd like to speak. He acknowledged them and made a note.

Graham said he hadn't seen the PBS documentary but he'd heard that the leaders of the Bosnian Serb Army, Radovan Karadzić and Ratko Mladić, who were still at large according to Galloway's afterword, had been arrested since the novel was published. "Interestingly enough, both of them have been caught now," he said.

To give the book club members a bit of background on the confusing geopolitics of the siege, Graham had asked Earl to prepare some material on the subject because he had once been a member of the U.N. peacekeeping force in Cyprus. But when Earl had to leave during the adagio, perhaps to meet a visitor,

Graham improvised the history lesson himself. "When Bosnia and Herzegovina declared its independence, the Serbs within Bosnia and Herzegovina, if I'm remembering correctly, rose up, with a little backing from their Serb friends next door, and decided that they didn't want to separate," said Graham. "And my understanding is they surrounded the city of Sarajevo and basically they shelled the city from the outskirts, from the hills. It went on for four years. They basically devastated the city. And then, if I remember correctly, they split the state in half didn't they, as part of the settlement?"

"Graham, that's great!" said Carol, confessing that she had never been able to fully sort out the roots of the conflict. "And it was the longest siege in modern history, surpassing the sieges of both Stalingrad and Leningrad."

Graham gave the floor to Richard again. "I wrote something down that Dragan, the baker, said, that I thought was the essence of the book," said Richard. It was on page 237 of the novel. He read it aloud, a passage that talked about how the city wouldn't die until its occupants were complacent with the idea of death.

I reflected on siege mentality and how it could change people. It could make you numb, it could make you heartless, or it could make you selfless. It is all about how we choose to live our lives. Richard's passage was an arresting moment. No one said it directly, but Sarajevo was a prison for those four years. How central that thought must be to the men with long prison terms—not letting the situation define you, not being branded a bad guy forever but someone who was paying his "debt to society" and could redefine himself.

"The heart of the novel," I said.

What makes *The Cellist of Sarajevo* so magnetic for book clubs is its many unresolved questions. Even though this was my second time reading the book, I was still confused about why Arrow, the counter-sniper protagonist, would kill the sniper not when he is about to assassinate the cellist, but rather when he is leaning back and smiling, eyes closed, listening to the music. She kills him at a moment when he is expressing his own humanity. Given Galloway's subtle wording, I wasn't even sure if it was Arrow who shot him. Carol was equally unsure. We needed other readers to help us sort it out.

Likewise, we needed a good book club debate to sort out who is good and who is bad toward the end of the novel. The men applauded Arrow for refusing to carry out instructions from her new handlers, who want her to randomly assassinate innocent civilians. As Graham said, she reclaimed her humanity in doing so. But even the inmates found it hard to fathom why Arrow, so skilled and well armed, allows those same operatives who had killed her previous handler to target her in the final scene. Was she, as Richard's passage had said, content to accept death and weary of the fight?

"How about Arrow?" asked Carol. "What did everyone think of her?"

Bookman, the inmate librarian, said, "Arrow realized that even the people up on the hill are stuck in her situation. A mirror image."

"I like that comparison," said Phoebe, whose sentences ended with the tonal uptick characteristic of some Canadian accents. "Arrow is constantly comparing herself to the people on the hills and trying to differentiate between the people defending the city and the people attacking the city. And more often than not, some of the characters come to realize that they're a hell of a lot more similar to each other than they would like to think."

This had to resonate with the men around the table: how war must blur the true goodness or evil of those who must survive in it and how prison does the same. Some of the men thought Arrow was a coward for her ultimate sacrifice at the end of the book. Some of them thought it was an act of goodness. It struck me that in that prison meeting room, each individual around the table had the capacity to recognize goodness. Whatever part of them had been bad was not apparent in our brief time together. It was not until later that that part was revealed to me, when I learned about some of their crimes.

Bookman wanted to explore the theme of sacrifice. "Each of the characters sacrificed something," he said. "Kenan, the one with the family, sacrificed his safety every couple of days to get water for his family and others. Arrow sacrificed her life to avoid being someone she didn't want to become."

"So do you think that's part of the theme of humanity," Carol ventured again, trying to resurrect her point, "that when we are truly human, we put ourselves out for the other?"

Frank responded: "I thought at the end Arrow just got tired of everything. She had all these options and she said, what for? Goodbye. That's the sense I got."

Then Donna pointed to the clock and the guys realized they had to rush to Count, so Graham took the floor. "The next meeting will be the second Wednesday of the month," he said, his voice easily heard over the after-meeting chatter. The book club members grabbed their copies of Jeannette Walls's memoir, *The Glass Castle*. They were all in a hurry, but still stopped to shake our hands and thank us on the way out. Carol told them that she was sorry she wouldn't be able to personally attend the Beaver Creek Book Club each month, given how interesting their comments had been.

Frank and Graham's first book club meeting had been a big success. Frank had found strong contributors and Graham had ensured that everyone who wanted to speak got heard. It was easy to imagine him using those same skills in a meeting of his street crew before his incarceration, or in a legitimate business meeting that might take place post-incarceration.

Frank and Graham asked us to stay until they got back from Count. When they returned, slightly breathless, Graham said "the guys" were asking him if it would be possible to get together in smaller groups first to discuss some of the issues, before meeting in the larger combined group. The book group was a hit! We congratulated them. As we and the other facilitators left the building, Frank shyly gave me a sheaf of typed papers—his journal about his reading in prison. He preferred to type rather than to write in the journal I'd given him.

On the drive back to the city in Carol's car, she and I talked about Frank's progress in his real estate correspondence course, Carol's longing for greater closeness with her siblings, what we had cooked for Thanksgiving and why there were lifers in a minimum-security prison. Roughly a quarter of the inmates at Beaver Creek were serving life sentences and, after a long time behind bars meeting milestones in their correctional programs, they each had earned the right to be there, even if they might spend years in minimum. I asked her why she thought the book club members resisted broadening the discussion to humanity and kindness in their own lives. Had Donna's presence made them guarded? Was it like Sarajevo and they had to self-preserve in hostile circumstances?

It would take them a while to trust, she said. She had seen it with every book club.

I reflected silently on whether some of the men had difficulty talking about kindness in the context of awareness of their own past crimes, when kindness had failed them. I opened a Google screen on my iPhone, then closed it, then opened it again. Sometimes I wasn't sure if I wanted to know what each inmate had done. I keyed in Doc's name. There was a hit. A man who shared the same name, a family physician. I slipped the phone back into my purse.

Carol was getting tired, so I took the wheel. Rain was sheeting down and it was dark. I had to focus on the driving. Not being familiar with her car's dashboard, and being fatally inattentive to gas gauges generally, I paid no attention to the fuel level. Just ten blocks shy of my house, at a busy city intersection, we ran out of gas. Carol insisted that I leave her there because roadside assistance was on the way and it was a safe area. I did so reluctantly, but felt guilty abandoning her. In my taxi ride home, I felt like Dragan early in the novel, looking out for himself.

9

I'M INSTITUTIONALIZED, BRO

Back at Collins Bay, the temperatures were dipping to five degrees Celsius overnight by early October and Ben was keeping the window of his cell closed. "Right now I am wrapped in three blankets and a sheet when I go to bed," he told his journal.

The previous month had brought plenty of ups and downs for Ben. When I read his journal, it progressed like a novel—full of cliffhangers and hopes. It made me want to read on, to find out what would happen next. "I been trying to get into the welding program and I just received a slip for an interview," he wrote one day in September. "This would be a positive step for me because it would be a trade I could do when I get out, and move on with my life." Twelve days later, this simple entry: "I found out yesterday that I didn't get in." He expressed no anger even though it was his last chance to get a trade before leaving Collins Bay. He was used to not getting a break.

That night he dreamt about being dependent. "I'm so used to doing things myself that the thought of depending on someone or others frightens me," he confided to his journal. "At times I worry how I'm going to adjust when I get out. Yeah, I got my diploma, but I don't want to be stuck in a basic 9–5 job paying me minimum wage." He hadn't given up hope, though. Within a few days, he was musing about jobs in the renewable-energy sector and his

105

support for the party in the upcoming provincial election that was promising those jobs. And by the end of that month's writing, he had decided to pursue a job in trucking.

Meanwhile his mind was on men who had some of the toughest jobs going: soldiers. For book club that month we were reading Sebastian Junger's *War*, an account of the journalist's fifteen months embedded with a U.S. Army platoon on the front lines in eastern Afghanistan in 2007 and 2008. Like Ben, some of the soldiers in *War* had difficulty imagining a return to normal life. He reflected:

> The book makes me feel like I'm in the action on the Korengal
> Valley with the platoon. As I hear the story of the soldiers and
> how the war has psychologically caused them trauma, I lay on
> my bed thinking *as much as we try or at least as much as I*
> try to suppress the fact that I'm institutionalized, I know I am.
> You don't spend 4 yrs. in one place and it doesn't affect you.

It was a Saturday morning as he wrote that, with its curious asterisks. Weekends were very different on the range from weekdays. "The feeling is a peaceful one because you don't have many inmates getting up in the morning on weekends. That is one of the unwritten prison rules: all is quiet until noon, and then the jungle is awakened."

When we met in mid-October, with a strong turnout of sixteen inmates, the men in the book club were disappointed to learn that Carol couldn't attend. Derek would be facilitating the meeting in her place. I didn't think much of it at the time. In fact, I could see why having a guy at the helm for a discussion about what it's like to be a front-line soldier would be good. As a Mennonite, Derek grew up in a tradition of pacifism and non-violence. But as a professional radio broadcaster, he could be agnostic on the subject of combat.

"The Second Platoon of Battle Company, 173rd Airborne," he said as we all got comfortable in our seats. "The Korengal Valley of Afghanistan, which is, as those of you who've read the book know, a valley near the Pakistani border about six miles long. One of the deadliest places on earth. It's a funnel of money and troops for the Taliban and Al Qaeda. The U.S. Army put these platoons—three of them—on a hilltop, without women, without hot food, without running water, without communication with the outside world or any kind of entertainment for over a year. It's quite a story. So I had a lot of thoughts about it and I'm sure you did too." Without women. He didn't say that as though women were army kit. He was reflecting the author's comment that these front-line units had no women soldiers at that time.

I looked over at Derek. He'd delivered a suspenseful introduction, but I knew that he was sleep-deprived and his eyes sagged in a way I'd never seen before. Without his energy to direct the discussion we could lose control of the meeting.

And then things took a turn for the worse. "*War* is not like a page-turner," Dread announced, his knit Rasta tam exposing more of his dreadlocks than at previous meetings.

Grow-Op agreed. "I only made it to the third chapter." Book club meetings that started this way usually petered out pretty fast.

But then Lenny, one of several new black inmates who turned up that day, gave the group something to discuss. "For the most part in war you're sitting around," he said. "You're hating on each other. And there's very few actual moments of real war. And then it sucks. You're not thinking about 'O Canada,'" he said, singing the title of the Canadian anthem. "That's not what it is. It's like 'oh shit' in a moment in time." He was able to capture in fresh words how Junger portrayed the platoon's long lulls and sudden firefights—trumping the language of the old adage about war being "months of boredom punctuated by moments of terror." He understood like a book reviewer, but spoke like a rapper.

"War is bad but it's not all bad," said Derek. "At one point in the book, I made a note, 'Why do men fight?' It does give them meaning and purpose and a sense of bonding with their brothers. They were protecting their tribe, their group, their gang, whatever you want to call it."

"It gives you insight into how loyal the soldiers are to each other, like how they risk their life to save somebody without any qualms," said Dread.

Junger's research on the military group dynamic is fascinating. In the book he cites a mid-1950s study in which paratroopers who were part of a tightly knit group were shown to experience less anxiety jumping out of an airplane than those who were only loosely connected. The bonded soldiers worried more about living up to the expectations of their peers than about their own safety.

"I compared it with being in prison," said Gaston, his brush cut almost bristling. "Because, again, you're isolated from women, they didn't have their families around. Nothing. And when there was no fighting, they didn't all get along. They were at each other. Which is similar to prison." However, he expressed regret that inmates did not bond in the same way as the soldiers. "There's so much bullshit around these places instead of convicts coming together."

Peter, Gaston's recent recruit, offered his own reflections on that point. "You know as convicts, we don't really need a reminder of what we can be reduced to, because we're in here, obviously. We're supposed to be civilized and advanced, and yet we still can be reduced back to that." "That" being the actions that landed them in prison.

The discussion was providing clues to how hostile the prison could be outside of our protected little book club. It was so abstract, it didn't make me nervous. On the contrary, I was impressed with how the men mapped the book against their own lives and how they had an impulse to seek improvements in prison culture.

Then, when there was a brief lull, I raised the topic of fear. "I was really interested in what Junger had to say about how the heartbeat rises during fear, how it obscures your judgment and ability to react," I said. "What do you think?"

"You think of your own person," agreed Ben. "Gunfire goes off and you freeze and the body reacts after." I certainly remembered that my brain overrode my fear response in those first few seconds of the mugging.

"There's *supposed to be* no fear," said Dread, who I'd noticed over the months often challenged Ben, his unit mate. Dread seemed to see Ben as teacher's pet. "I've seen guys who sacrifice their own life for the other guys in the group. Everybody has that in them. You don't have to be an animal to have that—just the love for your battalion members."

That's when Derek pointed out that Junger talks about courage being love. We sat there trying to wrap our heads around the idea. Dread said it was like running out into the road to save your child. And I reflected on Junger's point that the loyalty and bonding among the platoon was also what made the loss of a fellow soldier so psychologically traumatic. It created cohesion in the field for the military, but devastated the individual soldier in the long term. Some of the men in the prison, who had been in gangs, wore tattoos of fellow gang members who'd been gunned down. It was the same sort of thing.

Javier picked up on Derek's point. His ambered voice conveyed authority, and the others often fell quiet when he talked, perhaps because they liked the sound of it. Sometimes when the men took turns reading aloud passages from an upcoming book, they asked Javier to read more than one. "To me it seems a lot of these guys join up the army for a sense of security because when they first go to the army they're nothing," he ventured. "They're scared, and then they get teased, and then they get beat up and then they develop this killer, you know, instinct, right? They don't even know why they're going to war—they're just going there to fulfill some sense of family, some sense of security and when they get there they transform."

"What's interesting to me," said Derek, "is when it comes time at the end and their tour is up, most of these guys don't want to leave."

Ben jumped in, saying, "Because they have no reason to. They got immune to it."

"They got immune to it?" asked Derek.

"Yeah," continued Ben. "Just like you could be in here. Institutionalized. As in, like, 'Yo, I don't wanna leave.' Because you can't be somewhere four or five years and say you're not institutionalized. Just like how they are in the war. They're only there for fifteen months and they don't even wanna leave. Just because of going back to a normal settin' of life." Ben had been reflecting on this theme in his journal. Now he was trying it out with the guys.

"That's what the author says," continued Javier. "Like guys who've been in prison for so long, the only thing they have left is prison. They have nothing else to look forward to on the street. This is where they're shinin'. This is where most of their goals are."

Not everyone bought into Ben and Javier's hypothesis.

"I think I disagree with that," said a man named Quincy, looking directly at Ben, his voice rising, his limbs tightening as though readying for a physical fight. He was an average-sized inmate in his twenties who seemed to be anchoring a contingent of the new black attendees.

Then everyone began talking at the same time and Derek had trouble restoring order. "Hang on," he said. But they ignored him.

Carol, I thought. Where are you?

Eventually a nasal voice rose above the others. It was Lenny. He shored up Ben and the "institutionalized" side of the argument, then added: "If you go to the hole and stuff like that in terms of relatin' to prison, you go back to a baser humanity. And there's less anxiety because you're not held to a certain standard, you know what I mean." Was he saying that it was a relief to go to the hole, to segregation, because once you were there, expectations of you were lower? "The only thing that's expected of you in war," he went on, "is to take care of your friends and kill, right. I could imagine that providing some kind of security, not security but, um … " I assumed he was looking for a word like *belonging*.

But Derek filled in a different word. "Or is it excitement?" he asked. War, according to Junger is "insanely" thrilling.

"Yeah, that too, right," said Lenny. "I mean how many of us could say we'd been in a fight and not felt some kind of excitement in it? Like even when it's done, after you win, that's exciting and that can be addicting in itself. And this is on another level, right?" He looked around the room for confirmation.

But Quincy wanted to draw the discussion back to institutionalization. "Just a question," he said, swivelling in his chair to speak to Ben again. "What do you consider 'institutionalized'?" Then looking to Ben's supporters: "What do you guys consider 'institutionalized'?"

"I mean, you can't function outside," said Javier. "When you step outside, you can't function."

Quincy ignored him. "How long have you been in?" he asked, looking again at Ben in a manner that was challenging and unfriendly.

"I've been in 'bout four years, right."

"Are you saying you're institutionalized?" echoed Dread, always willing to gang up on Ben.

"Hell yeah," said Ben. "Because I'm getting up every time the same morning and—"

"That's just a set routine," said Quincy, responding before Ben had even completed his sentence.

"But mentally it bothers me," said Ben. "I could say that, 'Yo, I'm here and I'm only in this place right now for the time being.' But just that routine that I go by, day by day. I'm institutionalized, bro. I'm not going to deny it. I am. Because if I go to the caf and don't see my coffee in the mornin' I'm probably like, 'Yo, what the hell's going on?' I'm gonna freak out."

"When I first started my bit, it bothered me," said Grow-Op. "It doesn't bother me no more. That's the thing of being institutionalized. You get a routine and it's like a purpose." In the book, he said, the soldiers were nothing before they joined up. "Some of them would still be on the streets. So it's kind of like it's a purpose for them."

Everyone talked at once. I reflected on how Derek was proving that he had a knack for asking questions that were relevant to the men, even if it led to a verbal melee. This must be what it's like in an unsupervised argument in prison, I thought. If Carol had been there, likely she would have corralled the discussion sooner. But I was grateful for that brief window into their world, that glimpse of "the jungle" Ben had referred to.

There had been other book group gatherings at Collins Bay in which the men had taken control. Before I joined, during a discussion of Cormac McCarthy's post-apocalyptic novel *The Road*, the guys told Carol to be quiet until they had exhausted the topic they were discussing. These were brief glimpses into the way that disagreements can become dangerous in prison. I didn't feel personally threatened during the discussion of *War*, but I sensed that Ben might be vulnerable, and that Quincy's barrage of questions masked a rage that could erupt.

After the meeting, a new fellow came up to me and asked if he could be one of the book club members writing a journal. Word seemed to be getting out about the journal writing. He was a fidgety West Indian man in his twenties with eager eyes and densely tattooed arms. He introduced himself as Deshane. "I write songs and stuff," he said. I said he'd have to write about the books too, and he said he would. I had the chaplain search a blank journal that I happened to have in my satchel. It had gone through the X-ray machine earlier and the chaplain gave it the thumbs-up. I handed it to Deshane and watched him walk away happily, his small frame bouncing.

Then I spent a few minutes with Gaston. He must have been wondering if his personal campaign for self-improvement, which he'd pitched to Carol and me last month, was already more than he could handle. Carol had brought him a stack of classics of American literature that Dennis Duffy had recommended. As well, he had his prison job, courses and the next book club book to read. And now it was time for me to load him up with one more thing: a journal. He took it from me and smiled. "Okay," he said. "Okay."

Gaston made his first entry in his journal the following day, reminding himself to kneel while praying, vowing to lose five pounds and noting that he had started *Huckleberry Finn*.

IO

ABUSE OR NEGLECT?

THE SECOND MEETING of Frank and Graham's book club at Beaver Creek took place on a brilliant fall day. I loved how the terrain changed on the drive north from rolling moraine to the black soil of reclaimed marsh and finally to steep granite outcroppings. As always, I slowed when I passed a favourite field of mine on the moraine whose contours rippled crazily. That month, its cornstalk stubble rose and fell into the distance like a striped counterpane.

The night before, I'd reread Frank's journals, the neat typed pages that he'd produced on the Beaver Creek library computer. It was clear that he was now spending most of his prison days with books. He'd finished a 1974 biography of New York mobster Crazy Joe Gallo, by Donald Goddard, and was reading *The Best American Crime Reporting 2009*, a compilation of true-crime stories. And he was deep into *Mafia Wife*, the 1977 account of Barbara Fuca's experiences as the wife of a Mafia drug dealer. The "364" shelf of the Beaver Creek library—that section in libraries' Dewey system allotted to books on criminology and organized crime—must have been particularly well stocked.

Frank had also tackled a novel in Italian, *Lo Sguardo del Cacciatore*, and Elizabeth Wurtzel's five-essay book, *Bitch: In Praise of Difficult Women*. *Bitch* was an unusual choice for a guy in prison, I thought, given that it spends considerable time assessing tough celebrity bad girls like Courtney Love and Joan Crawford. He was also well into *The Panic Virus: The True Story Behind the Vaccine-Autism Controversy*, by science writer Seth Mnookin. The book hadn't convinced him. He distrusted vaccinations and was refusing to get the prison flu shot that season, not wishing to be a "guinea pig."

When I arrived at Beaver Creek that afternoon, it was visiting hours, and the reception area was a din of noisy reunions and whispered consultations. A woman holding a homemade cake appeared to be upset with the guards. I signed in and told the correctional officers that the warden had approved visits with Frank and Graham before each book club meeting. One officer found us a quieter space in the empty chapel. Like the chapel in Collins Bay, Beaver Creek's looked more like a public school classroom, with windows running along one side and what appeared to be a few school desks.

Graham and Frank came in wearing matching white waffle-weave long-sleeved shirts with blue short-sleeved T-shirts pulled on over top. It might be minimum security, but inmates still wore prison-issue. Frank was losing his voice due to allergies and had grown a salt-and-pepper beard. The facial hair was his contribution to "Movember," a movement in which men around the world grow moustaches during the month of November to raise funds for research on prostate cancer and other men's health issues. Graham was clean-shaven as always. He told me that even when he had been a biker, he had never worn a beard or moustache. Graham left to get Frank a glass of cold water for his cough.

Before we had a chance to even settle in our chairs, Graham began talking about a book drive he was organizing to improve the selection in the prison library. "Antiques" was how Frank described the existing library collection. Graham had worked out a scheme to approach women's book clubs in Toronto who might donate their books to Beaver Creek after they'd discussed them, using the local John Howard Society as the receiving dock.

Graham's strategy for how to get the donated books through prison security was to run them through the X-ray machine, then spread them out on the floor so that the dogs could sniff them for drugs. He had pitched the idea to the warden. All he needed was a staff member willing to supervise. I commended him on his initiative.

He also offered some advice on how to deal with book club members back at Collins Bay who repeatedly came to meetings without reading the books: stop providing cookies. A few, he said, showed up just for the cookies.

Now that Frank and Graham were in minimum, life beyond prison was tantalizingly close for them. Frank had begun studying for his real estate licence and Graham had received approval for three Unescorted Temporary Absences (UTAs), during which he planned to visit a university campus to discuss completing his degree. They wanted to know what kind of work Vince had found. Vince was a former Collins Bay Book Club member and protege of Carol's who had left prison some months before I joined the book club. I told them he was moving furniture. They were shocked. Graham said that surely, given Vince's financial services background, he would have found something in sales at the very least. It was as though Graham was calculating his own likelihood of success based on Vince's. Graham joked, "I've done more time in the hole than Vince did in jail."

"What am I going to do, Frankie?" he asked, looking at his buddy. He said that if all else failed, he would join his mother's fudge business. They laughed, and Frank's turned into a dry hacking cough.

We talked for a few minutes more, mainly about the parental neglect in the book we would be discussing that evening. Then they had to get their books and prepare for book club. By the 5 p.m. meeting time, darkness had fallen and I had to make my way alone across the prison complex to the programs building. It was as inky as that night in Hampstead nine years earlier, when I'd been mugged. There were no guards evident on the grounds.

I thought about what Frank had said in his journal pages about the prison, how there were no guards to prevent anybody from leaving the property and how the general atmosphere was relaxed. The main requirement of inmates was to stay within the marked perimeter and to show up on time for Count on their range.

Great. I picked up my pace, looking over my shoulder several times. I made it to the building and saw Graham and Frank inside. How strange that I now felt safe with a former Hells Angel convicted of extortion and a man who had shot up a restaurant.

This was the first meeting where the Beaver Creek Book Club would be flying solo, without Carol. I was curious to see whether Graham and Frank would fall quiet in deference to Phoebe. Donna and Meg were still there. So the other inmates hadn't objected to their presence.

That month's book was *The Glass Castle*, Jeannette Walls's bestselling memoir of a deprived childhood. The book opens memorably with Walls, by then a successful New York writer and editor living on Park Avenue, in the back seat of a taxi. When, from the taxi window, she spots her mother rooting through garbage in a Dumpster, she slides down in her seat. No longer able to deal with the hidden shame of her impoverished upbringing, Walls decides to tell it all, from her father's alcoholism and unstable work in a succession of mining towns to her mother's skewed priorities: ranking art supplies above food for the family. The story of the four Walls kids' upbringing amid abject poverty and neglect was often difficult to read, and I found her parents' betrayals (like stealing the children's money and not sharing food with them) horrifying. I couldn't stop thinking about the scenes where Jeannette falls out of the family's moving car and the parents fail to come back for a while and where the parents make the kids travel with the furniture in a U-Haul trailer whose back doors swing open on the highway. The father glamorizes these episodes on the lam as "Rex Walls–style" events. As the kids age, they figure out that Rex Walls–style isn't adventure but abuse. Graham told Carol in a letter that the book was "a great read," and that he had zipped through it in three or four days. One of the weaker readers, he told her, finished it in "two days straight. That's great though because it means the book club is encouraging guys to read a lot more, which is exactly what we were hoping for!"

Graham established his leadership off the top by taking attendance. It was the book club's version of Count. As he called out their names, gruff voices around the table barked "right here" or "present" in response. There were a couple of new faces, including Hal, a slight, gentle-looking man in his thirties.

Phoebe kicked off the discussion in a very English-teacher way by asking why people write memoirs.

"To excise guilt," said Tom, more as a statement of fact than as an opinion.

"Exorcise demons," added Earl, saying how some kids feel haunted by things that make them different from others. His voice was less gravelly than on the previous month and I noticed he was sporting a grey goatee.

"Help others," suggested a tall bespectacled middle-aged man whose name tag read BYRNE.

"Financial gain," said someone at the far end of the table.

And as we were all laughing at that comment, Graham said, "To tell their version of events, right? People like Cheney and Bush both wrote separate memoirs of the same events and they have very different interpretations of how things happened."

But the reasons they offered for why Jeannette Walls chose to write *her* memoir were more nuanced. "I think in Jeannette Walls's case," said Frank, "she was so successful and sort of hobnobbing and people looked at her a certain way, but this was a way for telling everybody, deep inside, I'm not really like that."

Doc agreed: "She was tired of being ashamed of her parents. There was a deep sense of guilt and she wanted to expose herself."

"I think there's a lot of healing that probably comes from putting that story down on paper," said Richard, who I had now decided was in his sixties—about the same age as Frank.

"I'd even be more cynical than that," said Tom. "I'd take it one step further and say that she's trying to profit off of the misery that her family endured." He'd done some background research on Walls, he told the others, and what he found out about her celebrity reporting made him dislike her. "And I really don't like anybody who's not proud of where they came from," he said. "To me that shows incredibly weak character."

"So you don't think she redeemed herself?" asked Phoebe.

"No I don't think she redeemed herself," he said, his voice oozing sarcasm, just as it had during last month's standoff with Carol.

We talked on for a bit about whether Walls, as an adult, did enough to offer help to her parents in New York. The men puzzled over why the parents were too proud to line up at soup kitchens when their kids were young and starving, yet once the kids were grown, the parents frequently ate at soup kitchens and other free-food programs and refused to take charity from their children.

Then Graham spoke up. "I know we're going there, but my terrible impulsiveness makes it hard to wait much longer. What I'm wondering is, who do you think bears more responsibility for the way those kids were treated? The mother or the father? We had this discussion earlier, me and Ann and Frankie."

"I was thinking it was the mother," said Mitchell, the only black man in the group. "But I think she got some mental illness."

Of course, I thought. All the signs were there: she slept all day and the children couldn't get her out of bed.

"But if Rex Walls wants to skedaddle during the night, Rex Walls–style, doesn't the mother have the responsibility to say, 'Hey I'm going to grab my kids, I'm going to go do something?'" persisted Graham. "I mean at one time Jeannette actually puts it to her mother and says, 'Hey listen, why don't you leave?'"

"She might have the responsibility," said Donna. "But did she have the capability?" Like Mitchell, Donna suspected that the mother was mentally ill, and she was diagnosing borderline personality disorder.

"I felt the mother's actions were more heinous than Rex's," I said. "When I put down the book the two images that stuck with me were the mother eating the chocolate bar under the blanket and not offering any to her children, who are starving, and the revelation that the mother owned that million-dollar piece of land. She conned her kids into thinking that their life was glorious and adventuresome."

"It's too complicated," said Hal. "They fed into each other—enablement or whatever. At times the father was worse. At times the mother was worse. How do you even pick in that situation?"

Doc weighed in by saying both parents were equally responsible. "It was really a classic story of codependency with rampant alcoholism," he said.

"I disagree with that," jumped in Frank. "Rex is not your classic alcoholic. He had a period of time there where he wouldn't drink. He would come through for them when he had to, and bring groceries. A real alcoholic is the father in *Angela's Ashes*," he said, referring to Frank McCourt's popular memoir of his miserable Irish Catholic childhood where the father would "drink the wages." "In *Angela's Ashes*, the father just showed up when he had nowhere else to go. *That* was an abusive father."

Richard said that he'd found something on page 61 that we should consider. I loved it when the guys noted page numbers. The passage described the moment when Jeannette and her brother Brian's chemistry experiment exploded, setting their "laboratory" in an abandoned shed on fire. Their father told them that in physics the zone above the flames was considered a borderline between turbulence and order. Richard said: "That's the metaphor for Rex's life."

"Order and turbulence," said Byrne. "Like when Jeannette is in the hospital recovering from burns. That was order." Her dress had caught fire while she was cooking hot dogs and she was in the hospital for six weeks after she received skin grafts. I recalled how she had enjoyed the three square meals a day and the nurse's concern and care. "And then Rex comes in," said Byrne, "and says we're going to leave the hospital Rex Walls–style and it's turbulence again." Rex was skipping out on the hospital bill.

Then Phoebe invited us to pile in with our favourite moment of Rex Walls at his lowest.

"Pimping his daughter out in the bar was pretty bad," said Earl.

"I don't think that was the worst," said Mitchell, as he poured himself a coffee from the coffee machine, claiming that Rex's worst moment was *after* pimping her out—when he denied that she'd been molested and claimed that the guy had probably only pawed her.

For Byrne it was the time when Rex came home drunk and smeared the mouth of the clay Shakespeare bust that Walls's older sister, Lori, had made for her Cooper Union art school application portfolio. "That was a very, very evil thing to do," said Byrne.

"His whole life was framed with excuses," said Richard. "He couldn't hold a job because the Mafia was mixed up in the unions and they wouldn't let him work." Almost everyone around the table broke into laughter, the laughter of recognition that Richard was bang on.

But for Graham, the father's greatest offence was risking the sexual abuse of the kids by his own relatives back in his hometown of Welch, West Virginia. "They'd lived in cars, they'd lived in pretty well every shithole you could think of, eating out of Dumpsters, but he leads the kids into a situation where they're likely to be molested," said Graham. He leaned forward on the table and thumped it. He had warned Frank and me before the meeting that he might not be able to check his emotions in the meeting when it came to Rex exposing his children to that danger. "You're gonna get me going and I'm just gonna go right off," he had said. "I can see it coming." Again I was seeing that strong moral code he had when it came to family.

It reminded me about something else we'd talked about, the three of us, before the meeting. We'd reflected on our own parents and whether we had any experiences comparable to those of the Walls kids. Frank said it wasn't unusual for kids to fall out of moving cars in the 1950s, especially if they were "old junkers." I said that before seat belts, many kids had scars on their chins from sitting on their parents' laps in the front seat and banging their mouths on the dashboard. I pointed to the scar beneath my lower lip.

"I smashed my head on the dashboard," agreed Frank.

"That explains a lot," said Graham.

I told the two of them that the way Rex taught his kids about geology reminded me of my father, who used to take us on rock hunts—sometimes on abandoned mine sites. "We were usually cold and wet, but we learned a lot," I said. But that was just the charming side of Rex, not the negligent side.

"Was *I* abused?" mused Frank. "My parents used to work, so they were never home. I'd be in the house all by myself. I was only eight or nine years old and I'd go to school myself, come back and have to let myself in. Sometimes I'd be walking to school and walk into a park and forget about school."

"I never lived in a place more than a year, I don't think," said Graham. I couldn't imagine living with that much uncertainty. I recalled asking my parents to promise that they wouldn't move until I finished high school.

"How many places did you live?" I asked.

"By the time I finished high school I probably lived in seventeen or eighteen different places," he said. He listed two remote Northern Ontario towns and two Southern Ontario cities. "And I lived in Winnipeg; Calgary; Regina; Blue Ridge, Georgia. Blue Ridge was horrendous, full of hillbillies. I was originally born in Montreal. We lived in Quebec City." Five provinces, and one town on the Georgia-Tennessee border. And in one city they moved five times. Sure sounded like life Rex Walls–style.

"But why?" I asked.

"'Cause my parents were always up to stuff. We were always on the move. My father drank lots, but in all fairness to my mother, she would step up and make sure that we had everything we needed."

Graham's family's nomadic lifestyle helped explain his questions to the book club members about the Walls parents. He asked the group whether they would describe the Walls parents' conduct as neglect or abuse.

For some reason, everyone looked to Doc for the answer. Maybe they were seeking the clinical definition. "To me, neglect is the absence of doing something," he said. "And abuse is the act of doing something that would be harmful. Neglect accumulates over time and becomes abuse."

"Which raises the question," said Richard, "can you be a negligent irresponsible parent, and still be a loving parent?"

"Yes, yes. I think you can love somebody but neglect them, deprive them of the basic necessities of life," said Graham.

This was difficult ground to map, but several of the men wanted to talk about the parents' love. A fellow named Jones said that even though he thought of Rex as a "deadbeat and a waste type of a man," Rex was redeemed somewhat by his Christmas present to the children one year when he had no money for gifts. He took each child outside one desert night to look up at the stars and gave them each a star for Christmas. Jeannette had expressed some skepticism and then decided on a planet: Venus, which shone brighter than anything else in the western sky that night. "I thought that was pretty decent of him," he said.

Bookman and Byrne both pointed to parental love in the form of education: how the mother, Rose Mary, and Rex brought home bags of books from the library and often home-schooled their kids at a level that was higher than that offered by the local schools.

"How much care they took in making sure that the kids were educated but they didn't give them a pair of shoes, you know what I mean?" countered Graham. "Or something to eat."

We plumbed the topic of the parents' selfishness: how the mother squandered food money on paint, and wouldn't sell the diamond ring that the kids found in order to buy groceries.

Graham said that he thought the author blamed her mother more, for not having the strength to leave Rex. He then asked the others whether they thought Walls had embellished her story in places. I was reminded of his skepticism at Collins Bay when we discussed *Three Cups of Tea*. The question prompted Tom to restate the moral question he had alluded to earlier: whether the author should have profited from her family's misery. He and others focused on the writer's shame, and pointed out that she seemed relatively content growing up and only appeared to develop shame when she achieved success.

Graham had handled the session masterfully. Over and over again, he spotted when guys wanted to talk, and he created space in the conversation to invite them in. If they'd forgotten their point, he had an admirable ability to remember what they'd been starting to say. Frank had recruited strong analytical readers. And Phoebe established herself as an agile facilitator. The details of the text were as fresh in her mind as if she'd reread the entire book the night before. I could see that the Beaver Creek Book Club was going to be just fine, even without Carol.

When the meeting broke up, I was without a guide to get back to reception. I would have to find my way alone past the men's living units. I hesitated for a moment before leaving the programs building, but Frank materialized beside me, perhaps sensing my discomfort. "I'll escort you back," he said. I knew I was safe with Frank. I remembered asking Graham once if he was ever afraid of his former gang members in prison and he replied jokingly that he was only ever afraid of Frankie.

Frank and I walked along in silence for a moment. Then he asked me if I would pass on a message to Vince when I saw him. I seemed to recall something in the volunteer training about not doing favours for inmates. They'd feel obliged to do favours for you.

"If I can," I said.

"Tell him, 'The Beggar-master says hi,'" he said.

"The Beggar-master says hi," I repeated, my throat suddenly dry like Frank's. Was this some kind of code? I wondered.

We parted at the reception building.

"Good night."

"Good night."

I drove home that evening thinking about Frank's message, wondering what it meant and knowing that I was scheduled to see Vince two days later. At Carol's urging, I would be meeting Vince for coffee for the first time since he left prison. He had robbed banks to feed an addiction but she believed that with lots of support he could stay out of trouble. Moreover she was proud of him. Even though he was a graduate of the Collins Bay Book Club, she was giving him the books that they were reading and he was reading along with them on the outside.

I turned on the windshield wipers. There was a light rain. What were the chances that any of the men could overcome, like Jeanette Walls, their difficult circumstances and would our book discussions really help counter the experiences they'd suffered in their own young lives? It was hard to imagine. That night at home I looked up two more of the men. I learned that Hal was only a teenager when he killed his parents and siblings and that a man with the same name as Byrne had killed his wife.

I had no difficulty spotting Vince in the Arbor Room at the university when I met him two days later on Remembrance Day. He hadn't shaved off the long goatee and moustache that many men grow in prison to look tough. Perhaps it was still necessary to look tough in his halfway house. We stood outside under a ginkgo tree and listened to the bugle and the sad tribute to the fallen soldiers: "They will not grow old as we grow old." After the service, we got coffees and sat down. He was gentle, with large dark eyes that rarely blinked and that communicated deep emotional pain. He told me his story, which included a traumatic childhood experience. I told him about my daughter's illness. We commiserated with each other.

"I have a message from Frank, but I don't know if I should give it to you," I said, warming my hands on the cup. "I don't know what it means and it might be an inappropriate communication."

"What is it?" he said.

I hesitated, then decided that the message was probably innocuous. "The Beggar-master says hi."

He laughed to the point of gripping his side to suppress a stitch.

"What does it mean?"

"The Beggar-master is a character in *A Fine Balance*, that novel by Rohinton Mistry. It's a really good book and I recommended it to Frank to read."

I laughed with relief. How innocent the message had actually been. How indicative of the culture of books that Carol was creating in the prisons. I should have read *A Fine Balance* that summer after all.

"The setting is India," Vince continued, "and the Beggar-master, he'd be like the pimp beggar for all the beggars. Frank always joked with me that he was the Beggar-master. So the message means that he's my master. Maybe when he gets out he'll find me some work."

It was only later that I picked up my copy of *A Fine Balance* and discovered that the street beggars in Mistry's novel paid protection money to the Beggar-master. I wondered for a minute why Frank had given himself the name, then concluded it was just an innocent joke.

11

JUST DO THE DAY

THE GHOST OF TOM JOAD shadowed us that November. He clanked in the prison gates and grew restless in the tents of the Occupy movement. He agitated at the prison overcrowding and watched as two men in the prison were stabbed with shanks. Or at least that's how I saw it after a month of reading John Steinbeck's rhythmic, angry prose in *The Grapes of Wrath*, the Collins Bay Book Club's November book.

Even though I didn't warm to Tom Joad, the protagonist in Steinbeck's Depression-era novel, I saw aspects of his story all around me during those cold, grey weeks, particularly at Collins Bay. That's the gift of a timelessly relevant novel. When I remarked on this to one of the prison chaplains, she reminded me that Bruce Springsteen had written a ballad about Tom Joad, champion of the homeless and jobless. The song is called "The Ghost of Tom Joad." Perhaps Joad, the parolee in Steinbeck's dirge for America, haunted everyone.

The collision between art and life started the day before book group with an incident at the prison. Collins Bay went into lockdown and the book club meeting was cancelled. It would be at least two weeks before we could reconvene. I joked with Carol that maybe the men had orchestrated some mischief to buy extra time to finish the book. It was a long read at 455 pages, even though Steinbeck wrote the Pulitzer Prize–winning novel in only one hundred days. At times I could only read it in short bursts because the story was so bleak: the Joad family is evicted from their tenant farm in drought-stricken Oklahoma and travels in a jalopy to California in search of work picking fruit, only to wind up in a migrant tent city facing more hunger and misery. Is prison better or worse than their predicament? Steinbeck asks. I guessed from speaking to the guys it was pretty much the same.

But the real reason for the delay at Collins Bay was more sobering. "A fellow was stabbed in the eye," a staffer told us. "An inmate on 6 Block. New arrival. One of those things out of the blue. Can you imagine being blind in a prison?"

Defenceless, was what I imagined. My mind went immediately to the stabbing scene in *The Grapes of Wrath*. Tom Joad describes how he and another guy were drunk at a dance and how the feeling of the knife in his body sobered him up. When the guy with the knife came at him again, Tom grabbed a shovel and hit him on the head, killing the man and landing himself in prison.

According to a staffer, an inmate had recognized the new arrival and targeted him—something to do with a shooting on the outside. The stabbing happened during changeover and that meant the lockdown wouldn't be restricted to just one cellblock. Guards would have to search the whole prison for weapons.

Gaston wrote in his journal that it was the second stabbing in the past week and that it looked like the inmates would be locked down for a long stretch. He predicted that the lockdown would once again delay his attempt to book a conjugal visit. For weeks, he'd been trying to arrange a seventy-two-hour Private Family Visit with his wife in one of the prison's two-bedroom apartment units because she was crumbling under the stress.

As for the first of the two stabbings, it had happened a few days earlier, on Ben's cellblock, 4 Block, the prison's toughest unit. Ben had sensed that something was brewing and scribbled a few lines in his journal:

Up waiting to go for breakfast, strange feeling in the air two small fights last night nothing much about it. One of them seems like it's not over. Went for breakfast, boiled eggs on Sunday. I came back on the range I see one of the guys in a fight last nite walking down the range all bloodied, I'm like man here's a lockdown for sure. (Ya he got stab up this morning). He got caught sleeping no good in prison don't matter how big you are. That's his own fault should have been up and ready.

Once the guards unlock the cells each morning, anyone still sleeping is vulnerable. The victim on Ben's unit might not have known that because he was a "fish," prison slang for a newbie. This particular fish had already annoyed the guys on his cellblock by trying to fit in too quickly, according to Ben. But he sealed his fate when he bumped into a man who "had seniority" and failed to apologize. Even Ben didn't sound sympathetic. Perhaps that was because he too had once been caught with his guard down and the incident landed him in Collins Bay. Carol had told me that Ben had been surprised by an armed home invader and had shot and killed the intruder. The incident was still unclear to me, though, and I assumed there were other extenuating circumstances that had led to Ben's conviction for manslaughter.

Two days after the bloodied inmate staggered to the guard post and collapsed, Ben wrote, "One inmate in the hole, the other in the hospital." Amidst the violence, he wrote a line about finding solace in the Joad family's strength. "The family, especially Ma, having that perseverance to keeping moving on no matter what is coming at you."

I'd seen the shanks that had previously been seized from inmates in Kingston prisons. One was carved from a toothbrush. Others were whittled down three-sided plastic rulers, filed metal blades or curved daggers and there was a hammer-shiv with a blade nearly ten inches long. Most were crude tools that would rip and lacerate. I couldn't imagine what horrible damage they would do, especially to an eye. Inmates fashioned the handles from scavenged padding, held together with a spiral of cloth-based adhesive tape. The grip styling struck me as familiar, but it was only later that I twigged. It had been borrowed from that most Canadian of icons: the taped hockey stick.

Even though I had grown accustomed to the prison environment, the knifings rattled me. My usual route to book club took us through what seemed to me less-supervised reaches of the prison. The Strip has a large guard station at the top and another halfway down. But at the second station we had to turn left and leave the main building through a door that the guards released. From there it was a long route along a narrow sidewalk flanked by a chain-link fence on the left and a thin stretch of grass on the right, as you made your way the hundred or so metres to the building that housed the chapel and the workshop. No guards were permanently stationed along the route. The previous month, a group of inmates from the prison workshop had passed us on that stretch. The sidewalk was so narrow that we had to accommodate each other by walking single file. They were men I didn't know, men who weren't in the book club.

I could have stepped out onto the grass and given them a wide berth, but I thought that might have been disrespectful. It's the same logic that made me reserve judgment about the two men in Hampstead before they attacked me. It would have been insulting to turn and rush to our little garden door. Also you don't run from a bear. It gives the bear permission to chase you. We passed each other single file without incident.

I refrained from discussing my renewed unease with Carol when I saw her at our women's book club meeting in Toronto that week. I didn't want to distress the others. As part of the next phase of Carol's efforts to show the men that discussing books could broaden their world, she had asked our women's group to read *The Grapes of Wrath* at the same time as the fellows in Collins Bay. We would make comments on the book to send to the men on a first-name-only basis and receive comments back. It was the first time the Collins Bay prison book club would read in tandem with a women's book club "on the outs."

Our women's book club had been running for six years and the members were affluent, well-educated friends of ours in their fifties and older. One or two were visibly nervous about communicating in writing with inmates, and some thought Carol was batty to even suggest it. But no one says no to Carol. So, with one woman altering her first name to protect her identity—"Could I just be Lillian instead of Lillian-Rose?"—the two wildly different book groups agreed to read three books together. In addition to *The Grapes of Wrath*, we would share Roddy Doyle's novel about an abused woman, *The Woman Who Walked Into Doors*, and American author Diane Ackerman's *The Zookeeper's Wife*, a non-fiction book about a zookeeper in wartime Poland who hid Jews in empty animal cages.

While the lockdown postponed the prison book club's meeting, the women's meeting went ahead in Toronto. We gathered at Lillian-Rose's art-filled three-storey brick house, which occupied a corner lot in a leafy downtown neighbourhood. She served a hot pear-and-apple crumble with vanilla ice cream, three cheeses with crackers, dried apricots, figs, wine and tea. We filled our plates and made our way to the living room, settling on comfortable chesterfields or in armchairs.

Betty kicked it off by saying she found the book incredibly powerful. "When the Joads were picking peaches for two and a half cents a bucket you got such a vivid sense of how utterly desperate they were," she said. "And I thought it was an appropriate book for today. It's about the haves and have-nots."

"The 1 percent and the 99 percent," said Deborah, who had lived in a commune in the '70s. The Occupy movement and its instantly viral slogan, "We are the 99 percent," were on everyone's minds, whether we sympathized with the movement or not. Two months earlier, Occupy Wall Street had taken over Zuccotti Park in Manhattan to protest social and economic inequality and the power of the richest 1 percent of society. As we sat talking at Lillian-Rose's, across town Occupy Toronto protesters were burning eviction notices, while not far from the Collins Bay prison, Occupy Kingston was manning its encampment. No question, it was Tom Joad's kind of scene.

Deborah told us that she had dined with Cesar Chavez, the farm worker who led the boycott of table grapes in 1968 in support of underpaid farm workers in California. Like the Joads, Chavez's family lost their farm and moved to California in search of work during the Great Depression. We went on like that for a bit, trading information about social upheavals, industrial agriculture, the history of organized labour in the United States and the origins of the Dust Bowl. But then we got down to how distressing and heartbreaking the story was. Carol and Ruth confessed they had cried while reading it.

Like Ben, we agreed that the one uplifting message was Ma Joad's philosophy of resilience and how it would help anyone, especially someone in prison. Carol found the passage and read it aloud. It was all about toughness born of persevering through hunger and illness and having the goal of just getting through the day, and it was narrated in Ma's folksy Oklahoma vernacular.

"You don't look back and you don't look ahead," summarized Carol. "You just do the day."

When we'd talked ourselves out, we drifted out into the evening, where the smell of decaying maple leaves reminded us that winter was approaching. We lingered and gossiped, offered each other rides home, calling goodbye as we parted, laughing and chatting. It was a stark contrast to the prison book club, where the men left in a frantic dash not to be late for Count.

While we were enjoying our pear-and-apple crumble at Lillian-Rose's, the lockdown and cell search was in full swing at Collins Bay. The guards searched Ben's cell that day and he had no way of knowing if they had found and read his journal. "I'll just clean up their muddy boot prints left on my chair and desk and organize back my books and keep on moving," he wrote in his journal, echoing Ma Joad's stoic message.

He didn't elaborate on what a search entailed. But I phoned Vince, and he filled me in. It's not just rifling through belongings. The first step, he said, is a body search.

I sensed he was holding something back. "You mean a strip search?"

"Yes." He said the guards order you to remove your clothes, open your mouth and move your tongue around to show that nothing's inside, then lift each foot to show that nothing is stuck to your soles. Finally they tell you to bend forward. Then you dress and sit in the common area while the guards comb your "house," jail talk for *cell*. They check the mattresses and pillows for cuts, examine toiletries, shake out clothes, open and shake books and take pictures off the wall. They pull the refrigerators away from the walls and ensure that the sealing tape on the televisions hasn't been tampered with. Until each inmate and cell is searched, prisoners remain in their cells twenty-four hours a day.

If the guards suspect that an inmate is concealing weapons or drugs in a body cavity, a doctor may perform a cavity search. It's hard to imagine hiding weapons in an orifice, but Vince said: "They wrap it in cellophane and shove it up their ——." He didn't say the word.

I shuddered at the image, but knew the searches had to be done. Also, I knew that the purging of any weapons from 4 Block would be a big relief for Ben.

The Collins Bay Book Club finally reconvened on the last day of November under grey skies after a night of heavy rain. I met Carol for tea a block west of the prison. She had bought several packages of chocolate chip cookies in a clear plastic wrapper for the men. I told her that Graham had advised us to stop bringing in cookies, and she agreed that it was good advice for future meetings. At prison reception Carol fished them out of her grocery bag for the guard, who inspected them through the plastic, then ran them through the X-ray machine.

As we walked The Strip and turned left to leave the main building for the smaller one where the book club met, I was thinking again about the stabbings, the long walk between the buildings past unfamiliar inmates and the guards' stab-proof vests. Now I knew why inmates taped magazines to their abdomens as body armor. I should have brought my back issues of *The New Yorker*. It was my ninth month in the prison book club and I was starting to regress into the post-traumatic anxiety that had followed my mugging in Hampstead.

Carol and I stepped through the doorway onto the narrow sidewalk. I held my satchel close to my body. The high walls flanking the prison walkway reared up like the brick garden walls lining our street in Hampstead. What would happen to the bag, with its precious tape recorder and notebooks, if I were attacked? I tried to calculate whether I'd be able to pitch it over the chain-link fence. My mind shot back to throwing the yellow purse. That first summer in England, I'd bought a bright yellow purse at a little shop in Highgate to replace my old torn brown one. It wasn't expensive, but it contained our family's passports and other identity cards, as well as the house keys. When the muggers came at me that day, some autonomic response kicked in: "While you are running, throw your purse over the garden wall."

It didn't occur to me that throwing the purse might provoke them. It was an involuntary reflex born of years of recurring dreams about lost purses and luggage. But that was why, when one of my assailants was choking me and the other was trying to grab my legs, they found only my cellphone and the car key. When I regained consciousness and stumbled into the garden yelling for my husband in an unrecognizable voice, I saw the purse on the pebbled walkway that led to the front door. Only then did I fully realize I had thrown it. For a moment, amid the shock of the assault and the joy of being alive, I felt heroic. I had saved our identities. I had saved the family.

On Collins Bay's narrow sidewalk, three unfamiliar inmates walked toward Carol and me. One was bald and heavy with tattoos climbing up his thick neck and a stoned look in his eyes. I couldn't look at the others. I just stared ahead, and then we were past them and at the building. Two guards waved to us from their post.

In the meeting room, some of the men had already arrived for book club. These were *my* inmates and I felt safer among them. They poured cups of coffee from the drip machine in the corner and came to sit in the circle. I watched the cookies disappear in four-biscuit handfuls. No one volunteered any comment about the stabbings or the lockdown and I didn't feel like asking about it. Instead, I made small talk about how the soil in parts of Oklahoma really is red. I explained to them that I'd lived next door in Texas for four years.

Carol started off the meeting with praise and encouragement for tackling *The Grapes of Wrath*. She pronounced it "wroth," the word familiar to her from the King James version of the Old Testament. "It was a tough read. If you finished it, I'm impressed. If you sampled it enough to get a sense of it, I'm also impressed." Four of the fifteen said they'd finished the book. Then unrelated chatter erupted among a few of the inmates in the corner but Carol put an end to it quickly. "You with us?" she asked, staring at them. The reaction was instantaneous. They fell silent.

Order restored, Carol reminded them that this was the first month her women's book club had read the same book as the men and that she would read aloud comments from Evelyn, Lillian and the others to start the conversation.

Gaston, his baseball cap on backward over his brush cut, interrupted: "Can I join your book club when I get out?"

"I don't see why not," said Carol, forgetting briefly that Lillian-Rose would have freaked out. Carol had no gene for risk aversion. But seeing my raised eyebrows, she corrected herself and said her preferred plan was to set up book clubs for members when they left prison.

I could see the men were curious about the women in our Toronto book group. Ben, his lanky form slung over one of the chairs, ran his hand through his dreads and asked whether "at least" some of them were young.

"Well, Betty's this young twenty-year-old redhead," Carol said coyly, shaving forty years off her real age. She read aloud Betty's comment, which described in anguished terms how trapped the characters were.

"I think she is very intelligent," said Dread, his dreads stylishly twisted with gold metallic yarn and partly stuffed into an overstretched black tam.

We were at risk of the men getting distracted by Carol's description of Betty, but then Gaston got to the meat of Betty's observation by disagreeing with her comment. "I don't think at any point the people in the book actually thought it was hopeless," he said. "'Cause they were continually going forward." He said it was evident in how they found a truck and fixed it up for the long drive west to California. The other guys nodded.

Ben agreed. More than anyone in the book club, he had internalized the Joads' determination. "Keep on movin' when life gets a bit hard," he said. He was resigned to a rudimentary determinism and said he wasn't complaining anymore about being in prison. "I think our life is painted out. In that day you just have to live for that day." I was amazed at how profoundly it had affected him.

The angle that really caught the men's attention, though, was Tom's decision to flout his parole restrictions in order to go west with his family. He wasn't allowed to leave Oklahoma. Carol asked if he did the right thing.

"Family comes first," said Deshane.

I looked over at Deshane. He was wearing basketball shoes so shiny they seemed plasticized. By then, he had shared with me that he had OCD and was doing time for manslaughter, aggravated assault and weapons charges. A sort of Cyrano de Bergerac at the prison, he fashioned himself a crafter of what he called "lovey-dovey" poetry for other inmates. "Guys who are not really good at romancing their girls with nice words, I just write something for them and they send it, acting like it's them, right," he had told me proudly. He didn't charge for the service.

Dread disagreed with Deshane, saying that crossing the state line would make Tom a wanted man and would bring heat down on his family. The men told us about the ROPE (Repeat Offender Parole Enforcement) squads in Canada that they said shadow parolees, especially upon first release, ready to haul them in at any sign of a parole violation. "Big jacked-up dudes," was how Peter described them, his face strangely red. It agitated the guys just to think of these posses. Dread and a few of the others argued about the differences between parole conditions today and in the 1930s. Most decided it was easier in the '30s. For a while they didn't need Carol to prompt discussion.

Then Ben wanted to talk about the humanity and goodness of the Joads. He pointed to the final scene of the book where the Joads' daughter Rose of Sharon, at Ma's prompting, suckles a starving man who can no longer take in solid food. She had just given birth to a stillborn child and her breasts were full of milk.

The room fell strangely quiet as the men considered the image of a woman breastfeeding a man. Their eyes grew wide. I figured some were just imagining breasts.

"Wow," said one man.

"She fulfilled her purpose," said Ben, looking around the room with his gentle downward-sloping eyes.

"No, no, no, hold on, hold on," said Dread, who, as usual, challenged Ben. "It wasn't even her idea, and it's not like she was a pervert. The guy was so sick he couldn't hold down anything, so the only form of nutriment he could take was baby's milk."

Carol pointed out to Ben and Dread that they were actually agreeing with each other, though Dread didn't look convinced.

Ben's appreciation of goodness and humanity made me hopeful for him. I had seen it in his journal before the meeting began. He had broken into a shy grin when I opened it, as though he had a secret. There was a card wedged into the crease. His journal page that day described how he had found a birthday card inside one of the books that our women's book club had donated to the Collins Bay Book Club the previous summer. He saw that the card was addressed to someone named Ann and contained a warm message from a friend. He assumed the "Ann" was me and he wrote in his journal:

[I] started thinking about friends and what real friends are: And that is someone that has no bad judgment about you, you are comfortable around them and speak, act and express yourself freely, then I said Ann is a "great friend." Thank you.

I let down my guard and we both laughed. It was just what I needed to feel safe inside. And I was glad that he felt encouraged by my friendship.

I came out of my reverie at that point to hear Carol telling the men that she and Ruth had cared so much about the characters, they had cried while reading the book.

"But it's not even a true story," said Dread.

"It's touching, but I wouldn't cry," said Ben.

"You cried," Dread goaded Ben. "You told me you did." The room erupted in laughter and loud talk.

The men wrote down comments for the women to consider. Peter was the only one to dwell on Steinbeck's left-wing politics. "I believe the book questioned the morals of a capitalist society and demonstrated how ruthless men in power are willing to be towards the masses," he wrote carefully in pencil. By that month, Peter had joined his buddy Gaston's classics reading project and Carol ordered a second set of the Professor Duffy–prescribed books for him.

Before we broke up, Gaston asked, "I have one question in regards to your women book club members. You say they're all in their twenties, but they seem to have older-generation names. I'm not sure you're being 100 percent honest." Carol and I burst into laughter. *Busted.*

I was once again sleeping over at Carol's island house so I could return to Collins Bay the following day to chat with Deshane about his poems. Poetry is a great vessel for anger, as Steinbeck had demonstrated in the book, and I wondered whether Deshane's "lovey-dovey" poems would have a dark underside. By the time Carol and I arrived at the house, the setting sun appeared as a glowing orange slit of light along the horizon beneath a lid of black cloud that covered the entire sky. It felt like the eye of the world closing.

At bedtime, Carol turned the thermostat down to fifteen degrees Celsius while I watched with dismay. This was probably a sleep strategy because, on previous visits, I had heard her up at night. I found an extra blanket made from the still-musky wool of the sheep from Topsy Farm next door and crawled under the covers with one of Bryan's many books on Churchill.

Long before the sun rose, I awoke shivering. As I walked to the car to catch the pre-dawn ferry, a coyote yipped in the field sometimes occupied by the Topsy sheep and their look-alike protectors, the white Pyrenees dogs. The sun rose as an orange wildfire, so that the hay wagons, bales, tractor and barn on the eastern rise appeared as black silhouettes. It had been a wet year on Amherst Island—nothing Dust Bowl about it.

At Collins Bay, two inmates joined the chaplain and me as we walked down The Strip: Joao, the blue-eyed boyish chapel cleaner and occasional book club member, and another guy, who wasn't in the book club. When we got to the narrow sidewalk, the men fell in behind us. The other guy was bigger than Joao and began insulting him, signing off with a smack to the back of his head as he split off to the workshop. Joao said nothing and the chaplain hadn't noticed, but it was my first concrete glimpse of bullying in prison, and evidence that the walkway could be lawless territory.

Deshane was waiting for me. As he handed me his journal, a sheaf of drafts fell out and he rushed to stuff them back in because he said he didn't want me to see rough work. One draft was a "Godly" poem for the chaplain, he said, but he let me hear two lines, which I admired. The couplet tapped into Delta blues and gospel, but its rhythm was all rap. He ended it with an admonition to let go of the past and let the devil keep "bouncin'."

I opened the journal. The first poem was called "Only You." He read it aloud to me, again in a rap rhythm, speeding over some words and landing hard at the end of each line, imagining that if love was "a crime," he would be doing "time" like C-Murder.

"C-Murder?"

"Yeah. The dude that got life. Got a life sentence."

Deshane was surprised that I didn't recognize the dude. C-Murder was an American rapper, convicted for fatally shooting a sixteen-year-old fan at a Louisiana nightclub. Unbelievably, the musician had managed to release an album while serving life at Angola, Louisiana's maximum-security prison farm, famed for its inmate rodeo. A life sentence was not a metaphor that most poets would employ to describe loving someone *forever*. I wondered how this image might strike the girlfriend receiving the poem.

"I didn't know I had it in me till I got arrested," Deshane said, referring to his writing ability.

I offered to get him some books of poetry, but he was quick to tell me that he wasn't interested in "old school" stuff. "I like poems that are more affectionate, about feelings, about pain," he said. "Do you ever go to Hallmark and they have a card for each thought? That's what I like."

It seemed safe to ask a guy who liked Hallmark cards more about the crime he had committed.

"I was defending myself—I got stabbed," he said. "But they said I used too much force. It was a handgun. The person got shot." Tom Joad said virtually the same thing. Deshane said that he had been at Collins Bay for five years and in lower security for a year, "but then they sent me back here, over some, say, 'security incidents'—and a butter knife was sharpened."

A butter knife was sharpened. The person got shot. Always the passive voice. A number of the men used it when describing their crimes, as though they had been mere agents of some force beyond their control. I liked them better when they owned up to what they had done and expressed regret. But I understood the instinct to self-protect.

From the corridor, the chaplain called, "Count." I quickly asked Deshane to write a poem about *The Grapes of Wrath* for next time and read him a sentence from the novel to show him how Steinbeck used rhythm to evoke powerful feelings. The line talked about tear-gassing the hungry rioters in California. When I looked up, there was an odd expression on Deshane's face. It was later that I found out that a police canine unit had captured him by tear-gassing him out of his hiding spot under a porch, after a police dog and pepper spray failed to dislodge him.

On my drive back to Toronto, I detoured close to the Occupy Kingston encampment, remembering that Ben had mentioned his admiration for the Occupiers. Using a park bandstand as a base and a patchwork of tarpaulins, the protesters had created a yurt-like central tent, like the Joads' tarpaulin shelter. Five days later they would be evicted, but not before their campaign had swept in two other prison-related protest groups: End the Prison Industrial Complex and Save Our Prison Farms. The people who end up in prison are usually not the 1 percent.

There and on the darkening highway, as I returned to Toronto, I listened to Springsteen's "The Ghost of Tom Joad" and thought about how Steinbeck might have seen the passing landscape. My gaze took in a line of Russian olive trees shedding their long silvery leaves—the last of the deciduous trees to give up their foliage, flaunting their resilience to poor soil. As Springsteen lamented, I saw that the sumac drupes and bulrush sedges had browned off and in the fields, dry yellow-brown stalks reminded me of arid stretches of Texas and Oklahoma.

12

CHRISTMAS IN PRISON

CHRISTMAS IN PRISON was like a poorly attended Visitors Day in a seniors' home. Many men at Collins Bay remained unvisited and lonely. And those who were visited couldn't count on their loved ones making it past inspection, where guards used frisk searches and sniffer dogs to detect contraband while visitors spread their legs wide to stand on two footprints painted on the floor. The drug-detection equipment was sensitive, and routinely picked up cocaine traces on paper currency because snorters' residue contaminates a large percentage of banknotes in general circulation. Some book club members said they didn't want to put their families through the ordeal.

The season was particularly painful for the fathers in the prison book club. When I talked to Gaston at the beginning of December, he broke into tears as I read in his journal that it would be his third Christmas in a row without his four children. "My son is eleven, and he thinks I'm at work and asks, 'Why isn't Dad coming for Christmas?'" he said, after I finished reading, his voice cracking. "The younger ones say 'Daddy' on the phone but they don't really know who I am. It's a horrible feeling. To be honest, Christmas is the worst time of all." No inmate had cried in front of me before, let alone a serial bank robber with a weakness for crack. I wanted to put my hand on his arm, but I refrained, respecting his dignity.

His remorse was not just as a father, but as a son, because his own parents had never missed Christmas with him. And, as if the holidays couldn't be more depressing, he hadn't spoken to his wife for several days. His journal said that she was frustrated about having to work full-time to support four young children on her own. In Gaston's view, she was the one serving time and he felt helpless. He wiped away his tears, self-conscious not just about weeping, but about a bright red infection that had developed on his nose.

Nor did he expect any presents from his family other than a Christmas card. He said that the restrictions on sending and receiving gifts were too onerous to bother. Three days after Christmas he planned to send his wife $110. It wasn't a Christmas present, just a portion of his pay from his CORCAN job. In the run-up to Christmas he focused instead on reading Robert Louis Stevenson's *Treasure Island* for his reading-the-classics project; *Small Island*, by Andrea Levy, for the book club; and, to feed his devotional needs, the Bible.

One bright spot during the season was "Christmas bag." As Gaston explained it to me, under a federal prison directive allowing certain privileges at Christmas, the inmate-run canteen expanded the variety of goods for sale to the inmates and the men were allowed to spend $175 over the two-week period around the holidays, up from $90 every two weeks during the rest of the year. The canteen managers also took inmates' wish lists into consideration in ordering Christmas stock. While some guys listed vitamin supplements and protein powders to boost their workouts, Ben and some of the Jamaican men asked for cayenne pepper, ackee fruit and salt cod so that they could cook Jamaica's national dish, ackee and salt fish, in the cellblocks' common kitchens. But, as I found out the next month, something in that season's Christmas bag would cause trouble.

Despite Carol's attempts to ensure a good mix of inmates from Collins Bay's ghettoized racial groups, of the fifteen or so men attending book club that day in mid-December, only three were white, and I noticed that they all sat together: Gaston, Peter and Grow-Op. In the five months since Graham and Frank had left for minimum security, the book club had failed to attract many new white inmates to replace them. The other members that day, including Ben, Dread and Deshane, were mainly men from the Caribbean islands or second-generation West Indian Canadians. As I scanned the room, I noticed a black fellow with a name tag that read ROMAN. He appeared to be influential. There was an air of deference in the others' attitudes toward him, or maybe it was just an alertness among the men in his presence. I didn't read the mood as a threatening one, but my antennae were up.

Even though it was only two weeks since my last visit to the prison, my fearfulness had abated somewhat, partly through a disciplined effort to rehearse my father's advice about expecting the best of people and partly through seeing the vulnerability of men like Gaston. Every time fear welled up, I imagined a button marked *No Fear* that I could press to stop the cortisol and adrenalin rushing through my body. Then I shifted my focus to the literature we were about to discuss. *Just think*, I told myself. *Sharing O. Henry with the men!*

We were surprising them with two humorous Christmas-themed short stories by the early-twentieth-century American short story writer and postponing discussion of Andrea Levy's *Small Island* for a month because the men had had only two weeks to read it. We knew that any men who had pushed to finish the novel would be disappointed, but when we asked those who had finished the book to put up their hand, only seven hands went up. Instead, Carol would read the O. Henry stories aloud in the meeting.

She began by explaining that O. Henry was a writer who knew something about life behind bars. He had served three years in prison more than a century earlier for embezzlement, and while in prison in Ohio published short stories under a number of pseudonyms. His real name was William Sydney Porter.

Carol read the stories aloud in her strong, steady voice. At the opening words of O. Henry's famous "The Gift of the Magi," the men fell into a storytelling trance. Even those who usually sat with their backs to the wall, their eyes watching for danger, took up her invitation to close their eyes and listen. I resisted the urge to close my own eyes so that I could take in their reactions. A man to her right turned his chair backward, straddled it and rested his chin on his arms. Beside him sat a man name Olivier, a soft-spoken sometime attendee who was serving a life sentence for second-degree murder. Olivier sat with his lids closed, his afro gathered with an elastic into a pouf on top of his head, a long-toothed hair comb embedded in it. He was lost in the moment.

Carol did not act out the voices of the characters. She let the men's imaginations fill in the details. But she knew which of O. Henry's archaic words and phrases she had to define for the guys as she read: *watch fob* and *meretricious ornamentation* for example. When I finally closed my own eyes, I realized that when the story was read aloud, I absorbed every word. Unlike with reading text on the page, there was no skimming.

"The Gift of the Magi" is an old Christmas favourite of mine. O. Henry imagines a young wife, Della Dillingham Young, who has only $1.87 on Christmas Eve. She sells her much-admired knee-length hair to buy a platinum watch chain for her husband, Jim, as a Christmas present, only to discover that Jim has sold his gold pocket watch to buy a set of jewel-rimmed tortoiseshell combs for her hair. Although their love was boundless, their gifts were useless, and they had sold the two objects they prized most.

"It's irony," said Ben in his sleepy voice. "She cut her hair and bought the chain link and he went and sold his piece to get her the combs, so it comes back as an irony for both of them."

"Amazing," said Gaston. "They each sold the one thing they valued most." When he said it that way, I recognized that each man in the room had unwittingly traded in something that he valued highly: his freedom.

No doubt some of the guys in the book group, like the husband in the story, had been to pawnshops or Cash for Gold outlets in the past to sell something. But they wrestled with the idea of whether they would do what the characters in the story did—sell the most treasured possession in their house to buy a gift for their spouse. Gaston asked whether anyone in the circle would sell his car or TV to buy something for his "better half" if he didn't have the money at Christmas. He wasn't sure he could do it himself.

Ben admitted it would be hard to part with a Rolex. "I'm thinking if I bought my Rolex watch for ten thousand dollars, and I know that's all I have, I could get eight thousand for it, but am I really going to sell it?" he mused. "Because it's a *statement* piece." To hear Ben the altruist say this gave me a jolt. Here was the guy who had pointed out the humanity of Rose of Sharon breastfeeding a starving man at the end of *The Grapes of Wrath*, and who had confessed during the book club's discussion of *War* that he was institutionalized. But now he was admitting that love had its limit, and that limit was a Rolex. He was being honest, at least.

With Ben in his camp, Gaston warmed to his argument and said that even though people today are still as romantic as O. Henry's characters, the world had changed. It was now a more material world. Dread agreed, saying that grand romantic gestures were part of an earlier age of chivalry and that the characters in "The Gift of the Magi" were "too unselfish." Dread had never claimed to be an altruist. But I wasn't surprised when Deshane, the "lovey-dovey" prison poet, challenged them both, asserting that romance was still with us, causing people to buy "stuff they wouldn't normally buy."

Peter then made a point that shone a new light on the story for me even though I had read it many times. An obvious point too. "My take is that the author is illustrating how possessions don't actually have a value," he said. "The value is the intent and the love." It reminded me of Ian McEwan's ruminations on stuff in his novel *Saturday*—how a character's household goods become disconnected meaningless objects after she dies.

With Peter's comment in our minds, we considered O. Henry's gloss at the end of the story: a comment on whether his characters were unwise in money, but wise in matters of love. Several in the room had a story to tell about mistakes they had made mixing love and money, but I couldn't hear them because so many were talking at once. Deshane said something about people doing "stupid stuff like co-signing for lovers," showing that the men were not so unlike O. Henry's characters despite their street-smart facades.

It struck me that, in some ways, the prison economy at Collins Bay at that moment in 2011 was a lot like the economy of 1904, when O. Henry's characters were counting their pennies. For those inmates with a prison job, the pay averaged $3 a day—yielding only about $700 annually—less in real terms than the average annual wage back at the beginning of the twentieth century. Only one of the book club members that I knew had been able to secure a coveted higher-paying ($6.90 a day) skilled job at Collins Bay's CORCAN manufacturing shop. That was Gaston. In that job, he was eligible for "incentive" pay of $1.25 to $2.50 an hour on top of the flat daily rate. Even so, he and other inmates who earned more than $69 a month were required to pay 25 percent of their earnings to the federal government for room and board. And Gaston saved as much pay as possible to send home to his wife and four children. The gap between the Dillingham Youngs' income and the inmates' income was narrow.

Before Carol read the next O. Henry story, the chaplain came in to open a window to dispel some of the heat in the room. Deshane muttered that he was sure to catch a cold now. It was cold outside and warm in the prison, which was a good segue to O. Henry's "The Cop and the Anthem," another of his best-known stories. Its hero is Soapy, a New York City hobo and drunk who tries in vain to get arrested before winter so that he can spend the cold months in a warm lock-up. After his small-time misdemeanours fail to result in a jail sentence, he lingers outside a church where organ music inspires him to go straight and apply for a job. In a twist, he is arrested for loitering. I was a sucker for old-fashioned twist endings, dated though they were.

"O. Henry has a thing for irony," said Ben.

The other guys got it too. "When he actually tried to stay out and do something good, he found himself in jail, right?" said one of the guys.

This was the third month in a row in which institutionalization had cropped up as a theme. First it was the soldiers in Sebastian Junger's *War* wanting to return to the front, then the parolee in *The Grapes of Wrath* missing the comforts of prison. And now Soapy yearning for a nice warm jail. But the men may have been sick of that topic, because instead they wanted to talk about whether short stories were experiencing a comeback. I confirmed that the short story was indeed enjoying renewed popularity and told them about some popular contemporary short story writers like David Bezmozgis, a Canadian whom *The New Yorker* had named among the top twenty promising fiction writers under forty.

At the break I took a moment to ask Deshane how his poetry was coming along. He took off his Celtics cap and repositioned it on his head. "Just fine, Miss," he told me. But I could tell from his evasive expression that the assignment of writing a poem about *The Grapes of Wrath* had either been forgotten or ignored as uninteresting.

He saw my eyes drop to the tattoos on his arm. The dark ink on the dark skin made them hard to make out. I asked him what they signified.

"This one is 'Can't Live Without Money,'" he said, a droll counterpoint to O. Henry's message in "The Gift of the Magi." "And these are just project buildings, like I've lived in," he added, pointing to a large tattoo of high-rise apartment buildings. "And this is 'Never Give Up' in Chinese." The Chinese character was emblazoned on one side of his neck. Barely visible at the neckline of his short-sleeved shirt were the initials of his family members. "My fams." Home and those he loves. A few words to live by. Deshane was a romantic, but with a love for money too.

Like many of the other men, he also had tattooed images of a smiling face and a frowning one.

"Comedy and tragedy?"

"Laugh now, cry later," he said. I could see now why so many of the inmates had that tattoo. The mantra was essentially "live for today, worry about the consequences later."

Several of the guys then gathered around me with their coffee. They had noticed my husband's Mercedes key, which I had forgotten to deposit in the lockbox at the prison reception and had stupidly taken out of my satchel while looking for another pen. My husband had insisted I drive his company car that morning because my old station wagon was unreliable in winter. It was as though the men had homing devices for the logo. I could feel hot breath on the back of my neck as they crowded around. They wanted to know if the Mercedes was mine. I wasn't surprised that they liked nice cars or gravitated to material status symbols, given how little they had. But how quickly they had forgotten the O. Henry parable. Their interest made me feel a little panicky. The last time a criminal paid attention to a Mercedes key in my hand, I was being strangled.

I was grateful that at that moment Carol summoned the men back into the circle. There was one more literary gift she had planned for them that day: a reading of T.S. Eliot's poem "Journey of the Magi," which he wrote as a kind of Christmas card in 1927, the year he converted from Unitarianism to Anglo-Catholicism. The poem operates as a metaphor for his own personal conversion. Narrated by one of the Wise Men in his dotage, the lines reminisce about how he and the other Magi travelled to visit the newborn Jesus, but along the way encountered premonitions of the death of Jesus and the end of their own Zoroastrian beliefs. It conveys feelings of alienation and of being surpassed by a changing world—themes that would resonate for some of the men at Collins Bay. Technology alone was evolving beyond recognition while the inmates did time.

Carol read it aloud. I recognized one line of Eliot's as the source for the title of Rohinton Mistry's novel *Such a Long Journey*, which the men had read in the summer. I caught Ben's eye. Carol read it a second time, more slowly, and urged the men to listen with their imaginations, not their heads. The opening stanza was wonderful for its gritty portrayal of the Three Kings not as regal bearers of frankincense and myrrh, but as put-upon travellers in winter, with obstinate camels and unreliable camel drivers.

"T.S. Eliot has taken a little bit of the story and tried to humanize it," explained Carol. "What picture did you get of the camel keepers?"

"They wanted their women and liquor," said Roman.

What stunned me was how quickly some of the men decoded the symbolism of other seemingly mundane sights along the caravan's journey. Drawing on their familiarity with the Bible, Peter, Dread, Roman and Gaston recognized the poem's foreshadowing of the crucifixion when near the end of their journey the Wise Men observe three trees on the horizon and men gambling for silver. It was Roman who pointed to the silver as a reference to Judas Iscariot betraying Jesus for thirty pieces of silver. And it was Peter who reminded us of the second meaning: how Roman guards cast lots to win Jesus' clothing.

Carol pointed subtly to the parallels between the journey of the Magi and the inmates' own journeys. In the poem, the Wise Man who is narrating recalls lavish summer palaces where women served them sherbet, Eliot's delicious image of earthly pleasures, and seems to recognize that those material preoccupations might have been the wrong path. Ben expanded Carol's point, saying that the Magi were also no longer comfortable praising different idols. He pointed us to the final lines about the Magi returning home and feeling out of place.

"That's what happens on journeys," said Carol. "You're forced to go one way or the other way. The question is, do we get wiser on our journeys or not?"

The journey. T.S. Eliot. And then a flickering memory intruded— of another king, another journey and another T.S. Eliot poem, "Little Gidding," from his *Four Quartets*. How sharply my chest aches when I think of it, because of my own journey with my father to the little church and farm in Cambridgeshire described in that poem. My father had come to visit me in Hampstead with a plan to spend one of the days driving to Little Gidding to recall his own visit there in the 1950s and to make a new pilgrimage with me, as father and daughter.

A short distance before we arrived, he had me stop the car on the side of the road, beside a gnarled hedgerow whose twist of hawthorn branches was choked with other plants, likely dog rose and bryony. My father said nothing about why we had stopped. We stood for a minute beside the tangle of the hedge and then returned to the car. A few minutes later, when we found ourselves beside the windowless stone facade of the church, which looked more like a tomb than a chapel, I understood something of the mystery that had gripped T.S. Eliot and my father.

And inside, as we read the poem aloud, I discovered the lines about the hedgerows white with snow, then white with hawthorn blossoms in May, and the lines about King Charles I fleeing the battlefield broken. But most of all I found new understanding of the lines about journeying and arriving at Little Gidding not knowing what you were looking for. Eliot makes it all intensely personal to the reader by using the second person, how *you* didn't know why you were there, or that the reason is beyond what you had imagined. And then Eliot's observation about how the reason changes when it is fulfilled and you know what it was that you came for.

As I looked around the room at the men that Christmas, I suddenly knew I was on a similar journey, and I was not yet sure what I had come for. It was not just to help with book selection, not just to encourage the men in their journal-writing, not just to discover books together and write this book, but to touch the web of meaning that connects our lives—the men to me, me to my father, me to my own elusive courage. The men's journeys ahead were precarious and would require much courage. And then that line in the poem about how the dead communicate with fire and how the things they couldn't tell you in life they can tell you now that they are gone. I felt my father with me in that sour-smelling prison room, everything he had given me through nature and poetry and the tiny ember of courage that he was fanning in me now.

I looked up and saw Gaston with a raised hand wanting to answer Carol's question about whether we get wiser on our journeys. "The Magi know that it is no longer acceptable, the way they live," he said. The comment settled over everyone, because it was the bare-knuckle lesson of prison. Something about the way each man had lived previously had led him to this place.

Before the chaplain could call Count, Carol told the men that we had gifts for them. It wasn't the fruitcake she made and distributed to friends each Christmas, which would never have passed prison protocol. When she told me she was buying them presents and asked for my suggestion, I recommended tree ornaments. She questioned whether the men would be able to hang them in their cells and whether a Christmas tradition might offend the non-Christian inmates, but she went ahead and bought lamb-shaped ornaments made from tufts of unwoven wool from Topsy Farm sheep. "They've been through the security screener," Carol said, as if to answer an unasked question. We told the guys that they could hang the lambs on the tree in the years to come—to remember us and the book club.

The men crowded around and she handed one to each. They cradled the balls of fluff in their hands. No one joked that the gift was silly or useless, at least not in front of us. They looked as vulnerable and innocent in that gift-giving moment as children on Christmas morning.

That giving season, Carol was agitated about people failing to open up their wallets in support of the book clubs cause. The inaugural Oysters & Champagne fundraiser for Book Clubs for Inmates Inc., at her condo in Toronto in late November, had yielded cheques totalling only fourteen thousand dollars from the many lawyers in attendance, despite the presence of the fundraiser's special guest, Ian Binnie, a newly retired Supreme Court of Canada justice, and

Vince, one of her first book club graduates. It was far short of the forty thousand needed to buy the books for the eight book clubs she had founded by that point.

Following her family's tradition of tithing 10 percent of earnings, Carol set the bar high for others, and was not above urging her friends to also be generous. Just six days after the fundraiser, she called one invitee who'd taken home a pledge card after having sipped her champagne and eaten her oysters. "John, John, John," she said to him. "Matthew 6 says that you cannot store up your riches in barns." She got biblical when she was trying to raise money. And saltier too. "It's a bit of a lousy trick to offer your wife as a volunteer instead of making a donation." John laughed and agreed to give five thousand dollars.

Five thousand dollars was enough to buy the books for one book club for a year. At that giving level, John was now a "Patron" of one of Carol's book clubs and would receive a card of appreciation from the inmates. The funds would purchase new books because it was important to Carol that the inmates all receive the same edition. That way, when one member wanted to discuss a specific passage, the others could find it easily. The book shipments also had to conform with prison security requirements and a uniform set of new books was less likely to be turned away.

Christmas came to Collins Bay eleven days after book group. The West Indian men got their cayenne. And in the week between Christmas and New Year, Gaston got his wish for a cell transfer. It was a smaller, colder cell, but he was more comfortable with his new range mates, who included another man from the book club. He celebrated by having one of his trademark high and tight haircuts.

Back in Toronto, I got my wish: to have my family around me—the best gift of all. My adult children had designed and baked a Mayan temple out of gingerbread. My son, an engineer, drafted the pattern for the components, and my daughter and my son's girlfriend mixed and baked the dough. It was a long-standing

Christmas tradition in our family to create a gingerbread house—each year a new architectural design. We ate roast capon with squash and Brussels sprouts while a fire burned in the fireplace. And we lit the brandy on the Christmas pudding. I was newly aware of the stark contrast between my Christmas and Christmas for those behind bars.

Then we sat quietly with the new books we had found under the tree that morning. Someone had given me Malcolm Gladwell's *Outliers: The Story of Success*, so that I could read it before the Beaver Creek Book Club discussion in January. I lounged on a living room chair, immersed in Gladwell's cleverness, while my husband was absorbed in Ian Kershaw's *The End: The Defiance and Destruction of Hitler's Germany 1944–1945*. A happy Christmas.

That evening, as I cleared up the dishes after dinner, I looked at the Christmas card on the fireplace mantel. Graham had given it to me on my last visit to Beaver Creek before Christmas. It was the first and only Christmas card I've received from an inmate, let alone a convicted drug trafficker and former Hells Angel. "Ann, Your friendship and support is the best gift anyone could ever receive," it read. "I am extremely grateful for both! I wanted to wish you and your entire family a Merry Christmas and a Happy New Year." The final letter in his signature ended with a confident three-inch-long flourish of the pen. I had known him for only nine months and he, like Ben, now counted me as a friend. I was moved each time I read it.

Still, I felt undeserving because I had come empty-handed that day. I had had no card for Graham. It was like Dread had said during book group: what if only one of the Dillingham Youngs had made a sacrifice to buy a gift for the other?

13

A BOOK CLUB OF THREE

THE MUSKOKA WINTER at Beaver Creek brought much heavier snowfalls than Frank was used to at home in Toronto. In his prison job as the grocery shopper for his unit, he had to carry bags of food from the on-site canteen along shovelled walkways between high snowdrifts. He observed in his journal in early January that only a few squirrels were active while the many other squirrels and chipmunks had disappeared. He surmised that the active ones were youngsters who might have been born that summer and hadn't yet learned about hibernation. I had encouraged the men writing journals to make observations about the natural world and I was pleased that Frank had begun to do so. The institution was readying its outdoor skating rink for the inmates and Frank wrote that he was hoping to be able to use it before he had to go for knee surgery later in the month. I guessed that the staff would be careful to count the skates after ice time.

Over Christmas, Frank had been denied a pass to go home to see his wife and two children, which he found particularly hard given that Graham had been granted a pass earlier on. The criteria for a pass to go home (an Unescorted Temporary Absence) were strict and often included soliciting the views of the community. But his pass to write a real estate exam in a nearby city had also been cancelled. "How can they justify a UTA for Graham and not for me?" he complained to me. "His withdrawn charges are probably worse than mine." But in his journal, he was philosophical to some extent about the disappointments, saying that at this late stage in his incarceration he chose to ignore those setbacks and that he didn't take it personally. He was even resigned about the outcome of his upcoming parole hearing in February. It helped that he had just read a book from the prison library called *Twenty Thousand Years in Sing Sing*, written in 1932 by Lewis E. Lawes, the former warden of the historic New York State prison. Frank described Lawes as a critic of nineteenth-century prison methods and took the position that many of Lawes's recommended changes still had not been implemented. He also observed that convicts with long criminal records had changed little since Lawes's time and still engaged in "cunning" to try to get around prison regulations.

In those snowbound and frustrated months, Frank's journal became a new focus as he read book after book and captured his thinking about each one in short book reviews. He'd finished the book on mobster Crazy Joe Gallo, which he'd first read thirty years ago, and found that he no longer revered Gallo for his glamorous life with movie stars, but instead despised him for his deeds, including his treatment of women. Ironically, I remember reading somewhere once that Gallo became a big reader in prison and could discuss the works of Hugo, Camus and others.

Frank liked the four books he'd just read that all pertained to women: *Nomad* by Ayaan Hirsi Ali, *The Glass Castle*, *Mafia Wife* and *The Woman Who Walked Into Doors*. He had an eye for plausibility when it came to female characters. He'd concluded that Lawrence Hill was better than Roddy Doyle at getting into the head of a woman. He'd noticed it when reading Doyle's description of Paula Spencer's sexual longings for Charlo. Paula seeing Charlo across the yard and falling for him—that was credible, he told me later. "But the other part about 'oh I'd like to rip his pants off' doesn't seem to be the way a woman thinks," he said.

A few days after Frank wrote those journal entries, I drove up to Beaver Creek to meet with him and Graham. The remote country roads that I'd negotiated in the fall looked different in mid-winter, making it difficult to recognize the turnoff to the prison. Worse, blown snow from snowplows had formed a thick crust over the road signs. A wrong turn could lead me down a bush road. Then it dawned on me that I now had a smart phone with GPS. I quickly identified where I was and soon found myself at the prison.

After checking in with the guards, I met Graham and Frank in the chapel. Graham was commiserating with Frank about not receiving passes home. Graham reminded him that it was always harder to get passes or parole back to your home community if that was where you'd committed the offence. The problem was, Frank's family home was not far from the spot where he'd committed the crime that had landed him in prison for his latest "bit." Frank had never spoken much about the incident and I didn't want to pry. All I knew was that the newspapers had called it a "brazen" daytime shooting in a restaurant.

But that day, because he had been denied passes, Frank wanted to tell his story. It took place more than a decade earlier. At the time, he was about fifty. As he told me, he'd walked into a popular Italian restaurant in Toronto to say hello to a waitress who was a friend of his. One newspaper account said the conflict erupted when the owner refused to serve Frank because the restaurant wasn't open at that hour of the day for business. But Frank told me that's not what happened. In his account, one of the male staff grabbed him because he didn't want him speaking to the waitress. Frank then fell on the ground and held a stool in front of himself for protection. The man threw it aside, followed Frank out of the restaurant and hit him. Frank left, but came back a short time later with a .40-calibre semi-automatic handgun and began firing. Staff and patrons ran for cover, and in the chaos of ricocheting bullets, one bullet hit the proprietor in the back and another hit someone in the foot. No one was killed. Other bullets struck other surfaces. I listened to his story intently. It was hard to imagine Frank wanting to scare people. He was so reasonable in all my dealings with him.

Frank evaded arrest for six years, though he'd been hiding in plain sight: in the Toronto Reference Library, where he often spent the daytime hours. At one point during that six-year stretch, he was on Toronto Crime Stoppers' most-wanted list. At trial, he was acquitted of attempted murder but was sentenced to eight and a half years for aggravated assault and weapons charges (including three and a half years for time served). A successful appeal by the Crown resulted in an increase of the sentence to ten years.

The following two hours were among the richest experiences I'd had with members of the prison book clubs. We became, that afternoon, a book club of three—chatting with the kind of informality that governs so many book clubs on the outside. We spun off topic constantly, but then whatever we discussed reminded us of other books we'd read. There seemed to be a stream of books that had become embedded in us like past experiences: memories, reference points.

I started off by asking Graham and Frank about *In the Garden of Beasts: Love, Terror, and an American Family in Hitler's Berlin*, Erik Larson's non-fiction account of Nazi Germany in the 1930s, told largely through the eyes of U.S. ambassador William Dodd and his naive and boy-crazy daughter, Martha. I'd missed the Beaver Creek Book Club's December meeting when they discussed *In the Garden of Beasts* because I had been at Collins Bay that day, so I was keen to find out how the discussion had gone. It was the book that everyone in my circle in Toronto was talking about that literary season. Larson portrays Martha as captivated by the Third Reich officers and the ideas of the period. He describes her affair with Rudolf Diels, chief of the Gestapo, and her rendezvous with Hitler, when a Nazi party official was seeking a romantic match for the German chancellor. Her father was slow to convey to Washington that something was not right in Berlin. Although the SA, also known as Brownshirts, controlled the streets of Berlin, and the Dodds witnessed Americans and Jews being persecuted, it wasn't until a year after the family arrived in the city, when the Night of the Long Knives played out gruesomely and Hitler eliminated his rivals in the SA, that Dodd expressed forceful concerns to Washington.

To my disappointment, most of the Beaver Creek Book Club members hadn't liked the book, according to Frank and Graham. There were too many dead ends, said Frank, like the unfinished story of the Jewish couple who lived upstairs in the ambassadorial residence. But the men nevertheless had a "great" two-hour discussion about it. You don't have to like a book to have lots to say about it.

"What did the men think of Martha?" I asked.

"She was a—" Frank began.

"Careful, careful," cautioned Graham, who was over at the coffee machine pouring himself a cup.

"Tramp," said Frank.

Frank said the book club members could have spent the whole meeting talking about her misbehaviour. But Frank framed his view of Martha through the lens of Malcolm Gladwell's book *Outliers*, which talks about the role that opportunity plays in success. It was the book we were all reading for their book club the following week. "When you're looking at Martha, it goes something like that book *Outliers*," said Frank. "I think it was maybe a bit of luck that she met all these people. Her father was the ambassador and she was taking advantage of it. I don't blame her. I didn't dislike her. I thought she was a good person."

"One of the interesting conversations was how Dodd was getting it on all fronts," said Graham. "The people in the State Department thought he was an idiot. The Germans thought he was an idiot." As portrayed in the book, the frugal Midwestern values Dodd had assimilated in his time as a University of Chicago professor put him out of sync with official Washington and the more lavish traditions of the U.S. Foreign Service. He came across as dull and monkish. Graham, Frank and I talked about how Dodd abhorred overspending and drove around Berlin in an old Chevy rather than an elegant ambassadorial vehicle.

"Dodd wasn't doing himself any favours by focusing on this question of people spending too much at the embassy," I said. "He was acting like a fussy accountant."

Graham said the best example of that was Fritz, the German butler at Dodd's ambassadorial residence. Instead of Dodd confronting the fact that Fritz was probably a spy, it was, as Graham riffed: "Fritz, count the cutlery." We guffawed. Graham rocked back in his chair and clapped his hands with delight at his own joke.

From that point on in our conversation, we ricocheted between history and books—books that weren't even on the book club roster. Graham spoke about how the winners of a given war write its narrative, and cited Al Gore's *The Assault on Reason* on the lies that countries tell themselves to justify entering wars. As we were exchanging facts about North American ports turning away a boat of Jewish refugees in World War II, I urged them to read *None Is Too Many* by Irving Abella, a Canadian book on that episode. When I was enthusing about Hans Fallada's 1947 novel, *Every Man Dies Alone*, about an ordinary couple in Berlin who mount a resistance against the Nazis, a book I'd just bought my husband for Christmas, Frank knew all about it. He'd read it, even though it had just recently been published in English for the first time, thanks to a translation by Michael Hofmann. Then when Graham got into American isolationism and Russia's effort to insulate its borders, both he and Frank got sidetracked by their enthusiasm for David Benioff's novel *City of Thieves*, which they both had just read.

"It's about the siege of Leningrad and a general's daughter is getting married and he needs a dozen eggs to bake the wedding cake," said Graham.

"The general had arrested two people and so he sent them out on this mission to find the eggs," continued Frank. "They get tied up with partisans and so they get into all these adventures until they find these eggs. I read it in one night. Or a day and a half."

"That was a good book," said Graham.

The men's knowledge of World War II was impressive. Frank had a strong grasp of German discontent over the crippling economic effect of the Treaty of Versailles. Graham raised the point that Hitler could have wiped out the British Expeditionary Force early in the war, but he inexplicably halted the German troop advance at Dunkirk. And when Graham turned to the topic of American isolationism in the 1930s, he noted that the United States had observed the same ground rules as inmates in prison who want to stay safe. "If it don't involve you, don't get involved," he said. "Stay out of it."

By the end of the afternoon, Graham was yawning and Frank seemed to be developing a sniffle. We said goodbye and I walked out into the sharp cold, my boots squeaking on the packed snow.

Just seven days later I was back for the January book group meeting on *Outliers*. Graham was away on an approved UTA, so he couldn't help lead the discussion. But Frank was more than prepared for it. He'd read it and two of Gladwell's other bestsellers: *The Tipping Point* and *Blink*. Carol had introduced him to Gladwell's earlier books back at Collins Bay.

When I walked into Beaver Creek for the meeting, I noticed one of Canada's best-known white-collar criminals sitting in the reception area, conferring with a group of his visitors. His green designer pullover and snow-white New Balance running shoes struck me as out of place amidst the Cookie Monster T-shirts and baseball caps of some of the other inmates. But perhaps it helped him feel comfortable in his new surroundings and normalize his get-together with old friends or business associates.

I spent about half an hour with Frank before the meeting and he said the opening of Gladwell's book had made him think about his own hometown in Italy. Gladwell talks about the Italian town of Roseto, whose residents immigrated en masse to Pennsylvania, where they proceeded to astound medical researchers with their low levels of heart disease. Frank was from another small town in Italy down near the toe of the boot: Vallelonga in Calabria. Like the Rosetans, his townsfolk favoured local produce, which Frank believes is essential to good health. Although he left there at age three and a half, he had a few memories of his hometown. "I remember we had a little square there and I remember wagons going up the street with horses pulling them," he told me. "I remember an old lady poking a big key into my stomach and pretending to open my belly button." Ninety percent of the town's population emigrated from Italy to the Toronto area in the 1950s in search of economic opportunity, according to Frank, leaving their houses locked up and empty.

Frank had first heard about Roseto when he boxed with a guy from Pennsylvania. Frank was involved in boxing for a decade, from ages nine to nineteen. Since reading one of Gladwell's other books, he had wondered whether boxing blows to his nose had impacted his brain, damaging his judgment faculty. "I'm thinking, gee, maybe that's why I did what I did," he told me. "I knew what I did was wrong, but I didn't really have any control over it."

Just before book club convened, I was startled to see Raymond, the white-collar criminal in the green pullover, ask Frank where the book club was meeting. "I invited him," said Frank after Raymond left. "He's written books. I told him he'd be an asset to the book club. And we can kick him out, just like anyone else." Frank had just been telling me that there were so many lifers in the book club, it meant spots for newcomers would be slow to open up. Perhaps something had changed.

The thesis of *Outliers* is one that would be encouraging for any inmate. Gladwell argues that it isn't just intelligence or innate talent that determines a person's success. Rather, as Frank summarized in his journal, hard work and luck play an even greater role, provided, as Gladwell would have added, a person also has a natural aptitude. As inmates, they might be in jail now, but assuming some degree of talent and a willingness to work very hard, coupled with a bit of luck, they had a shot at success.

Two memorable findings in Gladwell's book have become part of the modern zeitgeist. One addresses the role of luck or opportunity in determining which talented individuals get to be successful. Gladwell found research that shows that more top hockey players are born in the early months of the year. The reason is that those born soon after the January 1 cutoff date for eligibility in their age grouping are likely to be physically bigger than other players in the grouping who are born later the same year. That slight advantage, when kids start playing hockey at the age of five, leads to more coaching attention and more opportunities throughout their childhood and adolescence, which widens their advantage.

The other finding that has captured readers' imaginations is that individuals who possess innate ability in a given field can achieve mastery in that endeavour if they devote about ten thousand hours to practice. Gladwell cites the example of the Beatles' marathon gigs in Hamburg clubs from 1960 to 1962. The Fab Four played two hundred and seventy nights for up to eight hours a night, clocking more than two thousand hours toward their requisite ten. It occurred to me that any inmate with a five-year jail sentence automatically has ten thousand hours (at forty hours a week) to get good at something like yoga, writing or a foreign language. If he is also naturally gifted in that occupation, he could be a success.

We began the meeting by talking about the ten thousand hours. Tom, his long hair resting on the collar of his outdoor jacket, said that if he hadn't had to divide his time between playing catch with his father and practicing the piano for his mother, he might have had ten thousand hours on the piano, which must have been his preference. Earl said ten thousand hours sounded about right to him to be an excellent hockey player. He was from Brantford, a noted hockey town. "When we grew up there, every ice surface was rented every hour of the day. There was pond hockey, river hockey, road hockey. There was parking lot hockey! You go out as soon as it's light and you don't come back until it's dark again and when you take your skates off you can't even feel your feet." Brantford, of course, had produced Wayne Gretzky, known as "the Great One" in professional hockey.

Doc reminded the others that it wasn't just the ten thousand hours and the talent, but also opportunity that determined success. "You got groomed along the way," he said. "It was that stepping stone."

But Bookman, the inmate librarian, wasn't sure. He told a story about moving to Alberta as an adult and discovering that he had a gift for free climbing—rock climbing without ropes or other equipment. "I didn't do it growing up," he said. "I didn't get groomed. I just decided to do it on my own. I was thinking I never really had any talent for anything but after six months I was doing just as good as the guys that did it quite regularly. Not to blow my own horn, but I was really good at climbing walls." That news would not have thrilled the warden of a medium-security prison.

It was Dallas, the tall, dark-haired inmate, and probably one of the youngest men around the table, who brought the two ingredients of talent and hard work together in the most novel way. "There was something innate that made you *want* to put in the ten thousand hours," he observed. I wish I'd thought of that. Perhaps passion, interest and drive were innate. It appeared to set everyone thinking. Could drive be considered a talent?

It wasn't until about halfway into the meeting that Raymond spoke up. He hadn't read the book because he'd just arrived at Beaver Creek, but he observed there wasn't much consensus around the table about whether the book was good or bad. "It would be fascinating for me, given the socio-economic strata that is represented around the table and so forth, if you would rate the book on a one-to-ten scale and tell me whether you agree with the quote on the front of the book," he said. The blurb talked about the book being "explosively" entertaining, with "riveting" scientific information, and elements of self-help. The quote was attributed to *Entertainment Weekly*.

In one respect I had to hand it to him. The question evoked some of the most cogent assessments of the evening. As we went around the table, the book club members ranked *Outliers* at anywhere from three to eight, acknowledging that it was entertaining, though maybe not "explosively." The ranking averaged out at about six. Frank was one of the ones who gave it a seven for its "rudimentary form of science," but he argued that, like all of Gladwell's books, it failed to provide a clear solution. Richard, who'd majored in sociology, was not impressed with Gladwell's use of statistics and dubbed the author "the Michael Moore of the publishing industry."

A few around the table ranked it highly, based on its self-help potential. And these were to me the most poignant moments of the evening. Bookman had shared the section on practical intelligence with someone on his range who had difficulty communicating effectively. He said that it prompted the other inmate to study how to change that aspect of himself. And Earl said with hopefulness: "You might not have that burning drive or personality, you might not be Stephen Hawking intelligent, but you might have other things going for you."

Given the lukewarm ranking, Raymond asked how the book got to be a bestseller, or was everyone in the room crazy. Frank suggested that the reason for the book's success went back to some of the lessons learned in Gladwell's previous book *The Tipping Point*. Word of mouth. In particular, Frank likened it to *The Tipping Point*'s Hush Puppy anecdote, which described how a few cool young people in Manhattan in 1995 inadvertently started an epidemic desire for Hush Puppies, the previously uncool suede shoes with the crepe soles. Or, as Phoebe, the volunteer book club facilitator suggested, the book had likely caught on with young people because they were the right age to envision putting in ten thousand hours on something. On the other hand, Bookman joked, maybe it was just that everyone in the room *was* crazy, as Raymond had said. After all, he pointed out, everyone in the room was in jail.

The question of the role of nature and nurture in success cropped up over and over again. It was never more interesting than when Byrne mused about his own actions in life in the context of Gladwell's chapter on feuds and their underlying "culture of honour," tracking how cultural legacies are almost as powerful as genetic legacies and looking at criminal behaviour that results from those clannish behaviours. "Me being adopted, would I act like my genetic family in a situation of a culture of honour?" asked Byrne. "I don't know."

Byrne's question was particularly germane given the high-profile honour killing case then before a Kingston court: the parents (and their son) in a family of Afghan immigrants living in Montreal were accused of killing their three teenage daughters for dating and refusing to wear traditional clothing. The accused were convicted later that month. And by coincidence, the book in the centre of the table for next month's book club was Ayaan Hirsi Ali's memoir *Infidel*. It chronicled her early life in a nomadic Somali clan, and her political life in the Netherlands, where she became a target for Muslim extremists due to her opposition to the enforced submissiveness of Muslim women.

The men picked up their books and said goodbye, stopping to shake my hand or share a word. Tom looked at his copy of *Infidel* and said, "The fact that there's a foreword by Christopher Hitchens raises the book in my estimation."

And Frank asked me how Vince had reacted to his message, "The Beggar-master says hi." "Did he think of me right away?" asked Frank.

"Yes, and he joked that you're going to be his Beggar-master," I said.

14

ISLAND LIFE

According to Ben and Gaston, it wasn't until sometime after the New Year that the Collins Bay guards identified the potential risk of the cayenne pepper in the inmates' Christmas bags. The capsaicin in cayenne pepper is the raw form of the active agent in pepper spray. With a little alcohol and a few other easily obtained ingredients, the inmates might be able to manufacture an equivalent. Hell, they could just blow the powder into guards' eyes. The guards themselves had only begun carrying pepper spray canisters for personal protection the previous year. Once the danger had been recognized, the institution went into an eight-day lockdown for a spice sweep.

All the prisoners who had bought the brick-red powder were asked to give it back. Some did, but—surprise—some did not. "Seeing like they put everyone on their guard," said Ben, "everyone is either hidin', stashin', mixin', puttin' it away." He himself did not hand back his two packs. The guards had to find his forty-five grams the hard way—by searching his cell. They fined him five dollars, nearly two days' wages for an inmate with a prison job. Gaston said the guards searched with their helmet face shields down to protect their eyes.

The cayenne-pepper search impacted the Jamaican and other West Indian inmates disproportionately, because it was a key ingredient in their cooking. And I suppose that was a fitting atmosphere in which to read that month's book club book, *Small Island*, Andrea Levy's masterful novel about Jamaican immigrants in postwar Britain. Set in 1948 London, with all its deprivations, the novel examines how black Jamaican soldiers who fought for England as Commonwealth citizens find their "Mother Country" a less hospitable place after the war, when they return to live and work there. A white British couple, Queenie and Bernard, and a black Jamaican couple, Gilbert and Hortense, intersect in a boarding house in Earl's Court, and subtle social frictions based on class and race ensue. All four protagonists take turns narrating, and the dialects and sentence structure are unique and fine-tuned to each character. Given that at least half of the men in the book club had roots in the Caribbean, I felt it was an obvious choice when I recommended it for their book list, even though it was long, at more than five hundred pages. I figured that the men would find lots of readers on the outside who had read it too, because of its acclaim. *Small Island* had won the 2004 Orange and Whitbread prizes as well as the 2005 Commonwealth Writers' Prize.

It was cold on book club day, but there was very little snow on the ground. As we struggled out of our winter coats, I noted how stylishly Carol and Derek were dressed. Carol had new oversized pink plastic-frame glasses and a cardigan with a massive faux fur collar. Derek was wearing a pair of purple-striped socks that added some zing to his preppy attire. I was wearing the same ensemble I always wore: beige pants, my green tweed jacket, fully buttoned, and no jewellery.

I brushed some lint off my trousers and decided that it was time to buy another "prison uniform." That thought summoned a memory of the clothing I had been wearing the evening of the attack in London. When the trial was over, an officer from London's Marylebone police station called to ask if I'd like to retrieve the clothing that they'd taken for fibre analysis. The items were sealed in a paper bag emblazoned in huge letters: POLICE EVIDENCE. I walked out onto Seymour Street with my bag, passing shoppers with their more fashionable bags from Selfridges, which was just two blocks away on Oxford Street. Sure, their clothing might have been new and chic, but mine had been combed for fibres and DNA. In any event, I never wore those items again. They are still sealed in that bag somewhere in my basement.

Carol had asked Derek to take the lead for the *Small Island* discussion. Another potential volunteer was visiting the book club that day to see if he might become involved. His name was Tristan and he was a retired art teacher and artist. "As some of you know, I can't always be here," explained Derek. "So if you want Tristan to come back …" The implication was that the book club members had better be civil to one another. Derek looked meaningfully at Dread. Dread had a habit of conducting side conversations or picking on Ben. The book club ambassadors had brought in several new members and Derek welcomed them warmly. There was Michael, a man with a slight lisp from Toronto's South Asian community, and three white guys that Gaston and Peter had recruited: Colin, a young man from small-town Manitoba, Ford, a Maritimer with a completely bald head and Brad from Toronto, who gave off an air of cool. I wouldn't normally have paid such attention to race, but the novel made us all aware of colour that day. Gaston caught my eye across the circle and waved. I waved and smiled at him and he smiled back. He looked different somehow, but I couldn't put my finger on why.

"Okay, *Small Island*," said Derek. "What did you think? Ben?"

"I'm of Jamaican background," said Ben. "And I'm putting her up as one of my best authors." He had vetted the book in advance for Carol and me, and Carol had given him a copy of Andrea Levy's *The Long Song* to read as well. He thought Levy had perfectly captured what he called "that essence of Jamaica," especially in *The Long Song*, which was set in his family's home parish of Trelawny.

Javier, who was born in Jamaica, confirmed that the author had nailed the Jamaican patois, which he understood from his childhood in Montego Bay, when he'd been told stories about the mischievous Jamaican folk tale character known as Anancy, derived from Anansi the spider in African folk tales.

168

"Good book, obviously," said Peter, the first white inmate to offer a comment. "But I knew that we were all going to end up talking about race. I wrote down a couple of things that the author said." He read them aloud and both passages suggested that the British fought the war so that each could live with his own kind. "So it's not about hatred," concluded Peter. "It's about differences. And I think calling it racism is just putting a face on it."

To back up his point, he highlighted how the author also focused on class differences, reminding us of the scene in which a working-class British woman had been bombed out of her Hammersmith digs and was billeted in a posher area, to the alarm of a resident of her new neighbourhood. "As soon as you step out of your own demographic, you're treated differently, you stick out," Peter argued. "And it doesn't have anything to do with race."

In a way, Peter was driving at a truth: that Levy examines all the subtle snobberies that divide people, not just those related to skin colour. The Jamaican soldiers in the book consider themselves superior to those from smaller Caribbean islands, for example. And Hortense, as Ben observed in the meeting, was "uppity" compared to Gilbert. But I was aware of the fact that Peter's quotes from the novel about each living with his own kind came from the one white protagonist who is a racist: Queenie's husband, Bernard, who is the least likable character in the novel. In contrast, Queenie seems blind to race. Peter's comments made me feel a little uneasy and I could sense that the reaction would be heated from the black book club members.

"So you're saying those guys in the book weren't racist?" challenged Dread, whose oversized Rasta tam was a dramatic statement of Jamaican identity, even though he had to wear the same short-sleeved prison-issue blue shirt as everyone else.

"I found a lot of stuff in there offensive," echoed Javier, his deep voice assured, his earring glinting. "It opened my eyes to a lot of things that were going on back then. Like you're good enough to fight a war, but you're not good enough to shower in the same place."

Meanwhile Ben had been mulling over Peter's distinction between race and "differences" and was starting to see Peter's point.

"If I live somewhere, I don't want someone who is poor coming to live beside me," said Ben. "I'm gonna start thinking there goes the depreciation of my house."

Everyone laughed in snorts and explosive guffaws. Ben looked startled.

The scene that particularly bothered Dread was the one in which the education authorities dismiss Hortense's Jamaican credentials when she applies for a position as a teacher. "She went to apply for that job and they just look at her like she's crazy," he said. That scene had bothered me too. The education official hands back Hortense's letters of recommendation unopened and resumes her desk work. It was brutally dismissive.

"That's a terrible scene," agreed Derek. "Where she just gets treated like shit. It's heartbreaking."

And then Levy makes it hurt even more, I reminded everyone, by having poor Hortense accidentally walk into the closet as she leaves the room. Ever sensitive to how the scene might make the men feel about themselves, Carol observed that she'd always been quite aware of the high level of education in Jamaica, and that it was apparent in the number of very competent readers from Jamaica in the book club. Like Derek and me, she added her voice to the chorus of readers in the room who found the treatment of Hortense appalling.

Javier said Hortense reminded him of his own cousin. When she moved to Canada with multiple degrees from schools in Jamaica, she couldn't get a job. "She was told she was overqualified," said Javier. "I think eventually she just lost hope. Her spirit was really broken down."

Derek asked the Jamaican guys in the book group if they or their families had experienced racism or rejection upon coming to Canada, even though Canadians prided themselves on their multicultural society. Javier, who immigrated when he was fourteen, said he thought that Canada was racist, but not like the "full-out racism" of America.

Albert, an American, confirmed that things were worse in the U.S., saying that when he was growing up in New York State and

Oklahoma, "the only white people I seen in my neighbourhood were police and mailmen." Canada, he said, "personally I don't see it that racist."

Another Jamaican-born newcomer to the group with a slow, halting manner of speech said: "I experienced racism mostly with the cops, right? Every time I get in trouble they tell me their intention is to send me back, right? Because we're messing up the country, is how they put it, right?"

If you are a Jamaican, "you're black, you're violent, you're thieves," said Dread.

I wanted to ask about racism in the prison, but I didn't have to. Another newcomer from the West Indies raised the issue. "There's a lot of racial stuff day to day within the prison," he said. "You have less of a chance to do certain things in the situation where you're black. Look at the amount of blacks in CORCAN. It's a small fraction." I recalled how disappointed Ben was when he didn't get into the welding program in the CORCAN workshop.

"I'm a CORCAN worker," responded Colin, the new inmate from Manitoba. "Yeah, there is a lot of white people working in CORCAN. There's also six black guys. Over there, unfortunately, they do look for very specific skill sets. But could they hire more black offenders? Yes, I think they could."

"I've been in prison since 1996," he went on. *Fifteen years.* Sometime later he told me about his crime: he'd murdered an elderly lady during a robbery of her house. "I've also seen a lot of what everybody's talking about in prison, but not white towards black. Black towards white. When I arrived here at Collins Bay I was put on 4B, and I had black guys calling me: 'Hey white boy, hey white boy.' So I started repeating it back to them: 'Hey black boy, hey black boy.'" But Colin soon realized that it was just the black inmates' way of breaking the ice. "Now we'll joke around, throw in a racist comment here or there, but done in a prison-friendly way."

Derek wrapped it up by thanking the men for being honest and listening to each other. There was no time for Carol and me to linger after book club. She and I were rushing off to a local hall in Kingston where she was hosting her first volunteer-appreciation-night dinner. She wanted to thank the book club leaders for the many hours they had devoted, without pay, to the six Kingston-area federal prisons where she had started book clubs. Sixteen of her volunteers attended, all people who loved books and seemed to have some of Carol's toughness. Among them were a retired head librarian and a lawyer. We laid out poached salmon with mango salsa, chicken wrapped in prosciutto and a special emerald-green cold-pressed olive oil for dipping that Carol had brought back from her recent trip to Italy. Carol was fastidious about even the smallest details, insisting that each fork and knife be paired and wrapped in a paper napkin.

When Carol and I returned to Amherst Island that night, we placed the appreciation-night leftovers in the fridge and retired to our bedrooms. It had been a full day and I needed to get up early to meet some of the Collins Bay Book Club members the next morning.

It was still dark outside when I left Carol's for the prison. There was just a hint of pink at the horizon as I wheeled my luggage across the limestone paving stones and gravel driveway to my car. As I opened the trunk, I had a strong sense that someone was nearby. Carol was still asleep, there were no lights on in the neighbouring farmhouses and it was quiet, yet I had an uncomfortable feeling that I was being watched. I threw my bag into the trunk and darted into the driver's seat, quickly pulling the door closed and locking it. In my nervousness, I backed out of the long drive on an angle and the car's wheels went off the gravel grade briefly. Carol would see the tire marks on the grass when the sun came up.

No one in sight. I began to relax as I put the car into drive for the ten-kilometre trip to the ferry. Then it appeared. About three hundred metres beyond Carol's driveway, where Topsy Farm's summer sheep pastures flanked both sides of the road, an animal that moved like a giant hare bounded over the fence on my right, hopped across the road through the beams of my headlights, then leapt over the opposite fence into the pasture to my left. I slammed on the brakes. The animal circled back, stopped and turned to stare at me, tall rabbity ears pressed together exposing white furry linings. Not a hare. A coyote with a plush grey-brown coat. He looked well fed. "Hi, boy," I called to him through my now-open window. He stepped closer and stopped, staring, ears still pressed together. Here was the night stalker of Topsy Farm lambs, taking in my scent, my sound. He stood there for five seconds. Then he bounced, still hare-like, in a wide circle around my car, crossing the road behind me, springing into the field to my right, charging parallel to me and then hopping back into the car's headlights. His eyes flashed red in the light as he turned to look at me before he completed his circuit and loped over a rise near the water. I was awed by his playfulness and his beauty. Were they his eyes that had watched me earlier? I smiled the rest of the way to the ferry that would take me to the mainland from Carol's small island.

I was able to meet individually with each of the book club ambassadors that day: Dread, Ben and Gaston and, for the first time, Peter. I felt certain that, once again, I would hear even more interesting observations from the men during our private conversations than I had in the larger book group.

When Dread and I sat down, he complained to me that he got less time to speak during book club and that Derek and Carol didn't coax him on as they did with the others. "I notice these things," he said. "I'm a very analytical person."

So I told him I wanted to know everything he had to say about the book. I found out how he admired Gilbert for respecting Hortense and not forcing himself on her the minute she arrived in London, how if it weren't for Hortense's money, Gilbert wouldn't even be in England postwar and so *he* wasn't *her* "meal ticket," as someone else in the book club had said, how he believed Queenie had a good heart for taking care of Bernard's aging father, Arthur, and how Gilbert wasn't dumb. "Gilbert tried to get a good job, but no matter what he did, he ended up being a driver," said Dread. We talked about all the evidence that supported his observations. One thing was certain: Dread knew that book inside out.

When Dread had to leave and Gaston walked into the room, I still couldn't figure out what was different in his appearance. Something made him look more put together. "Sorry if I'm talking a little funny at the moment," he said. "I've got my new teeth in there." That was it. Where two teeth had been missing, he now had a full smile. Also his nose infection had healed, so it was no longer pink and swollen.

His journal revealed that he had hoped *Small Island* would change his thoughts on some of the Jamaicans he encountered in the prison. Before reading the book he ranked them as "ignorant." I suspected his views did not change, especially after some of the Jamaicans in the book club meeting accused CORCAN of deliberately depriving black offenders of opportunity. "There's nothing racist about CORCAN," Gaston told me. "I've worked there for a year and a half. They hire these guys, give them a chance, and they come in with their pants hanging down to here, they don't tie up their shoes and they don't want to get dirty. Some have never worked in their lives."

Discipline was big for Gaston, and no more so than in his daily prayer. Over and over again in his journal he talked about the discipline of getting down on his knees. Now he wanted to tell me about an entrepreneurial idea he had to take the pain out of kneeling for prayer. "What I came up with was the Personal Praying Pad," he said. Inspired in part by seeing Muslims praying on their carpets, he had designed a prototype praying cushion for Christians, with a slot in it for reading materials and even a carrying handle. He had conducted market research to find the most appealing colours and words for the design, asking respondents, "If one word could represent God to you, what would it be?" I suggested that his invention might qualify for CBC TV's new reality TV show, *Redemption*, in which recently released offenders with entrepreneurial ideas took part in job skills competitions. The final contender would win a hundred thousand dollars in seed money to launch his start-up.

But why was prayer so important to him, I wanted to know. "I'm nothing like what I used to be, and I know that's directly through prayer," he told me. "I was extremely self-centred, egotistic, selfish, ignorant, a womanizer, alcoholic, drug addict, money-hungry, greedy." The words came pouring out of him in a wave of self-loathing about the man he had been eleven years earlier. "If you woulda known me before, you wouldn't believe it. I mean I was in the gutter. The worst of the worst. Shelters, homeless, nothing. No food. No one would even look at me because I burned so many bridges, lied, stole, cheated. I was a piece of garbage. I would think, Do I kill myself today or do I try one more time?"

In one serious suicide attempt back then, he walked onto train tracks and waited. A policeman yelled at him to get off, but he wouldn't move. Backup arrived just as the train was approaching and the police pepper-sprayed him to force him out of the train's path. That time, he spent three days in a mental health unit. "I always had a good heart," he said, softening. "I was brought up well. But unfortunately drugs and alcohol encase it in cement."

"You had a lot of self-loathing," I said sympathetically. I was familiar with the concept because my daughter's anorexia involved bouts of very low self-esteem.

His conversion had come soon after that, when passersby found him in a ditch, left for dead, with two broken ankles and cracked ribs. It was around the same time that he'd lost his two teeth. Someone smashed him in the face with a golf club. He'd been "ripping off bikers" and screwing around with the girlfriends of guys he thought might be connected to the Mob, he told me. Someone took him to a church called Word of Life near Niagara Falls and he heard what he thought was the voice of God. "I fell on my knees, started crying out of control and started speaking in tongues. The next week I got baptized in a tank in front of the congregation."

Religion also became a bond for Gaston and the woman who would become his new wife. He met her just at the point where she had been excommunicated by her family's Anabaptist Christian congregation for conceiving a child out of wedlock. Together, they found a new church.

Being "godly" is why he avoided arguing in the book club meeting on *Small Island*, even though what the men said about racism ticked him off. Quite apart from his feelings about what some of the men had said about CORCAN, he told me he once saw a gang of eight or nine black offenders swarm and beat up an older inmate. The *Small Island* discussion really had brought some of the racial divides in the prison to the surface. He took a deep breath, looked down and then looked at me with renewed calm. "What I've learned is I'm supposed to love my enemies and clothe them and feed them and forgive them.

"I'd like to hear more about your thoughts on my praying pad," he said as we shook hands and parted.

"Of course," I said.

Ben poked his head around the corner. Here was a man who seemed the opposite of the black inmates that Gaston was describing. In his free time he had been reading *Things I've Been Silent About*, the memoir by the Iranian-born author of *Reading Lolita in Tehran*, Azar Nafisi. His journal notes showed that he was moved by her pain when her father was imprisoned—a chastening moment in the book for him. And he mentioned a book that she referenced, "*Jane Eyre* or something," he said. "She's more on the feminist." Maybe he meant "more *of* a feminist" or "more on the feminist *side*," but I loved his way of expressing it.

I thought of it as more about class than feminism, except for one or two defiant speeches by Jane. "*Jane Eyre*," I said. "It's a novel set in the Victorian period in England. Jane is an orphan who ended up in the house of a man as governess to his children. And he became attracted to her." Ben emitted a soft laugh, the kind of sound that indicates that the storyteller has held the listener in a momentary trance. How quickly that alchemy happens. We are hard-wired to have stories told to us orally.

"But I wouldn't want to ruin it for you, Ben," I said. "It's one of the great works of literature that you might enjoy reading."

My last visitor of the day was Peter. We had a good debate about how Andrea Levy structured the book. I said that dropping in Bernard's large section at the end of the book threw me off. I wasn't prepared to start caring about another main protagonist. And I was itching for a chronological story. But Peter didn't mind the things that bothered me. "Through the book club that's one of the things I'm learning to appreciate," he said, "the jumping back and forth in time, instead of a chronological story."

I invited him to talk about why he was in Collins Bay, if he didn't mind telling me.

"I don't mind at all," he said. "I'm in here for a robbery." It was his local convenience store, where he bought his cigarettes every week. "I don't actually remember the robbery because I got hit with a bat. He busted my head open and broke my arm. But I had this little tiny penknife, right, so I guess I stabbed him in the leg. I remember afterwards going to hop a fence and I couldn't because my arm hurt."

Peter had a history of drug use, with some binges that cost up to thirty thousand dollars a go, and he believed those binges had permanently impacted his brain. "I'm talking about actual thought processes, the way you perceive things," he said. He told me the redness in his face that I'd noticed back in November was psoriasis.

I presented him with a journal to record his impressions of the books he was reading with the book group and with Professor Duffy. He made his first entry a day later, on January 27, and expressed his concerns about how much to share with me. "Do I trust her? More importantly, do I need to in order to give what she asks…. Evidently, with pencil to paper and little inhibition the answer is yes. I am curious and as I said eager, to see where this may lead." He ended it with his signature.

On my drive home I reflected on how intelligent and articulate Peter seemed. I, too, was looking forward to where his writing might lead.

15

A DIFFERENT KIND OF PRISONER

LIKE SALMAN RUSHDIE, the author Ayaan Hirsi Ali has lived some of her life in the shadow of death threats from Islamic fundamentalists. In November 2004, a Dutch Moroccan man killed Theo van Gogh, the filmmaker who produced her short film *Submission 1*. The assassin issued his threat against Hirsi Ali in a note that he attached to Van Gogh's body after he stabbed, shot and nearly decapitated Van Gogh in broad daylight in the cycle lane in front of the Amsterdam East borough office. In her 2007 memoir, *Infidel*, Hirsi Ali tells her life story, from her birth into a Muslim family in Somalia—where she survived female genital mutilation and brutal beatings by her family—to her escape from an arranged marriage, leading to her asylum in the Netherlands and re-emergence as a feminist activist and parliamentarian who spoke out against Islam's treatment of women and against her adopted country's approach to multiculturalism. She saw Muslim women as trapped in a cage. And when the death threat forced her into hiding, she became a different kind of prisoner.

I was instantly in tune with the author's world of ever-present threat. In the months after the mugging in London, I had been on constant alert for danger. Parking garages remained particularly frightening. I would sit in my car until a woman or couple walked by so I could tag along with them to the lift. At home, I kept our windows' metal security grilles locked day and night. Before nightfall, I closed our curtains so that no one passing in the lane could see into the house. It was like Hirsi Ali's description of piling furniture and suitcases against the door of a Frankfurt hotel when she was in hiding and suspected the desk clerk had recognized her. Of course, mine was largely an imaginary threat triggered by post-traumatic stress, whereas hers was much more real and infinitely more deadly. Nevertheless, I heard reports of chokehold robbers continuing to attack other women in London, so my fears were not entirely abstract.

It must have been Carol who suggested *Infidel* for Frank and Graham's Beaver Creek Book Club, because the book was new to me. As the men were reading it in their prison bunkhouses up north, I too was discovering the book for the first time, propped up in bed while the warm light from my bedside lamp illuminated the pages just enough so I could see but my husband could sleep. Some of the author's images were so disturbing I had difficulty falling asleep after turning out the light. One such image was Hirsi Ali willingly assuming an agreed-upon submission pose for beatings from her mother.

When I checked in for book club at Beaver Creek's reception in February, I noticed several "personal protection alarms" (PPAs) hanging on hooks behind the security desk. I asked a guard whether I was required to wear one when I was walking alone across the complex in the evening. I'd never worn one before, remembering that Carol had said it would signal to the men that I felt uneasy around them. He didn't answer my question—simply handed one over. It seemed easiest just to accept it. Much bigger than my pocket alarm in London, the five-inch-long plastic box had a button that when pushed would instantly summon the guards. I attached the alarm to my waistband where it was almost invisible under my jacket. I didn't like the feeling. Wearing the device ironically made me more aware of potential threats.

As soon as I sat down with Graham and Frank for our pre-meeting catch-up session, I showed them that I was wearing it. I didn't want to insult them by letting them think I was afraid of them. I wasn't. Graham and Frank didn't even react. "If it goes off, you'll know," said Graham. "The cops will be here."

Graham was sniffling noticeably. He said he had a cold and joked that it was because Frank had made him walk outside without a shirt. He loved to tease Frank in ways that made Frank out to be the boss. Graham was physically bigger, but his jokes about Frank made me think that maybe Frank had some authority in prison that I didn't fully understand.

Frank was walking with a limp in the wake of his knee surgery for torn cartilage. He wouldn't be back on skates on the prison's outdoor ice rink for a while. Before the surgery, he had managed to get in one skating session on the bumpy natural ice surface. And he was surprised at the skates' high quality, even though the size eight boot was too narrow for his foot. Some of the other inmates organized hockey games, Frank explained. But Graham told me he avoided those. "Hockey games in prison—they play by prison rules," said the former Hells Angels enforcer. "They're bad. Anyway I don't like people hitting me."

We talked about membership changes in the book club. Although Graham had been away for Raymond's debut appearance at the book club meeting for *Outliers* the previous month, he'd heard some grumbling about how Raymond had managed to get into the book club so swiftly, when there were four or five inmates on the waiting list.

"You have to keep in mind, Frankie, that there's other people on the list that you bypassed letting him in, which caused some very hard feelings," said Graham.

"But those guys don't know nothing about the list," said Frank. "It's your list."

"They know because they've come to me and said, hey listen, their buddy's on the list and the next thing Raymond jumps the queue, as they put it to me, and all of a sudden Raymond's sitting at the table."

"You know why I did that? 'Cause I think the guy is going

to be beneficial to the group. He's got a lot of experiences."

"I'm sure his input is valuable. But at the same time ..." He described how some members of the book club had complained that Raymond had dominated the meeting last month.

I told them that I didn't think Raymond had done so. Frank agreed, saying that Raymond's comments were helpful. "But if it comes with attitude and that," said Frank, his tone changing sharply, "we don't have to take his crap." All his normal warmth fell away at that moment. It was uncharacteristic of Frank, but inviting new members is a contentious issue for all book clubs.

Despite his comment about Raymond, I noticed, as we talked about what we were reading, that Frank's values were often gentle and moderate, particularly when Graham was pronouncing on matters of geopolitics and regional conflicts. That afternoon, because Graham had been reading more of Al Gore's *Assault on Reason*, he wanted to talk about the threat of a nuclear weapon in the hands of the then-president of Iran, Mahmoud Ahmadinejad. "I mean clearly this book is relevant to all the stuff that's going on now in Iran," he said. He told Frank and me that he thought Israel would be justified in striking out first, given Ahmadinejad's controversial anti-Israeli statements.

"Let me ask you this, if you live next door to a guy, Frankie, and that guy told you that I've got the gun and as soon as I get the bullets on Monday morning I'm going to come over to your house and I'm going to shoot you, would you wait till he got the bullets Monday morning?"

"No."

"I wouldn't neither. Ahmadinejad's got the gun. Once he gets the bullets, he's coming."

But Frank said these issues were "distracting from the real issues like pollution. We are damaging our environment. And that's where the war should be." He thought the money spent bombing other nations could be spent building better recycling plants. "Who knows how many geniuses got wiped out in Iraq," he concluded.

It was only one segue later in the conversation that we wound up talking again about Frank's shooting incident in the restaurant.

I asked Frank whether there had ever been a restorative justice initiative between him and the man who had been seriously injured. Traditionally, restorative justice brings victims and offenders together, after the offender has been apprehended, in the interests of helping the victim to explain how the crime affected him and helping the offender repair the harm. Frank replied that "somebody," presumably an acquaintance of his, had reached out to the restaurant owner during those six years when he himself was on the lam. "The owner said he didn't want no problems," said Frank.

I was imagining how that might have played out when Graham suddenly gripped the arms of his chair and was overtaken with explosive laughter. "I'm not sure," he managed to say between spasms, "that was ... really a ... restorative justice process. I'm not sure ... that qualifies." The effort of talking while convulsing over the hilarity was causing his eyes to brim with tears and causing me to laugh too. "That might not be the technical definition: 'Yeah, he told me he didn't want no problems.' Problem solved. I can't imagine why." By then Graham was so hysterical he was gripping his chest with his big paws. He was implying, of course, that the restaurant owner might have felt threatened by whomever had approached him on Frank's behalf.

Graham's helplessness in the face of his own laughing jag was infectious and watching him laugh made me laugh more, even though I was thinking about how Frank felt and ultimately how the shooting victim must have felt. Frank smiled but didn't actually chuckle. The chaplain opened his office door to look at us. "I'm the one who went overboard," Frank said in a subdued voice.

As we gathered for book club I could see that Raymond was back, looking natty in a Roots Canada sweatshirt and an elegant scarf. Clearly he'd liked the discussion enough last time to return. Graham opened the meeting by inviting the members to forward any book recommendations to him, so that he could submit them to my Book Selection Committee and to Carol. And, for the benefit of new members, he introduced himself as the moderator "so everyone gets to talk and nobody hogs too much time." Frank and I made a point of avoiding each other's eyes. Raymond was the only new member.

Phoebe opened the meeting in a very Carol-like fashion by addressing the elephant in the room. "Obviously the subject matter of *Infidel* is one that is very sensitive in nature," she said. "Politics and religion are always controversial and this has both. Let's make sure we're respectful in our view. People are easily offended." I had no idea if there were any Muslims in the group. She suggested that before getting to some of the more touchy issues, we could discuss each of Hirsi Ali's family members in turn. It was an approach that Carol had recommended to Phoebe when the men were discussing novels. But this was the first time I'd seen her adapt it to a memoir.

The first character up for discussion was Hirsi Ali's bullying brother, Mahad, who enjoyed privileges and freedoms while his two sisters, Ayaan and Haweya, did the housework under the strict eye of their mother. Characterizations followed in rapid-fire, with no need for Phoebe to prompt anyone. Mahad was the stand-in disciplinarian when the father was away, said Frank. He was the subject of Hirsi Ali's contempt, said Raymond. A fellow who never amounted to much, said Tom and Graham. A kid who succumbed to peer pressure, said Byrne. A thief who stole their mother's money, pointed out Doc. Except for an incident in which Mahad told his mother to stop beating Hirsi Ali, the men concluded that he was unremarkable and spoiled by his position in the household.

"The male is everything," observed Earl, about the Somali Muslim households portrayed in the book. "As the boys grow older they don't have to do any chores, don't have any responsibilities other than being *the man*. It almost encourages you to be a bully. You've got this whole systematic abuse. It doesn't matter whether it's brothers, uncles or strangers."

And we shouldn't be surprised, Raymond suggested. "The question you have to ask is, what's the incentive for a male steeped in the Islamic culture to evolve, to have an awakening, to have a realization that there's an escape from that oppression when you're the beneficiary of the oppression?" He knocked on the table to stress certain syllables, so that everything he said seemed iambic or dactylic, like someone whose ear is tuned to poetry or music.

Their verdict on Hirsi Ali's younger sister, Haweya, was more complex. Haweya followed Hirsi Ali to the Netherlands, but failed to adapt in the way her sister had. She was unmotivated, seemingly depressed, then began hearing voices. For a while after returning to live with her mother in Nairobi, she seemed better, but the mental illness returned and she died following a psychotic episode and miscarriage. There are gaps in the narrative that leave the reader wondering how much the family concealed.

Earl blamed Haweya's mental illness on the genital mutilation. "She was held down and mutilated and after that, clinical depression set in," he said. His tone implied, wouldn't anyone go crazy after such a horrible event? I admired his empathy for how awful that would be for a woman.

We all volunteered other theories. Byrne said Haweya felt like an outcast after having two abortions and Phoebe pointed to the passage about Haweya's feelings of guilt surrounding those episodes. I suggested it might be a chemical imbalance. Dallas and Raymond said it sounded like bipolar disorder or schizophrenia. Haweya's risky sexual activity would fit with a diagnosis of bipolar, according to Tom. Whatever the reason, it was Doc who observed that circumstances had resulted in role reversals for the two sisters. Hirsi Ali had been a devout Muslim as a teenager but then broke away from the religion when she was older. Haweya, who had been more rebellious as a teenager, couldn't make the dramatic leap that Hirsi Ali had, and instead returned to her faith, or some new version of it, influenced by psychotic episodes.

For Raymond, Hirsi Ali's failure to help her sister consistently through her mental illness struck him as "huge selfishness." "This was symptomatic of a much bigger problem with the book, even though it was provocative and valuable as a read," he said. "You barely pierced the surface of the emotional depth of this woman." He couldn't believe that such an intelligent woman failed to see that her sister was in jeopardy, or to plumb her own "trauma" over breaking away from a faith that had governed her entire life for years. "I really don't know if this woman knows how to love," he said. "I think she's devoid of a huge number of feelings."

The men were horrified by some of the details of genital mutilation, which Hirsi Ali tells us is a practice that predated the Muslim faith, but is performed on almost every Somali girl in the name of Islam. In describing her own ghastly mutilation at age five, she gives us the image of an itinerant circumciser tweaking her clitoris, then cutting it off, along with her inner labia—like a butcher cutting through meat. He then pushed a sewing needle through the outer labia to stitch up the area into a virtual chastity belt of scarred flesh, leaving openings for urine and menstrual flow. The circumciser worked on Mahad and Haweya too.

"I did not know that they sewed them up," exclaimed Tom.

Phoebe was unafraid of speaking candidly about the procedure. "The point is to get rid of sexual desire," she said. "But it doesn't take away that desire." And Hirsi Ali claims that it doesn't eradicate sexual pleasure, either, though she describes how much pain accompanied any remaining pleasure. The mention of desire prompted Earl and Frank to remind the others of how amusingly male desire featured in the book and how Hirsi Ali was taught that if she uncovered any skin she would be so "beguiling" it would cause traffic chaos.

As for the parents, we discussed the much-talked-about estrangement between Hirsi Ali and her father after she skipped out on her arranged marriage by claiming asylum in the Netherlands. Phoebe asked why the father's reaction had been more violent to her foiled marriage arrangement than to her rejection of Islam. "The marriage was a business transaction for the father," Frank said. "He was now in debt to the man she ran away from." The father's honour had been tainted. Frank's close reading always produced insights for the rest of us.

Finally we tackled some of the more controversial questions. On the issue of her ability to break free, Bookman argued that it wouldn't have been possible if she had not at one time been extremely devout, searching within Islam to find answers to key questions. "It became an issue of why she couldn't find those answers," he said.

And Raymond, whose scholarship in the Jewish faith was deep, was again a helpful contributor. "The book is about the rejection of the *dictates* of the Koran. It's not a rejection of the essence of the religion. And in her rejection of those dictates she makes a big point of its anti-American, anti-Semitic bias." He thought she was still a God-fearing woman, though she described herself as an atheist.

Frank agreed. "If you asked her today if she's really an atheist, she would say no. She was just revolting against all the man-made rules. To tell you the truth, reading this, I almost question my Catholic upbringing." He confessed he couldn't see the point of repeating the same prayers and rituals over and over.

"There's a great passage," says Raymond. "And I can't find it right now, where she specifically says she wants to be a woman of integrity, how she wants to adopt all the greatness that Islam represents in all of its multi-faceted nature but does not want to be constrained by the strictness."

"It's on page 281," said Byrne. Pages rustled. He read it aloud, the passage about finding her own intrinsic moral compass and no longer relying on a holy book to tell her what was right or wrong, good or bad. The lines he read spoke to everything that I believed about goodness and kindness. And it shone through that day in the men, whose own judgments about members of Hirsi Ali's family spoke to their own moral compasses, and their own innate awareness of right and wrong. As Graham said to me: "If your daughter or wife chooses to wear a burka and that's part of her belief, I don't have a problem with that, but if you're forcing her to wear a burka, I do have a problem with that." Contained in that response was a deep natural morality and an instinct to honour women's rights.

With just fifteen minutes to go before our time was up, Phoebe posed a question that would get good traction in any book club: what role did the Western novels that Hirsi Ali read as a girl play in her later rebellion.

Tom didn't think her early reading was important. He thought the Harlequin romance novels that Hirsi Ali and a friend had giggled about as girls were passing fantasies. But Raymond challenged that view, arguing that reading torrid romances fed her determination to marry for love, rather than to submit to an arranged marriage.

His view aligned with Phoebe's. Two specific passages stood out for her about the importance of Western books for the author. She directed them to page 94, where Hirsi Ali talks about romance novels saving her from submission. But it was clear the men had already flagged those passages in their own books. Bookman asked Phoebe to read from higher up on page 94 where Hirsi Ali says that reading romances made her feel wild and free, and aroused her sexual desire. And when Phoebe then pointed them all to page 118, Doc was already on that page and suggested the line at which she should start reading. It was exactly the section that Phoebe had been hunting for, where the author describes being fascinated with the ethical choices that characters faced in Western novels. In *Dr. Jekyll and Mr. Hyde*, for instance, Hirsi Ali discovered that good and evil could reside in one human being.

"Or page 69," said Bookman. There was a rustle again as everybody found the page. He read the passage about how even trashy books introduced her to new ideas of freedom and equality for people of different races and genders. The men talked about how the books allowed Hirsi Ali to experiment with freedom and moral choices in a way that wasn't possible in her real life, by standing in the shoes of characters who were free to make life decisions.

I thought about all the books that Hirsi Ali had read at the Muslim Girls' Secondary School in Nairobi: *Wuthering Heights*, *Huckleberry Finn*, *1984*, and works by Jane Austen and Daphne du Maurier.

"They plant the seeds of rebellion," said Graham.

I considered how lucky Hirsi Ali was that her family was living in Kenya at that point in her education, because her mother was able to enrol her in a school where she had access to good books and she had the opportunity to learn English. And Tom must have been thinking the same thing because he asked why the other girls in Hirsi Ali's school didn't react as she did.

"We all read a book," said Graham. "But we get different stuff out of it."

I cannot begin to tell you how so many of the men's statements that evening thrilled me. They brought the book to life for me in ways that I hadn't begun to discover on my own. And while Graham often intervened to invite some of the quieter men to speak, Raymond had not "hogged" the meeting. Indeed Graham had often agreed with Raymond's points. The new member, it seemed, was going to work out.

After the meeting, Graham told me that some of the men had been asking to read a wider range of genres, particularly science fiction.

"I'm not crazy about science fiction," Frank said.

"Neither am I," said Graham. "But if that's what everyone else wants to read, I'll read it too," he said, with an equanimity that proved his leadership yet again.

They both preferred non-fiction to fiction, and sci-fi seemed to them fiction to a factor of five. "I think non-fiction is stranger than fiction," said Frank. He liked the way non-fiction wasn't neatly tied up like a work of fiction. For example, now that he'd read *Infidel* and Hirsi Ali's other memoir, *Nomad*, he was ready for more. "I'm interested in what happens to this woman," he said. "I'd like to keep track of her in the future."

He turned to me. "How do you pick the books for your Toronto book club?"

"We usually select books around a theme," I said. "So one year all our books were by Indian authors, and before I joined the book group the women spent a year reading African authors. This year we're reading a smattering, including three books in tandem with the Collins Bay Book Club."

I asked Graham and Frank what they'd been reading outside the book club. Frank had finished *Power Concedes Nothing* by Connie Rice, *Every Man Dies Alone* by Hans Fallada and Jhumpa Lahiri's *Namesake*, and was now starting *The Elegance of the Hedgehog*, the bestselling novel by Muriel Barbery. Graham was reading two books at the same time: Erik Larson's *Devil in the White City* and Yann Martel's novel *Life of Pi*. He read one in the morning while doing cardio on the exercise bike, and the other at night. So many literary works.

I walked back to reception with Phoebe, the portable alarm banging against my thigh. I decided I wouldn't wear one again.

That evening I sat down with Frank's journal. It was full of admiration for Hirsi Ali. He described her as remarkable for her achievements and for risking her life to shine a light on what Muslim girls experience. He went on to describe how he was eager to get home sooner than his "stat date" in May. He had a parole hearing in a few days and he'd managed to persuade his parole officer that an old police report that had been dogging him should be put aside.

I took off my reading glasses and put his journal on the table beside me. How many different types of prisoners there were in the world. Prisoners in cells, prisoners of religion and prisoners of those threatening violence. Even prisoners of fear, as I once had been. With each book club I was gradually liberating myself.

Something else occurred to me that night. I was discovering my "opinion compass," much as Hirsi Ali described discovering her moral compass. Although I had always had a strong sense of moral direction, I had never been a highly opinionated person—usually more interested in exploring the facts on either side of an argument than in landing on one side or the other. I think partly I owed this tendency to the non-opinionated, apolitical discussions around our family dinner table when I was growing up. For a judge, my father seemed completely non-judgmental. And my training as a newsmagazine journalist taught me to deliver just facts, not an editorial point of view. But as I saw the men express their views, listen to each other and sometimes alter their positions as a result, I began to find my own views sharpening into opinions. And I liked it.

16

THE WOUNDED

THAT YEAR the Turner Classic Movies television channel showed several vintage films on prison pets. I watched *Birdman of Alcatraz* for the first time and *Caged*, a 1950s Oscar-nominated film set in a women's prison where a kitten becomes a pet. It made me wonder if the men at Beaver Creek or Collins Bay were allowed to keep any animals. I knew that feral cats roamed the prison grounds at both Bath, a minimum-security prison twenty kilometres west of Collins Bay, and at Warkworth, another medium-security prison in the province. And some U.S. jails had introduced programs in which inmates trained rescue animals to make them more adoptable, while gaining skills for their own re-entry to society. But when I asked Ben about it as we were waiting for the February 2012 book club to start, he said the only animals that entered Collins Bay were birds. I wasn't surprised, given that the prison, like Amherst Island, was on an avian flyway. On one occasion, he saw an owl fly in and perch on the bleachers in the yard. From his description, "big and brown with a white stomach" and a pale face, I guessed it was probably a short-eared owl. "He looked scary to me," said Ben. "Are they prey or predators?"

"Predators," I said, describing how they hunt talons-first and holding up my hands to illustrate. I told him I was planning to go owl watching with Carol on Amherst Island after book club.

In the weeks leading up to that February meeting, Peter wrote at length in his journal, documenting his reactions to the books that he was reading, and observing that literature had "elevated something inside" him. In one observation, he noted that Edgar Allan Poe effectively establishes his characters first "to make his tales more believable and subsequently more disturbing." Writing in pencil in a neat script with a backward slant, Peter also captured other aspects of his life in prison. For the past year, he had been learning a style of street fighting from an inmate who was a professional in mixed martial arts. That, he said, explained his "bruised shins and black eyes." He had enrolled in and dropped out of a restorative justice program, saying that it was a good program but that he was past having the ability to forgive. In one stunning passage he talked about an emotional numbness. "I know my past sadnesses and remember why, but cannot recall how it felt," he wrote. "I can describe its weight, its overwhelming nature, the mind-tricking effort required to subdue tears, but cannot for the life of me, feel it." I recalled that he had been homeless for a while in high school. He also dedicated some space in his journal to describing the lack of variety in the weekly meal plan in the cafeteria: baked chicken thigh for dinner every Tuesday, cooked the same way every time; on Sundays, a piece of cake (with no icing) for dessert. He experimented with saving the cream centres of Oreo-type cookies and using them on Sunday nights as icing for the cake.

As the February book club meeting drew near, Gaston's journals indicated that he was not inclined to finish that's month book, which would be a first for him. Some of it was circumstantial. He was preparing for a parole hearing seeking a transfer to a halfway house. And six days before book club, his wife arrived at the prison for a weekend Private Family Visit. But most of all, he was finding it troubling to read a novel about alcoholism and domestic abuse.

We were discussing *The Woman Who Walked Into Doors*, the fifth novel by Booker Prize–winning Irish author Roddy Doyle. Thanks to Carol's initiative, Roddy Doyle himself had agreed to answer all of the men's questions by email. And once again the women in the Toronto book club to which Carol and I belonged were reading in tandem with the men and exchanging comments. When Carol and I gathered with the men in late February, I was revved up for a great discussion. Tristan was there too, filling in for Derek, who was away.

When Carol had handed out Doyle's book to the men a month earlier, she described it as another example of a male author putting himself in a woman's shoes, like Lawrence Hill's *The Book of Negroes*. In this book, the shoes are those of Paula Spencer, a woman in Ireland who marries a local tough named Charlo. Charlo subjects her to physical and verbal abuse, and her own alcoholism clouds the picture. There is a riveting scene in which Paula could blurt out the real reason for her bruises to a nurse at the hospital, but doesn't, because Charlo is on the other side of the curtain, hearing all. Carol told the men it was a rollicking read about "a poor Irishwoman who's just got everything going against her. But she's a heroic character and I think you'll find her inspirational."

I think I'd first read it in England, with one of my two book clubs there. While I understood why Gaston found some of the material later in the book difficult, I admired the early chapters, where Doyle beautifully captures the chemical rush of a teenage girl's crush and the confusion of a young woman in love. At the last Collins Bay Book Club meeting Carol had asked the men to read aloud from that scene to kick-start their reading, and it was strange to hear Paula's words, so familiar to me, in the mouths of the men. It was Gaston who had started off, reading aloud the bit from chapter 2 where Paula describes the collapsing feeling in her legs and her lungs when she first sees Charlo. Colin took over from Gaston, reading the passage about the fabulous plumes of smoke from Charlo's cigarette and how they danced to "My Eyes Adored You." Gaston and Colin were both too young to get the nostalgia kick from the description of Charlo's 1960s stovepipe pants and loafers. But I got it, being essentially a contemporary of Paula's.

When we discussed the novel in our Toronto ladies' book club a month earlier, some of the women had strong opinions on whether I should have recommended it for the men. Lillian-Rose asked bluntly who screened these books. If an inmate had engaged in domestic abuse, she said, wouldn't the book provoke, disturb or even excite them? Ruth said that since Carol and I were not psychologists or therapists, how would we handle it if the material brought out something in a book club member that he hadn't faced before. But Carol and I explained that the men had managed well with other books about abuse and neglect, like *The Glass Castle*. In fact, every prison book club that had read *The Glass Castle* had absolutely loved it, Carol said. "Many of them have been through anger management programs and a lot of them have more self-knowledge than just about 95 percent of people I know," said Carol. "I think it's a way to unpack what is really evil and have a frank talk about it."

The discussion of Doyle's novel was the longest and most thoughtful of any Collins Bay Book Club discussion I had participated in to that point. We began by analyzing Charlo. Shockingly, the guys didn't see him as all that bad. Gaston pointed out that Charlo was a good father and not abusive toward his kids. Ben said he had a certain rebel appeal and only changed to become "unstable and moody" when the jobs dried up and he couldn't find work. Dread tried to counter Ben's point that Charlo changed. He argued that Charlo's violence was "in his DNA," and then he joked that Ben was confusing the fictional character with his own reminiscences. The two bickered briefly.

"I'm talking," said Dread, trying to make some space to be heard. "It's this aggressiveness," he said, referring to Ben again. "You see what I mean, Miss?" Everyone laughed.

"Are you feeling abused again?" joked Carol, whose sense of humour usually got the conversation back on track.

"Slightly," said Dread, feigning hurt.

Peter, who came in late, a little out of breath from jogging across the prison grounds, was the only one who slammed Charlo outright. "This kind of abuse is actually beyond abuse, in my opinion," he said. "I don't even know what you call this. But I think it's his own sense of inadequacy that causes the abuse. He's looking in the mirror saying, I'm not much of a man. He beats her so he can be the bigger man, but the more he beats her, the worse he feels and it just gets into that cycle. And I think that's highlighted in the end, when he sees how strong and independent his daughter is." What a strong, clear insight, I thought. Where had that come from?

"That's very helpful," said Carol. "Because I think that we would all agree that there's some lack of self-esteem here in both these characters." How about Paula, Carol wanted to know. What about her background?

Colin offered his précis. He said that while her family was really tight-knit, they lived in a relative state of poverty and she suffered from lack of privacy.

Carol probed further: "And what do we know about her parents?"

Peter said that we didn't know a lot but some things were being insinuated. "Tough love" was how Ben described it.

But Dread speculated that it was worse than that: the insinuation was incest. "The author never really explored it," said Dread. "He just gave you a hint of it, then left it alone." Dread had given the book a close read, I could see, as had Albert, who remembered the incest scene clearly with Paula and her siblings sitting on the father's knee and playing a game.

"Yeah," said Carol. We recalled how Paula's father had beaten her older sister, Carmel, with a belt. I remembered how Paula misfiled that in her brain as okay because fathers were different then: cruel to be kind.

"I think right from the start, Paula had a rotten deal," said Peter. "I don't think she was just a victim of Charlo. She was a victim of life. She was born into what she was born into and she didn't have a lot of options available, even before Charlo. She was basically told she was stupid, right off the hob, and then she realizes that she was poor."

That whole question of victimhood was perhaps the most thought-provoking question of the day. Carol advocated that Paula was admirable because she didn't see herself as a victim. She eventually fought back. But Dread disagreed forcefully, saying that if she didn't see herself as a victim, why was she longing for hospital staff to ask her where the bruises really came from. It went to the heart of the question: do you need to see yourself as a victim in order to accurately sort out right and wrong and accuse your abuser? It was a hard one, because in the second half of the book, Paula's ruminations are so muddied by alcohol and perhaps head injuries, her memory so incoherent, the reader has difficulty knowing if she's a reliable narrator. I recalled how in our women's book group, Deborah said that Paula's scattered, out-of-sequence memories accurately portrayed the non-chronological way that abused women with "traumatic memory" speak, and that Doyle had captured the way these women present clinically.

Carol looked over at Tristan, who hadn't said anything yet, and asked: "Were you going to say something, Tristan?"

"No."

"Well, I'd like you to come into the conversation at some point," she said. It was only his second meeting as a volunteer and he seemed a bit tentative. Nevertheless, he responded to Carol's prompt, suggesting that Paula had some responsibility for her situation, but that it would be hard for her to squeal on Charlo.

Peter then drew our attention to the scene where Paula tries to sort out in her own mind why the abuse was happening. "It started with dinner," he said. "Charlo came home, saying dinner wasn't made. She said, well you weren't there last night, so he said, well put on some tea and she told him to make his own fucking tea. And that's when he drove her and that's where it goes to the scene where she wakes up and he's over top of her and he says, you fell." Then he described how Paula's thoughts returned again and again to that night, asking herself whether the abuse might never have started if only she had just done what she was told and made Charlo his tea.

"However, was she for some of you a heroine?" Carol asked. "Was she an admirable person?" Certainly Paula is heroic when she finally throws Charlo out of the house.

Dread offered that Paula was perhaps heroic because she didn't pass the abuse along to her kids. She took care of her family, even through her own alcoholism. But since the beginning of the meeting he had been wanting to talk about Doyle's writing style and so he took advantage of the fact that he had the floor to redirect the conversation. "I kind of disliked the style at first because it's all over the place," Dread said. Carol asked him what he thought the author was trying to show with that mixed-up storyline, and the answer came to him: he said that it was Doyle's way of mimicking the mind of an abused and alcoholic character.

It seemed like a good moment to share the comments about the book from the women in our Toronto book club. I handed the sheet of comments to Carol. She read the comment from Deborah, who, as it happened, had worked as a therapist with abused women and with abusers. Deborah was pondering why women stay in abusive relationships. "So often they have childhood histories of abuse or emotional neglect and stay in abusive relationships, particularly if they have children, because they cannot imagine how to disengage and become independent," she said. From that Toronto discussion, Deborah had left some unforgettable images in my head of the abused women she'd helped—women "with no teeth, with half of their faces bashed in, with one eye blinded, with hair pulled out that won't grow back and too poor to buy wigs." They were not images of women who had power.

To Deborah's question, Dread provided another answer: "'Cause she's being abused, she internalizes it and tries to blame herself and see ways that she could have made things better, when the fault is not with her." He had a way of talking that was a rapid, run-on monotone, as though warding off interruption.

"I agree with him," said Colin. "My parents were like that. And my mother was complacent toward the actions that my father was doing to her. Like she would just pretend things weren't happening or try to change the topic and act like something else was happening. I see a lot of similarities to my mother and father's relationship as I do with Paula and Charlo."

"She was in a state of denial," said Carol. "I mean, is there anybody here who hasn't known about domestic abuse in their own family or in a family close to them?" From the response around the circle, domestic abuse was well-known to many.

"I was raised in an abusive home," said Parvat, a new member with long hair and hooded eyes. "I read books about what to do and what not to do when I get into a relationship and have children." So he'd tried self-help. And as I found out later he'd needed it because his experience was more traumatic than most. He told me his father had dangled him from the balcony by his feet when he was a young child because he had tried to prevent his father from hurting his mother. Parvat and his mother had lived in a shelter for victims of domestic abuse for a time.

"I salute you, Parvat," said Carol in a maternal tone, referring to his self-help initiative.

Peter told the others that when he attended the family violence correctional program in prison, they said that one in nine women are abused. He was not happy about being in the program, saying his partner was bipolar and would throw things at him, then call the police when he walked out. In the program he was told that yelling back in an argument or walking away was abusive, advice that he was not sure he agreed with. Despite that view, Peter was keen to see more domestic abuse prevention. "I believe most abuse is learned," he said. "If we could break the cycle." The men suggested greater access to psychologists and psychiatrists.

"I think that you are enormously wise about your pasts and about how you move forward," Carol said to all the men. If only Lillian-Rose and Ruth from our ladies' book club could have been in the room to see how sensitively the men had navigated the issues in the book, I thought.

When I'd originally recommended the book, I'd forgotten how much sex it contained, as Paula recalls her first encounters as an adolescent. Correctional Service Canada prohibits pornography, but not sexual content, in prison materials. Stieg Larsson novels, for example, aren't censored, despite the sexual violence. And *The Woman Who Walked Into Doors* was well within the rules. But I realized during the meeting that I was more comfortable talking about violence than sex with a roomful of male prisoners.

Before the meeting was over, Ben had one question about the sex. "There's a statement he made about eating fries off her knickers," he said hesitantly, seeming to want an explanation.

Dread said to Ben, "Why would you remember that?" Then he looked at Carol and said, "He's disgusting, Miss."

Everyone laughed.

Then Dread got the last word. "Your new name is Knicker Fries," he said to Ben.

At coffee break, the men took time to write some responses to the women in the Toronto book club. One that stood out was the comment from Michael, who was serving time for his role in a drug trafficking operation. "The book captured the feeling of numbness abuse can have on a woman," he wrote in non-cursive round letters. "Paula became a zombie by absorbing constant pain with little feeling. Her maternal instinct became her salvation." He was talking about what finally gave Paula the courage to throw Charlo out of the house: the prospect that Charlo might turn his attentions to her daughter.

They also scribbled their questions to Roddy Doyle: Why did you write this novel? Did you witness this as you were growing up? Do you believe that abuse is learned and carried from generation to generation? Was holding back the abuse content of the book done for the purpose of maximizing the impact? (Doyle spends the first half of the book giving us Paula's memories of her adolescence and early relationship with Charlo, and leaves the description of the abuse and alcoholism for the second half of the book.)

Parvat came up to me afterward. He was keen to tell me about the book he was reading to learn about how to better communicate with women. "It's called *The Five Love Languages*," he said. When I looked it up later, I saw that the author's prescribed five ways to express love are gifts, quality time, physical touch, acts of service and words of affirmation. These were certainly good ways of forestalling an abusive relationship. But it also struck me that, except for physical touch, these were the graces that Carol was bestowing on the men. No wonder they respected her.

That evening, after a rough ferry crossing over choppy water, Carol and I went owl watching on Amherst Island. Snowy owls arrive on the island most winters in search of voles and I'd never seen one of these majestic birds, with their enormous white mass and exotic yellow eyes. We drove to the south shore of the island, past a flock of black-and-white bufflehead ducks bobbing in the shallows, where the lake was free of ice, and past a flock of snow buntings. And there, atop a telephone pole perched a bird that looked like an elongated marshmallow, with eyes the colour of Meyer lemon rind and a rounded head. It was a snowy. He tolerated us for a moment and then drew his wings up sharply, pushing off from the pole with feathered feet so massive they resembled paws. With slow-motion balletic strokes of his wings he pulsed the air and tilted into the woods. We took separate cars back to Carol's, and I travelled alone along a side road at sundown where some short-eared owls swooped in spurts over a field, their pale, disc-like faces seemingly sewn on to their bodies. It seemed to me that Amherst Island was a wildlife sanctuary first, and a settlement of humans second. And predators were more visible than prey that day.

I cooked chicken for our dinner that evening, to which Carol had added a salad. I pointed out to her that she still had an ash mark on her forehead leftover from the Ash Wednesday mass she had attended earlier that day. She rubbed it away. That evening she told me that charitable donations were starting to come in as people honoured the pledges they'd made at the fundraiser. It came as a huge relief. She would be able to buy the books for the coming year.

The next morning I set off early from Carol's for the prison to visit Ben. The sun seemed to rise with unusual speed that day, as though it were a school play where the stage crew had mishandled the hoist.

It was Ben's last month in the book club. We would miss him terribly. He had noted down a few pages from *The Woman Who Walked Into Doors*, about how Charlo brainwashed Paula. He read to me from the part where Paula remembers Charlo telling her that she wasn't fit to look after the children because of her alcoholism and stupidity. "He broke her down," said Ben, looking up at me.

Then he read from another section in which Paula imagines running away, trying to wrest back control over her life. He was struck by Doyle's description of how in Paula's nighttime dreams she could never run away, how she couldn't breathe or move. "That description, like wow. Just fighting something. You're trying to sleep. You're trying to not let it in, but you have no control over it."

"The control issue makes me think about what it must feel like a little bit to be in here," I said.

"That's one of the worst things," he said. "You might be in the yard and then you're coming back in here. You know it's a thing that you just have to do. It's terrifying just to think about it. So you try not even to think about it."

He would wrestle back some control in fifteen days, when his family would pick him up at the front gate of Collins Bay Institution and drive him to his halfway house. He had requested day parole in a Toronto halfway house near his aunt's place. His girlfriend lived in the Toronto area, and had just put down a deposit on a loft under construction north of the city. This time, the authorities were giving Ben a full month, not just seventy-two hours, to gather his financial records and present them to his parole officer.

I looked down at his journal again. On January 5, he made a note in his journal about reputation and that it was important. His own reputation in the prison, he told me, was as someone who's quiet, who gets along with others and attracts others. I pointed out that he never reacted when Dread provoked him in book group. And I remembered how he didn't respond angrily when the men ganged up on him about being institutionalized when we were reading *War*. Why did he put up with that? "No, I don't succumb to nothing like that," he replied. "I can't, while I'm in this place. I should not basically say how I feel. Like, I still hold my feelings, but act nonchalant about that."

The chaplain called, "Count," and Ben had to leave. He would be in touch with Carol's organization when he got out, he said. He would be taking all his book club books with him when he left.

"When you get out, do you see yourself reading on an e-reader?" I asked him. Some of the other men were interested in trying one.

"I'll think about it. But I still want that good smell of a book and turning the pages. Even building your own little private library."

"That's great, Ben. That's great." We shook hands and he walked toward the door.

In a women's book club on the outside, we'd probably have a festive send-off for a member who was moving away. Champagne, maybe, and certainly a card or present of a book. But at Collins Bay, men disappeared from book club abruptly, never to be seen again. Those stepping down to minimum usually told us. Others just evaporated. Some were deported and some wound up in solitary for a spell. One nearly died from a heroin overdose, we were told.

As Ben walked away from me, holding his journal, I wondered if he would be the book club member who would start a book club on the outside.

17

THE SUSPECTS

IT WAS THE SETTING MOON that woke me on March 14, its beam shining through the slats of our bedroom window shutters just before dawn. To be woken by the moon felt as though the earth had been bumped off its axis. When I sat up, my copy of William Boyd's novel *Ordinary Thunderstorms* slid off the bed, reminding me that it was book club day at Beaver Creek. When the sun finally appeared, it marked the beginning of a record-breaking March heat wave that would bring hail and, yes, thunderstorms to Toronto and the areas just south of Beaver Creek.

Carol did not usually accompany me to the Beaver Creek Book Club, but this time she was planning to meet with prison officials to accelerate the launch of a book club at the adjacent medium-security prison, Fenbrook Institution. So she had scheduled that meeting to coincide with book club. As she sat in the passenger seat answering emails, her cellphone rang. It was an Anglican chaplain calling from Cowansville Institution, a federal prison in Quebec's Eastern Townships. He had heard about the book clubs and wanted to start one in his prison. He was telling her that it would be an English-language book group—20 percent of the inmates spoke English only. She turned to me grinning widely and explained that this was the second call in a week from people wanting to start book clubs in federal prisons outside Ontario. The first call had been a former CSC employee wanting to start one in Stony Mountain Institution, the men's medium-security prison in Manitoba where Graham had spent some time. Carol's ambitions made her hungry to expand quickly, but her board was more cautious and asked her to make sure the funding would be in place before venturing out of province.

As we drove onto the Beaver Creek grounds two hours later, Carol fished her lipstick tube out of her purse and again expertly applied the colour without looking in a mirror. It was a trick that always made me laugh.

The next two books at Beaver Creek were mystery novels about criminal suspects in Britain and India. William Boyd's *Ordinary Thunderstorms* was set in London in 2009, and Vikas Swarup's *Six Suspects*, an Agatha Christie–type mystery, was set in New Delhi in 2001. Both explored ideas of dramatic reversals of fortune and overturned stereotypes about class and criminality.

Ordinary Thunderstorms was the latest novel by Boyd, author of the Booker Prize–nominated *An Ice-Cream War*. Technically a thriller about corruption in Big Pharma, this new novel twisted the literary formula. Adam Kindred, the protagonist, is an innocent man who stumbles upon a body and, through a series of naive decisions, finds himself on the run and homeless, sleeping rough by the Thames. After the disintegration of his marriage and the loss of his job as a cloud scientist in the U.S., Adam is in London for a job interview. He is eating lunch at a restaurant when he notices another diner has left behind a plastic business file with his business card visible. When Adam attempts to return the file to the owner's Sloane Avenue address, he finds the man with a knife in his chest begging him to remove it, which Adam does. That fateful decision makes him a prime suspect and soon, despite his innocence, he is hiding out in bushes below the Embankment at Chelsea Bridge. Evading the law drives him into ever-deepening circles of homelessness, begging and, eventually, a stunning criminal act, upending everything the reader thinks he or she knows about Adam.

Adam's decision to help the victim by removing the knife from his chest tested the book club members' patience. "Anybody who's been in prison knows don't touch the murder weapon," said Graham. "Don't touch the murder weapon. Leave it right there, right? Hands up and back out of the room."

"That does seem to be the litmus test for cons, doesn't it?" said Earl. "We all just back right out of the room. No way, I'm not touching that."

Carol countered that she might very well remove the knife if asked. But then, she'd never been in prison as an inmate.

Raymond, who in prison parlance was a "commercial criminal," and not a violent offender, instead focused on Adam's actions *after* pulling out the knife. In his view those choices simply strained credulity. "Adam went from this towering professional with great ethics and great academic history to a subterranean culture and immerses himself to the point that he can't escape it without going to the lowest common denominator of that culture," said Raymond. There was something about the ramped-up volume of his voice, and the slow pacing of his sentences that made me think he was used to being listened to by underlings. He had, after all, been the founder of a major public company before his conviction for fraud.

Someone pointed out that there is a turning point in the novel when Adam enters the Belgravia Police Station to turn himself in and assist police, but changes his mind, thinking that the circumstantial case against him is too great. Again, Raymond protested that the guy had a plausible defence and should have just picked up the phone and called a lawyer. My mind went immediately to the name of the top criminal defence lawyer whom Raymond himself had called to handle his own case.

But many of the other book club members had had experiences that ran counter to Raymond's, quite apart from what calibre of lawyer they could have afforded. "Many of us in this room have been to neighbourhoods," said Graham, "where, if you happen to be there, the police don't really give a shit what your explanation is."

"You may well be able to explain your way out of it," agreed Earl. "But not before the cuffs are on, you do the perp walk, you get the picture in the paper and everything else happens first. Maybe you get to explain it all later and you get a walk. But maybe you don't." Tom nodded. He said he knew people who had made the same choices as Adam.

Unfazed, Raymond continued his critique, protesting that the characters were "contemptible," the plot "predictable" and Adam's transformation "inconceivable."

But then Graham gave Jason, a new inmate in his early twenties, the floor. Jason told the others that they were being too critical and made a case for thinking about the book as a parable. "I think Adam's transformation ties into the whole theme of the book, which is social identity and how we're all interconnected. We're not so different from each other. Anyone can go from one position to another position like that." He snapped his fingers. Then he suggested that everyone turn to the final chapter where Adam reflects on how two lives can overlap without being observed. Jason read aloud the passage, which talks about an invisible network of almost-realized encounters between individuals. I hadn't seen it before, but now I could imagine the slender threads that connected the novel's Big Pharma executives and Shoreditch prostitutes, the police and the criminals. It struck me that crimes are Venn diagrams where the desperate and the privileged intersect.

"I think you're both right," said Graham, telling Raymond that, yes, the events seemed implausible, but that he'd seen situations where well-off people made terrible mistakes and chose to disappear.

And yet, as Byrne pointed out, despite those overlapping lives, none of the characters in the book seemed to care about each other. "From the top CEOs to the lowest bum on the street, they didn't seem to give a heck about each other," he said. Tom and Graham and Richard all came up with examples from the book that supported that view. And Carol suggested that it was a way for the author to show how it feels to be homeless in the world.

At that point everything changed. Doc arrived, apologizing for missing the early part of the meeting. His wife had been by for a visit. He had a totally different take on the book, saying that it reminded him of Guy Ritchie crime comedy movies like *Snatch* or *Lock, Stock and Two Smoking Barrels*. "It's that British farce where you've got a whole bunch of different characters that end up being intertwined," said Doc. Boyd was having us on by tampering with the conventions of thriller writing. And layered on that, said Doc, was the sense of resignation that overtakes those stuck in poverty in Britain.

Once Doc pointed out that it could all be intentionally comic, some of the more bizarre scenes made sense, including the one that Frank had written about in his journal earlier. It was the scene in which Adam's homelessness has driven him to kill and eat a seagull, but then he looks at the lights across the Thames and feels "Christmassy." "Absurd" was how Frank described it. Equally unlikely, in Graham's view, were the scenes in which Adam begins dating the female police officer who was initially assigned to the murder investigation and who fails to recognize him, and in which Adam takes a nap soon after leaving a murder scene. "Does anyone remember when Adam crawled into the bush and went to sleep?" he asked the others. "Like, you're on the run here because they think you just murdered a guy and, 'I think I'm going to take a nap in the bush.'"

That nap hadn't computed for anyone in the room. Frank told me later: "I just know from experience, when you're under that kind of pressure, like, I didn't sleep for three days after my incident." In his case, he said, "I was having a good day. Next thing I'm wanted. And then I hear I'm wanted for attempted murder. And I didn't turn myself in. And I couldn't sleep. I mean I tried. But I'd wake up and see the thing on the TV. You can't sleep. There's no way." He didn't leave town because his wife was pregnant, and, like Adam, he evaded arrest for some time. Frank appeared a little depressed that day at the book club meeting. The parole board had denied him day parole and had told him that, upon his release in May, he would have to reside in a halfway house. It wasn't clear whether the house would be in Toronto, close to his family, or not.

All it takes is one person with a definitive insight to turn around a book club meeting and that day Doc was that person.

As Carol and I drove back to Toronto, we noticed two very large bright lights side by side in the western sky soon after darkness fell. They looked like twin headlights or a double star. In fact they were Jupiter and Venus, weirdly close to each other, like two worlds that might collide. Another Venn diagram.

Three weeks later, the board of Book Clubs for Inmates convened at the law offices of board member Brian Greenspan, one of Canada's top criminal defence lawyers, to meet with Graham, who was out on an Unescorted Temporary Absence. It was Carol's idea to recruit Graham as an adviser to the book clubs operation, even as a member of the board, if it was allowed. I happened to be looking out Brian's boardroom window when Graham came walking toward the building. He looked so much bigger in the city than he did in the prison and it was strange to see him in street clothes, including a crisp polo shirt with a crest. He came with a gift box of fudge from his mother's confectionery business, for the board members. One person at the table made a point of explaining to Graham that the wires visible at her waist were not a "wire," but were attached to a Holter monitor for monitoring heart activity. Everyone laughed. For an hour, Graham impressed those present with his command of statistics on the prisons and his insights into the problems that afflict them. He suggested strategies for how to proceed with a new book club at Manitoba's Stony Mountain prison, drawing on his familiarity with the institution. The only question was, could an inmate serve on a charitable board?

Graham had come a very long way from that winter morning when he was arrested for drug trafficking and extortion. On that day, he'd been in the basement of his house, which had security cameras at every corner, linked to monitors in his bedroom and basement, giving him wraparound views—"a fortress" in his words. He first noticed a figure in black running across one monitor, then, as the screen split to display views from different cameras, he saw what looked like a municipal truck parked outside. The land line rang and he ignored it. Then his cellphone rang and his wife answered. She called out to Graham that it was the RCMP and they were outside with an arrest warrant. "They said, 'Are you going to come out?' and I said, 'Yeah, I'm going to come out, hang on a minute,'" recalled Graham. "I said, 'What are you arresting me for?' and the officer said, 'Well, I can't really tell you that till you come outside,'" Graham opened the door, put up his hands and was covered with red dots as an RCMP tactical team aimed the laser scopes of their guns at his torso and an officer guided him to the vehicle. "They were all over the place in their little grey-and-white outfits hiding behind the cars and everything," he recalled. "But they were nice to me when they took me in, and they were nice to my wife." He always referred to her as his wife because he was arrested two months before their planned wedding day. Sometime later the RCMP must have told him that the man he'd been extorting was a police agent.

I wondered what the arrest had been like for the two men the London police apprehended after I was mugged. The detective in charge of my file had been reluctant to provide me with many details of their investigation in case they required me to testify. They didn't want to influence my testimony in any way. However they did talk about arresting one man on a weapons charge later on the day I was attacked.

Some time later the detective asked me whether I would be willing to try to identify my assailants from a lineup of suspects or, as they said, "a police identity parade." The very idea was just about the worst thing I could imagine. Not only was I reliving the trauma but I felt an enormous sense of responsibility. The outcome could affect someone else's life for years to come. However, I wanted to be helpful and so I said yes. And that was how I found myself in a small outbuilding at Southwark Police Station on the south side of the Thames. There were several other people in a waiting room. We all looked at each other curiously. I didn't know whether they were other witnesses, plainclothes police or lawyers for the accused. I looped my arm through my husband's. I felt sick. A policewoman advised me that I had a right to ask the men in the parade to stand.

When they called me, I walked alone into a long chamber and confronted a lineup of black men who all appeared to be staring at me. They couldn't see me, of course, because the one-way glass concealed me, but from my side of the glass, I still felt like the one on parade. Unlike in the movies, they were sitting, not standing, and there were no height lines. The parade seemed calculated to make the witness focus on the individual's face, not the build or height. I moved hesitantly along the walkway studying each face. One fellow was wearing what looked like a 1970s shrink top over his sweater. The man next to him appeared to be beset with uncontrollable twitches and facial contortions, though it was impossible to know if these were involuntary Tourette's-type movements or were designed to distract. I asked two of the men to stand. The moderator asked if I could identify an individual while he was still seated. I replied simply: "I understand it is my right to ask them to stand." I took a long look, allowing my mind time to reach back into that evening. I returned to the lineup and checked each face a second and third time. I turned and spoke softly to the moderator and then returned to the waiting room. The detective in charge said I could go. I relived the attack in my mind all the way home in the back of a police-driven vehicle, feeling haunted throughout by the eyes of the men in the lineup, and also wondering again about what their mothers were feeling. It was impossible for me to separate the idea of the desperate men from their role in someone's family.

I was thinking about the suspect lineup on the drive north to the Beaver Creek Book Club on April 11 because our book that month was all about suspects: Swarup's novel *Six Suspects*. And so when I looked around the table at the book club members, I found myself newly aware of minute details in each man's appearance and conscious of wanting to memorize their features. There was Richard, one of the older men, with his grey close-cropped hair, his moustache and beard, his blue eyes looking out from behind black-framed reading glasses, his intelligent-looking face; Pino, a relatively new member, a hunch-shouldered man with a long thin nose and an angled scar on his chin, who appeared to be in his seventies; tall, slim Byrne with short grey hair and wire-rimmed glasses, and a habit of scratching his head and chewing his nails; Tom with his walrus moustache, dirty-blond hair that hung to his shoulders, brown eyes and long, pointy fingernails; Earl with his grey goatee, blue eyes and Nike ball cap; Raymond with his bored expression, expensive-looking watch, long hair and grey socks with a red stripe at the cuff; Doc with his freckles and colourfully striped knit beanie hat; Frank with his deep dimple, nearly bald head and dark grey sweatshirt; Graham with his great size, eyes that seemed to change from blue to grey and short-cropped blond hair; and Hal with his high-pitched voice, hazel eyes and grey zip sweatshirt.

It was Ben who had recommended *Six Suspects* the previous August during the book club meeting at Collins Bay when we'd reviewed the books we'd each read individually over the summer. I had bought it back then based on Ben's recommendation and now I was finally having an opportunity to discuss it with men who had also been suspects. Swarup is best known as the author of *Q&A*, which Danny Boyle made into the hit film *Slumdog Millionaire. Six Suspects*, a whodunit bristling with social satire, explores themes of poverty, wealth and corruption in India. Playboy Vicky Rai has just been acquitted of killing a barmaid who refused to serve him a drink. But at a party to celebrate his victory in court, he is murdered. There are six suspects in the case: a Bollywood actress, a mobile-phone thief, an American tourist, a bureaucrat, a politician and an indigenous man from the Onge tribe of India's Andaman Islands. All six were at the party, all six hated Vicky Rai and all six were carrying guns. Swarup had manufactured an interesting premise but, in the end, none of the book club members was very happy with how he resolved the mystery. Frank and Graham in particular said they felt cheated of the opportunity to at least string together some clues.

For Indian readers, the book's premise would certainly bring to mind the high-profile 1999 murder in New Delhi of a model and sometime barmaid, Jessica Lall, who was shot at a party, allegedly when she refused to serve a drink to the son of an Indian MP. At one point in the Lall case, there were twelve suspects, though all were acquitted at trial. It was only upon appeal that three suspects were convicted, including Manu Sharma, the son of an Indian National Congress MP. Swarup intentionally based his plot on the Lall case, capitalizing on the perception in India during the attenuated legal process that high-society individuals appeared to be above the law—a different kind of untouchable.

It was Swarup's experiments with multiple narrators that the men wanted to discuss first. The Bollywood actress's thoughts are conveyed through her diary entries, the politician's section is a series of telephone calls, the tourist and the thief speak in the first person, while the remaining suspects are described in the third person. To all those voices, Swarup adds a framing narrative by an investigative journalist who is phone tapping—a possible reference to the phone-hacking scandal in Britain, which at that time was in its early stages. Frank and Tom both said they liked the literary technique and Phoebe said it reminded her of *The Cellist of Sarajevo*, although she thought the device worked better there. For Richard, the formula reminded him of the Paul Haggis film *Crash*, where very different lives converge because of a traffic accident. Or *Six Degrees of Separation*, said Raymond.

Then Phoebe, who had taken a back-seat role as facilitator that meeting, pointed out an interesting theme that she had come across in a reading guide for the book. It was the theme of dual identities or identity confusion. She listed examples: a poor girl, who is a doppelgänger for the Bollywood actress, begins usurping the actress's career; the corrupt bureaucrat Mohan Kumar puts on Gandhi-like wire-rimmed glasses and comes to be known as Gandhi Baba, then comes to believe Gandhi's spirit has possessed him.

"I always find these academic revelations mundane," said Raymond, somewhat rudely.

But several of the others were intrigued by the idea of duality in the novel. "The really poor guy finds the briefcase and becomes really rich," said Earl, twigging to the theme. "The sexy starlet finds the girl from the dirt-poor village and brings her along. A big part of their culture is about balance too." And, as Richard observed, the starlet was simply exploiting her double without sharing any of the benefits with her.

"The underlying theme is corruption at every single level," agreed Doc. "Everybody does anything for money."

And, in Graham's view, the author was most pessimistic for the few innocents in society, like Eketi, the indigenous man. "Look what happens to that guy at the end," said Graham. "Tortured, beaten, enslaved."

Pino, the new guy, argued that the book's main theme appears close to the end of the novel. He waited while the men thumbed through to the book's last chapter, then read aloud a section from the investigative reporter's narration about how the middle class must be the conscience for the other classes. The irony is what the reporter does to right that wrong by taking the law into his own hands.

"So let's go round the table and rank the book on a one-to-ten scale," suggested Raymond.

"Oh no," groaned Graham. "Not the one-to-ten."

"Number! Number!" insisted Raymond, who hadn't liked the book and gave it a three.

Frank gave it an eight, Graham a six and a half and Doc, who said that he enjoyed the realism of its portrayal of India, gave it an eight as well. "Just because," he said, "Raymond would hate that." He had started to tire of Raymond's strong opinions.

It was after the meeting that Frank and Graham added one more intriguing layer to the book analysis, though it was in jest. The deaths in the novel are less troublesome to Indians, Frank told me, because Hindus believe in reincarnation. "So they don't care!" he observed.

"You've always got such a positive outlook," said Graham laughing.

"Well, I believe in karma," said Frank. "I don't think you can do bad deeds without eventually it will come back to you. I don't mean going to jail or anything. I mean it comes back to you in life. When you feel guilty about something, it's already gotten you."

"You carry it all around with you," said Graham.

"Yeah, and that's the biggest weight."

18

GOOD IS MORE CONTAGIOUS
THAN EVIL

IF IT WEREN'T for what I came to call "the Plexiglas lockdown," Parvat said he wouldn't have finished the March book for the Collins Bay Book Club, *The Zookeeper's Wife*, by Diane Ackerman. A piece of Plexiglas from the CORCAN workshop had gone missing in early March. Plexiglas, which was not detectable by a metal detector, could be fractured into equally undetectable and lethal shanks. Over on Unit 7, Peter used the time to read too. He was always well equipped for lockdowns with an emergency pack of supplies to deal with the lack of access to the showers or the canteen. The pack contained a sponge for hand-washing in his cell sink and snacks to bridge between mealtimes because of his high metabolism: oatmeal, sugar, apples, peanut butter packets, cream cheese packets and crackers.

Even during a lockdown, though, inmates still could be released from prison. On March 7, Ben wrote his last diary entry at Collins Bay: "I'm out tomorrow. My aunt is picking me up. I'm not sure where I will be going yet."

When we gathered for the Collins Bay Book Club meeting later in the month, I was expecting the discussion to be gripping. *The Zookeeper's Wife* tells the heroic true story of Warsaw zookeepers

Jan and Antonina Zabinski, who audaciously hid more than three hundred Jews in their empty animal cages and the closets and basement of their house on the zoo grounds during the German occupation of Poland in World War II.

The zoo's animals disappeared in three phases: German bombing destroyed some of the zoo enclosures, sending some of the animals scurrying and galloping through the streets of Warsaw; soldiers then killed the big cats and other more dangerous animals in case they might escape too; and finally the director of the Berlin Zoo looted some animals for his own collection, then sponsored a shooting party to kill the remaining creatures on the zoo grounds while they were still penned up.

Jews found their way from the Warsaw Ghetto to the zoo because of Jan's position in the Polish Underground, but it was Antonina's bravery and ingenuity at deception that kept them safe. Complicating the matter was the risk that their eight-year-old son, Rys, might accidentally blurt out their secret to the German officials who regularly came onto the grounds. Such a blunder would have led to the execution of everyone involved. Recognizing that risk, the family gave the stowaways animal names, so that even if Rys slipped up, the Germans would think he was talking about animals.

Only ten thousand of the more than three hundred and fifty thousand Jews who lived in Warsaw in 1939 survived there by the end of the war. The actions of the Zabinskis to save three hundred of them has been recognized formally by Israel, which includes them on the list of "The Righteous Among the Nations"—those who showed extraordinary courage to rescue other human beings from the Holocaust in the face of widespread indifference by their countrymen.

The Zabinskis' story was a little-known episode in the resistance and I had recommended *The Zookeeper's Wife* with hopes that the men might empathize with the courage of the zookeepers. But I also hoped that the author's rapturous descriptions of the zoo gardens would transport them briefly out of the prison's enclosed world.

Her evocations of the scent of lilacs and lindens transported me, as though being a naturalist gave her an animal-like heightened sense of smell and a poetic language for conveying it.

"Peter, what did you think?" asked Derek, whom Carol had asked to lead that month's discussion.

"It was a good read," said Peter, referring to his notes. "I think the author was trying to say the zoo itself was just an inherent spot for goodness. It represents life, nature." As opposed to the Nazis' murderous campaign, he explained. His comment made me recognize how extreme evil can occasionally provoke extreme good. One becomes necessary in the face of the other. His choice of the word *inherent* stayed with me too. The zoo celebrated life forms in all their diversity. And while some animals kill others for food in the wild, I could think of no animals, other than human beings, who killed out of cruelty or ideology. I remember the Canadian realist painter Alex Colville saying once, in reference to his depictions of animals, that he didn't believe that any animal was evil or capable of malice.

Parvat tucked his long hair behind his ears and expanded on Peter's idea, arguing that the Zabinskis had a heightened degree of empathy because they were more in touch with nature. "It was easy for them to care for humans, 'cause they were caring for animals," he said in his somewhat sleepy voice, with its cultivated cool. And Antonina went beyond just caring for animals, I thought. The way Jan Zabinski described it, his wife had an uncanny sixth sense in which she seemed able to intuit what the animals were thinking. In one scene, Antonina appeared to understand that it was the moving fingers of human hands that scared the lynx kittens. In another she discerned that their baby badger was sociable and benefited from long companionable walks.

The men were intrigued to discover in the book that the Nazis' eugenics program extended to animals as well as humans. The Nazis despised animals that had "degenerated" from racial purity, and sought to rebreed extinct animals that they considered noble and pure, including European bison, aurochs and forest tarpans.

Some of the animals that the Germans looted from the Zabinskis' zoo were taken expressly for that purpose. "A little twisted," commented Gaston, in a dry understatement.

Meanwhile, Peter highlighted some of the more startling details of the book. He reminded the men about the passages describing how Jews altered their appearances to avoid detection. "Re-skinning, for example," he said, "having your foreskin surgically brought back over again." Specifics like those are what readers take away, he said, when reading books on the war. He also talked about the Nazis creating anti-Semitic children's literature. "These little things are just as atrocious as the bigger things."

The men puzzled over what it was about Antonina that gave her the power to defuse situations when the SS were on the property snooping around. "She could talk to these SS guys and get them to back off," said Derek. "I mean the power that she had was extraordinary." I recalled one scene in which a German soldier questioned Antonina about a fire near their barracks. She coolly deflected the blame by pointing out that the haystacks near the barracks were often used by German soldiers to entertain their girlfriends and smoke. It reminded me of the scene in *The Guernsey Literary and Potato Peel Pie Society* where Elizabeth invents an alibi that deters a suspicious German patrol.

Peter proposed that maybe Antonina's power derived from her ability to read and calm people, as she did animals. Joao recalled that the author attributed some of it to Antonina's Aryan features. Parvat took a different tack by observing: "Women tend to have a certain power, especially attractive women." Dread disagreed, saying her power wasn't sexual. In my view, some of Antonina's charisma derived from her determination to make life fun by filling the house and grounds with other animals: rabbits, badgers, muskrats, dogs, hamsters, pigs and even cats that would nurse baby foxes. It was a way to stay sane in the face of terrible uncertainty.

Carol, looking particularly cheery in her oversized pink plastic glasses and long mauve scarf, jumped in next. "Maybe I could throw this out as a thought," she said. "The book was about sacrificing yourself and your safety for others." I loved Carol's predictability in always raising the theme of helping others.

Peter took Carol's thought a bit further by suggesting that the Zabinskis' courage was a more complicated gamble than simply putting their own safety at risk. "The author pointed out that there was cumulative responsibility," he reminded us. If Polish citizens were found to be harbouring Jews, the penalty would have been immediate death for them, their family, their employees on the grounds and their neighbours. The severity of that punishment was far more extreme than in many other countries, where the consequences for sheltering Jews was prison. "That's a whole different ball game," said Peter.

"It's really something to put all those people at risk," said Carol.

Then Peter made a breakthrough comment. "I think that the people that are actually at risk catch on and start to do it as well," he said. "The overall good is more contagious than the evil. Then those people say, 'Yeah, she's putting us at risk, but we should be helping too,' and it just goes around." The humanity in that statement, the innate goodness, thrilled me.

And, as Michael pointed out, Antonina anticipated that eventually the war was going to end, and they just had to hang on a little longer.

"I have to say that I really wondered if I'd be able to be as courageous as Antonina," offered Carol. "I had a very—I had a funny feeling I wouldn't be."

"I wouldn't risk my family," intoned Dread, without any of Carol's hesitation. Dread had two children. "Even though I know it would be a courageous thing, I wouldn't do it."

"It's hard to turn people down," said Peter. Several of the other men said "yeah."

"But nowadays nobody would do that," said a new member whose name tag read TONY. "Back then, there was more sense of family, belonging, tightness." The comment sounded very much like Dread's comment when we had discussed O. Henry's "The Gift of the Magi," and he observed that grand romantic gestures were part of an earlier age of chivalry. Tony's remark implied that ethical decisions could go in and out of fashion. As I saw it, the whole point is not what others would do, but what you or I would do when confronted with an opportunity to save the life of another human being. But I realized that in prison, minding your own business is part of the survival handbook. So there were no heroes that day in the book club, and I suppose I included myself in that number. I wasn't sure I could put my family at risk. But Derek reminded us that no one knows what they would do in the instant when a desperate person is standing on your doorstep begging for help.

"You know," said Carol. "As I was reading this I was thinking about you fellas. Some of the people that we encounter in this story are people who have lost their home and they are moving through from one safe place to another. Are you going to be able to find that thing called home when you leave here and what effect has that had on you, being placed here for a period of time?" Something about that question made me uncomfortable, but I couldn't put my finger on it. Perhaps it was the question's implication that family and friends might drift away.

Tony said he would always know where home was: Toronto. His hair seemed to be slicked down with oil and his head was large in proportion to his body. "The last time I got out, after six years, so much had changed. Stores locked up, an old club taken down. But I know the streets will be the same."

Dread wasn't sure it would be quite so easy. "You have a record, people will stereotype you and it's not going to be easy," he said.

"A child or a wife can affect where home is or was," said Brad, the only one of the white inmates who wore his hair long. His voice sounded shaky and I wondered whether he had lost a family member.

"There's a difference," said Parvat. "We had an option of coming here or not. We got caught. The Jews got removed out of their places of home." An important distinction. And then his thoughts took a twist. "For some people, being home is doing drugs and eating once every three days. In here they're eating three meals a day, so some people love jail better than out there."

I passed around a piece of paper and a pen and asked the men to write down comments to share with our Toronto women's book club, which would meet two weeks later to discuss the same book. Then Carol had an exciting announcement. Roddy Doyle had emailed back answers to the men's questions about his novel *The Woman Who Walked Into Doors*. Carol asked the book club members who had posed the questions to read his responses aloud. It was Michael's question that evoked the most interesting reply from the author: "'Do you believe that abuse is learned and carried from generation to generation? I suspect that Charlo himself was a victim of abuse,'" Michael read, with his slight lisp.

Then he read aloud the author's answer:

> "'I don't know' is my answer to that question—and 'possibly' and 'probably.' But I'm reluctant to say 'Yes.' Paula says 'I don't know' quite often in the book, because the possible reasons for Charlo's behaviour seem too neat and simple; and they seem, almost, to excuse his behaviour. If abusive behaviour is learnt, what then of the men or women who hit their children although they themselves were never hit? It happens."

Doyle's point hit a chord, and the men talked about it as they said goodbye and walked down the hall. Gaston and Peter lingered for a moment at Carol's request. Carol went to the chaplain's office and came out with a stack of Professor Duffy's selected security-cleared classics. She gave them each an armful: *The Heart of Darkness* and *The Secret Sharer* by Joseph Conrad; two sci-fi novels by H.G. Wells, *The Island of Dr. Moreau* and *The Time Machine*; Charles Portis's western *True Grit*; and J.D. Salinger's *The Catcher in the Rye*. Peter had already read *The Catcher in the Rye* and said he was not inclined to read it again. Carol told him the books were his to keep, and he was delighted. "These will make a wonderful beginning to a book collection," he said. He told Carol, though, that it was likely he would be transferred to a halfway house just before or after our next meeting. It would be a loss for the book club and a personal loss for me, given his fine journal writing.

Later that afternoon on Amherst Island, the mercury climbed to twenty-eight degrees Celsius in the rare March heat wave and Carol and I brought our pre-dinner drinks outside. Hers looked like a martini, mine was a cold pilsner. A summer haze hung over water that would normally have sheets of ice, and grass was greening where normally a foot or two of snow would lie. Carol was surprised to see dark pink rhubarb shoots breaking through and made plans to weed the asparagus bed in the coming week. We breathed deeply and could smell earth. Dozens of pairs of mergansers floated in the narrow channel between the island and the mainland, like couples promenading. The males roughed up their rakish crests and bobbed their chests impressively into the water in their annual courtship ritual, while the females barked and cronked appreciatively. American robins pecked without success at the still-frozen earth, not far from the month-early scilla and crocus that were opening their throats to the warmth. The scene was soothing after a day in the prison. I couldn't help thinking that the scene would have delighted Antonina, the zookeeper's wife.

With the weirdly early spring, birds were already nesting willy-nilly around the garden. Carol had found a mourning dove nesting in her bird feeder, meaning that she and Bryan would have to avoid that area until the hatchlings fledged.

But that afternoon the surrounding chaotic birdlife failed to distract Carol. She was preoccupied with thoughts of recruiting new book club ambassadors from among the Collins Bay Book Club members to help bolster attendance and encourage the slower readers to get through the books. She'd been disappointed that only nine of the twenty-three members had shown up for book club. Her comments revealed again what I had learned about Carol: partial success was never enough. It was not enough that she had founded a book club in a prison. It had to be a *good* book club and the members had better bloody well show up.

I agreed that it was discouraging that only Peter and Parvat, and perhaps Michael, had finished the book. I mostly understood why Gaston only managed to get to page 100. He'd had his parole hearing to prepare for, college courses to finish and classics to read, as well as the book club book. And also, he told me after the meeting that, lately, he'd been more eager to read "positive spiritual books" because the themes of war and domestic violence were depressing. I told Carol we should keep that in mind for book selection. But what about Dread, who hadn't cracked the spine? He had offered no excuse. I said to Carol that perhaps with the departure of Ben, his buddy and foil, Dread no longer had an enthusiastic reader on his unit to encourage him along. I also reminded her of Albert's stunning excuse at the meeting for why he'd come without his book read, and, in fact, without his book: "We got flooded in 4A Block," he said. "When I woke up there was a couple of inches of feces and urine water in my cell." And floating on top was his copy of *The Zookeeper's Wife*. Derek had remarked that that was better than 'The dog ate my homework,' and we all laughed.

And what about the empathy that I'd hoped the book would elicit? It was there in Peter's remarks, and sometimes Michael's and Parvat's. But it was less evident among the others that day. How different from the unrestrained empathy that the members of our women's book club often expressed.

Within a week Carol had wrangled a meeting to deputize new ambassadors: Peter, and also Michael. She coached them on using their intuition to identify likely readers. Some might already be readers, she said, but others might just be desperate for something to counter the loneliness of prison. She wanted ten to fifteen men to show up every time. She reminded them that one inmate had had a good outcome at a parole hearing in which he and one of the parole board members discussed at length a book he had read in the book club.

Dread, a veteran ambassador, shared his philosophy with the new appointees on how to encourage readers who were having difficulty getting into a book. "The book is not a predator. It's a prey. You have to go after it. It's not like a Sidney Sheldon read. Sidney Sheldon books are predators that go after you." *Predator and prey.* It was the second time in a month that an inmate had made that observation, making me think that some inmates saw the world that way in prison, and possibly even outside it.

After the meeting with the ambassadors, I sat down for individual visits with Gaston and Peter. Gaston arrived with the news that he'd been granted day parole and would be out as soon as a halfway house could find him a bed. Of the classics prescribed by Professor Duffy, he'd finished *The Adventures of Huckleberry Finn*, *Treasure Island*, *The Red Badge of Courage* and Timothy Findley's novel *The Wars*. Dread announced that he had a parole hearing the following month. Two of Carol's ambassadors were already moving on.

Peter had proudly brought his journal along to our meeting. In the two months since I'd given it to him, he'd written ninety-three pages. His entry about *The Zookeeper's Wife* on March 11 in particular was notable: "The zoo, the animals, their influence, need of care, played a huge role in the family's resilience, determination and logistical operation," he wrote. "I found the animals' respect for each other really quite remarkable and something I would have never imagined." He then turned his attention to the animals that appeared at the prison:

> The geese, that sometimes come in the hundreds, eat the grass, shit the grass and go on their way. The grass is so similar to the way it goes in, it may very well just keep on growing after it comes out. Seagulls. Pigeons. And crows that are sometimes large enough to prey on the pigeons. These crows have a calculating look to them. In the summer of 2010 we had a hawk on the premises. Its behaviour and the behaviour of everything else in reaction to it, was simply awesome to watch. I came

to realize that the resident bird population here is not unlike the resident and employed human population here. Predator, preyed upon, and scavenger. But, among the human element it is difficult to discern which is which.

I read that passage several times, noting yet another reference to predators and prey. Here was a man who was becoming more aware of the natural world through his journaling. Also, he was thinking like a writer. With my encouragement, he had even begun paying attention to the smells of the prison and writing about them. And he seemed to have absorbed some of Diane Ackerman's descriptive powers. On March 29 he wrote:

Ann brought up the "prison smell." Jails and prisons all smell the same, not unlike hospitals in that manner. It's very difficult to describe. The cleaning chemicals most certainly contribute. The floors, every square foot, are cleaned every single day and the vapors of such over the years likely linger in unseen crevices and no doubt permeate the concrete itself. The lack of sensuous stimulation is in fact what the prison smell is—an absence of other scents. No breeze with smells of trees, flowers or gardens. No scented candles or potpourri. No ashtrays, empties or leftovers. No perfume. No rubber, asphalt or exhaust. There is not even a whiff of your meal before it arrives. No smells of spring with earth's exhalation after winter. No wind off the water in the summer and no thick lingering aroma that accompanies autumn's dropped leaves or its unmistakable departure when the cold air seals it down.

Unlike nearby Millhaven, a maximum-security prison, which had wire fencing through which the inmates could often see deer and other wildlife, Collins Bay's high walls blocked the view of the outside world. From Peter's perspective, that meant the inmates' awareness of what lay beyond the walls was perceived mainly through sound: traffic, train horns, the occasional police siren and even what he described as "the high-pitched revolutions of speed bikes." He concluded that the deprivation of the senses reduced him and the other men to animals.

He also wrote in depth about *Les Misérables*, which he'd borrowed from the library. How had he had time to do that, while reading the classics *and* the book club book? He thought Victor Hugo's writing had a peculiar rhythm, which he initially attributed to translation, then realized it was the author's narrative style. He wrote in his journal:

> Instead of reading, it was more akin to having been read to. The narrator is gently authoritative, like a benevolent grandfather insinuating what is good, and what is questionable. The ultimate message may be that no person has the right to condemn another and that every person does have the right to not only give, but also to receive goodness and love from another.

These were the very themes we were exploring in *The Zookeeper's Wife*.

Our women's book club met four days before Easter at Evelyn's condo, and her fireplace mantel was festive with decorative eggs and tiny rabbit figures. We settled into her comfortable sofa and chairs to talk about *The Zookeeper's Wife*. After some initial quibbles from two members about the author's occasional digressions from the main story to elaborate on points of research, Ruth warmly championed the book for finding a radically different way to talk about war. "I found it incredibly personal," she said. "I think it was because my house was a zoo." During the years when Ruth's five children were young, she and her husband had a menagerie of pets—two dogs, a cat, a raccoon, an iguana and a rabbit—while simultaneously taking in one or two troubled teens at a time and providing them and their families with counselling. She was a family counsellor who had founded an organization in the 1980s for families with wayward adolescents. Some of the kids were involved with prostitution or drugs, were robbing their parents, had come out of juvenile detention centres or their parents had just given up on them. "Our house became a safe place for them for a little while and I would work with the parents," said Ruth. If her own kids weren't comfortable with a particular guest, the visitor was invited to use the family's Arctic sleeping bag to sleep outside in the back seat of their car. In the summer months, the whole human and animal menagerie would move to the family's lakeside cottage. "I thought, Antonina is a kindred sister," said Ruth, still beautiful in her seventies.

We talked about the book's description of how Poles helped Jewish citizens disguise their faces with bandages and dye their hair blond to evade detection, and I told them about how Peter said the penis re-skinning was what caught his eye.

"Can I just read you one thing because I found it profoundly moving?" asked Deborah, who was wearing a rustic necklace of Indian silver and rough stones. She read from chapter 20, the passages where Ackerman describes the heroic actions of the zoo-keepers' neighbour, pediatrician Henryk Goldszmit (who wrote children's books under the pen name Janusz Korczak). Goldszmit ran an orphanage for Jewish children in the Warsaw Ghetto, where he invented plays and other distractions to soothe them. He repeatedly turned down invitations to escape because it would have meant abandoning the children. The men at Collins Bay had talked about the same passage. Deborah tried to read the sentence about how Goldszmit anticipated the fear of the children on deportation day, and then joined them on the train to Treblinka—all two hundred or so of them. "Because—" Her voice quavered and she stopped, then restarted with tears in her eyes, explaining that the doctor had gone along because he felt he could help them stay calm. She read aloud Ackerman's quote from Goldszmit's writings describing his belief that just as you would sit with a sick child through the night, you stay with children during an ordeal like deportation. Her hand moved to her throat, and she sat looking down at the page. She managed to read on, to where it describes him at the Transshipment Square marching hand in hand with some of the children, while the other children and ten other staff members walked behind, all under German guard and how none of the children cried or cowered because he was with them. After that, she was unable to read further.

I reflected on Henryk Goldszmit and the Zabinskis and the difference between their sacrifices. Goldszmit was a Jewish man protecting dozens of children from suffering, but unable to deliver them from their fate. As non-Jews, the Zabinskis' odds of survival were greater and their opportunity to save lives was greater, but their actions risked endangering more lives, including their own. The risk calculations were very different in each case but both involved a level of heroism that I had difficulty imagining.

The women's book club gathering was often more emotional than the men's. Now the women were eager to hear what the men had said about the book, and I passed around the men's comments. Lillian-Rose read aloud Parvat's observations about how, thanks to the book, he now knew that the Nazis' Aryan breeding program extended to animals as well. They admired Peter's comment about the zoo as a natural place to mount a defence against Nazi programs to extinguish life. So I told them about what Peter had said in the meeting: that the zoo was a place where goodness could reside, and that goodness was more contagious than evil. The women looked at me with slightly dazed expressions, absorbing the beauty of Peter's thought. No one spoke.

We closed up our books, sampled a Quebec-made blue cheese called La Roche Noire that Evelyn had set out and laughed as Carol told us about the time she babysat a Vietnamese pot-bellied pig in their house. The pig toileted on newspaper in the corner of the living room, rather like Antonina's badger, who used her son's training potty. "Vietnamese pigs love to have their bellies scratched and to watch TV," Carol informed us.

"Rather like some husbands we know," joked Betty.

We air-kissed one another good night and drove or walked home. When I opened the front door of our house, our elderly

Maine Coon cat, John Small, staggered sideways as he came to greet me. He was eighteen years old and declining, but still dignified and kind. He bore the name of my ancestor, a minor official in the first government of Upper Canada who had shot and killed its first attorney general in a duel. The original John Small was tried for murder and acquitted. I gathered my cat into my arms. He smelled of urine and age. I carried him to a chair and sat and stroked him so that he would know he was cherished. He looked up into my eyes and the darkness of them told me he was in pain. I would have to make a decision soon about when the pain should stop, and I couldn't bear to contemplate that.

19

RECONSTRUCTING A NARRATIVE

O**N MY WALK FROM THE PARKING LOT** into Collins Bay prison that May, a cloud of stone dust hung between me and the entrance. Either it was construction or a jailbreak. As I drew closer I could see that a restoration company was working on the prison's limestone walls. Behind scaffolding and netting, the company was drilling out disintegrating limestone blocks and replacing them with new stones from a nearby quarry. In the worst areas, every third stone needed replacing because water seepage had hollowed out its core. The new blocks appeared to come from a different seam of rock in the quarry. They were beige, not the cool grey stone mined in the 1930s when the penitentiary was first built by inmate labour. I stood at the entrance and looked up. If not for the razor wire at the top of the walls, the workmen's exterior scaffolding would have made an ideal escape route.

Inside, as I watched my satchel go through the X-ray machine, I wondered if earlier in the day Peter's scheduled transfer to a halfway house had occurred. He didn't want to go, having heard stories about other inmates being unable to meet their parole conditions and sensing that his own temperament would make it hard for him to comply with the rules. He would have preferred to serve out his sentence and bypass parole.

Peter's plan was to turn himself in to Kingston police even before arriving at the halfway house, a strategy that would likely land him at the temporary detention unit at Kingston Penitentiary and allow him to return swiftly to Collins Bay. On the eve of his release, he wrote a note to hand to the police to explain everything. In anticipation of being dry-celled (a two-day feces watch for prisoners who might have swallowed contraband), he planned to swallow a "package." It was a dummy package containing only a pencil eraser and a note saying, "I don't enjoy being humiliated. Do you?"

How ironic that he might end up in Kingston Penitentiary on the very day that we would be talking about it in book group. That sunny May day we were discussing *Alias Grace*, my favourite novel by Canadian author Margaret Atwood, in which Atwood brilliantly channels the voice of a young Irish maid in the 1840s. A work of historical fiction, it draws on the true story of a sixteen-year-old Irish immigrant servant named Grace Marks who was convicted for her role in the 1843 murder of her employer, Thomas Kinnear, and his housekeeper, Nancy Montgomery, on Kinnear's farm north of Toronto. Her accomplice, James McDermott, another servant on the farm, was hanged for the murders. Even though Grace Marks was wearing the dead woman's clothes and was on the run with McDermott when she was arrested, she pleaded not guilty. In the novel, Atwood creates a fictional character named Mary Whitney as Grace's friend and the source of Marks's alias while on the run. The real Marks was spared the gallows, spending nearly thirty years at Kingston Pen and in the "Lunatic Asylum" in Toronto. Ever since, people have debated the guilt and sanity of Grace Marks.

What's more, Marks was now back in the news. Just two weeks before our book group session, the federal government announced that it planned to close Kingston Pen, which since 1835 had been home to some of Canada's most notorious murderers. A maximum-security prison with 346 inmates as well as others in the 130-bed psychiatric unit at the time of the closure announcement, the penitentiary's current occupants would be distributed among prisons like Collins Bay. The local paper, *The Kingston Whig-Standard*, published a special section about the prison and its most high-profile inmates over the decades. Among the photographs of more recent lifers, such as the serial child murderer Clifford Olson, who had died the previous year, and sex killer Paul Bernardo, was a drawing of a female inmate from the nineteenth century: Grace Marks. As Carol and I walked into book club, she was carrying a copy of the *Whig* to show the men.

The image of Grace Marks in the paper fascinated the book club members, but Brad and some of the other men also took a strong interest in the photo of the late Roger Caron, the infamous 1970s Canadian robber who wrote a book on the 1971 prison riot at Kingston Penitentiary, *Bingo!: The Horrifying Eyewitness Account of a Prison Riot*. The rioters had taken six guards hostage and had beaten and tortured two "undesirable" inmates to death while controlling the prison for four days. After the inmate killings, the army was called in to restore order. When Brad suggested I read it, I thanked him for his recommendation, but resolved in my own mind not to do so until my visits to prisons were over.

As I scanned the room, I could see that only one of the original six book club ambassadors was present: Gaston. Gaston confirmed that Peter had been released that morning. Frank and Graham were at Beaver Creek. Ben was in a halfway house. And Dread couldn't attend. I wondered who among the other book club members might shine in their absence.

Carol called the meeting to order. Dressed in black pants and a black vest that closed with snaps over a blue shirt, she blended in with the dark prison-issue clothing that day. But despite her usual admonition of "no fancy jewellery," she was wearing her glittery sapphire-and-diamond wedding ring. The longer she was in the prison, the more relaxed she had become. "I guess the first question you might want to ask is, 'Do you think she did it?'" said Carol. "Let's go around the circle." These were men who had an insight into motive and had first-hand experience of courtroom procedure, so I was interested to hear what they would say.

Joao, whose gentle, slightly startled blue eyes made it difficult to believe that he had once killed another human being, piped up first. "I think she did it," he said. "I had a girlfriend that was probably worse than me. She spent more time in jail than I have." He had seen bad girls, so he wasn't giving Grace a pass just based on gender.

Gaston wasn't sure. "At the beginning I would have said McDermott all the way," he said. "And then as you get further into the book you find that Grace is a little smarter, more cunning. Although she was pretty young—fifteen or sixteen at the time. But she was twelve years old when she started work, so she grew up pretty quick. With nothing. You know someone who has nothing could probably be persuaded to try anything because she wanted out so badly." From the eruption of comments among the others, I detected agreement.

"So for you, the jury's out?" asked Carol.

"The jury's out," said Gaston. "I can see both sides."

Then Brad advanced another theory, and because he was a close reader, he had everybody's attention. "There were certain things or comments that indicated that she might have a mental illness," he said, his long blond hair pushed back behind his ears. "Schizophrenia, another personality. Quite possibly she actually did it. But she had a whole other side that she wasn't completely aware of. And she went for thirty years without confessing. I mean how long can you keep up the facade of 'I don't remember, I don't know' unless you really don't?"

"I sensed that too," I said. "Perhaps dissociative identity disorder."

Carol then turned to Tony, who had come in late to the meeting.

"I think she's definitely guilty of accessory," said Tony, sitting forward in his chair, his voice strong and confident, his hair slicked flat on his head. "But I think she's very manipulative, number one. Number two, I think that she not only used Mary Whitney as her alias, but it was kind of like her alter ego because her friend Mary had this vivacious joy of life that Grace was so envious of. When Mary died it was 'Oh my God what am I going to do?' She was left with this void in her life."

I had forgotten that Grace envied Mary.

Tony went on to trace the trajectory of Grace's further disappointments when she arrived at Kinnear's farm, concluding, "In actuality, I think she had a bigger part in it."

I said that Atwood's Grace reminded me of the Toronto teen who was jailed in 2009 for counselling her boyfriend to murder her perceived rival. She came to be known in the press as "the puppet master," and she received the harsher sentence, even though she did not physically carry out the act. A few of the guys agreed with me. They knew the case well.

"It was either Stockholm syndrome or she was down with it," said Parvat, adjusting his L.A. Dodgers baseball cap. I noticed for the first time that Parvat, convicted for dealing cocaine, breathed audibly through his nose in the manner of James Gandolfini's Tony Soprano character. The air whistled slightly on the intake and sometimes he sniffed, as though the cocaine business had made him more conscious of inhalations.

"So am I the only person who thinks that Grace wasn't guilty?" asked Carol. The room went silent. "I thought she was incredibly complex, smart as heck, very manipulative," she continued. "But she grew to be that and learned all that through living in the prison. So would anybody join me in saying that she's not guilty?"

No one could bring themselves to agree with Carol's argument that Grace was innocent, particularly Colin, who said he had done time with plenty of inmates, later exonerated as wrongfully convicted. Unlike them, Grace never protested her innocence, he said.

Derek was interested in finding out how the mid-nineteenth-century prison life depicted in the novel compared with prison life today. He quoted the passage in the novel in which Grace describes inmates fighting over a piece of cheese. "Does that still happen?" he asked.

I think he knew what the answer might be, given that just a month earlier an inmate at Toronto's Don Jail had admitted to murdering another inmate who had stolen his partially eaten bag of Ruffles potato chips. The guys in the book club all jumped in, not only to confirm that this kind of thing happens, but to offer their own examples. Joao reported that another inmate had threatened him just because he had a cup of coffee. And Colin, who was rumoured to have had a relationship with a female guard at a previous institution, told the group: "There's so much pettiness in prison it's unbelievable: the lady guard that's talking to you more than the other guy and that guy's jealous. Guys get seriously hurt." I knew from his tone that he meant physically.

It is easy to imagine why these petty jealousies erupt. Inmates have so few possessions. Peter had once told me that he had been denied access to an electric keyboard that his mother had sent him, so he drew a keyboard on paper and practiced his music on that.

There wasn't time to get to the question that had been nagging at me all through the discussion: was it true that perpetrators of violent crimes blank out about the details of the event, as Grace claimed, or do they remember every detail? I resolved to put the question to Gaston in my visit with him after book group.

We sat down together in the chapel storage room. I noticed Gaston was missing one of the new teeth that he had proudly worn last time we met. I asked him whether he had clear recollections of his bank robberies. He said he had spoken to some twenty murderers in prison and all of them had vivid recollections of their crimes and there wasn't a day in their lives when they didn't think about them. As for himself, he said he could relate every detail about every holdup, including what was said and what the tellers looked like. He especially remembers the botched jobs.

"Tell me about one of those," I said.

He related the story of his own bungled getaway from a bank robbery in Toronto. One of the packs of money the teller had given him contained a dye pack that exploded as he and his accomplice were trying to escape in their car. The dye pack's cloud of red smoke and pinky-red dye powder filled the vehicle before they had even left the parking lot. The force of the blast was so powerful that it shot out the window and fifteen feet into the air as Gaston sat holding the cash in the passenger seat. The driver aborted their planned escape route and steered the car to the closest exit, careening down a narrow pedestrian walkway through a too-tight stone gateway to the street.

"I had the door open trying to save all the rest of the money but get the dye pack out," he told me. "But the driver hit a post, which hit my arm. I thought it was broken for sure. And I still didn't want to drop the big pile of money so I held this money in my lap. There's people on the sidewalk scrambling to get out of the way and I'm like, 'This is insane.' I'll never forget it." What he remembers most as he was yelling in pain and the car was speeding down the sidewalk was the panicked eyes of a pedestrian.

I knew what he meant about the eyes. His story reminded me of the look of awful intent in the eyes of one of my assailants as he ran toward me in the lane in Hampstead. In an art therapy session to help deal with the trauma of the attack, I was asked to draw the incident. Working with oil pastels, I took a piece of dark construction paper to represent the twilight and sketched two eyes, wide open and full of menace. "Yes," said the art therapist.

"Yes, that's it," I said, pushing the sketch away from me.

Dread poked his head in the chapel storage room door and apologized for missing book group. He'd been appointed range rep and had had to visit an inmate in the hole. I put the question about Grace's amnesia to him too. He said he wasn't sure about amnesia, but he'd seen lots of cold hearts in prison. There were fellows "worse than Hitler" with "many many demons" who slept soundlessly, in his experience. "Some people will do these things and brag about them," he said. "They're coming from generations of cold people. Their dads are killers, their brothers. Human beings kind of evolve like that."

But Dread also wanted to talk about Atwood's style. He was full of praise for the author's writing. "She transports you like an avatar to what's going on," he said, laughing wildly. "And I think her writing is kind of Hemingway simple. But it's beautiful at the same time." He told me he felt he knew Grace completely. "And I know the type of person she is." He understood her affection and concern for her siblings, her ignorance and her hunger to learn more. Dread was responding as I had to the novel.

He confided that he would be leaving the prison in early July. He didn't want the other men to know but said I could tell Carol. I had assumed he was moving to a halfway house. But sometime that summer, the chaplains told Carol that he had been deported to Jamaica. News clippings revealed that a person with his name had already been deported from Canada on four previous occasions. Of all the book club ambassadors, Dread had been the least known to me. Almost a ghost.

That evening, Carol and I took the ferry to Amherst Island. It struck me that her house and Kingston Pen were both built at about the same time and both constructed of local limestone. Just thirty metres from Lake Ontario, Carol's property attracted water snakes from the lake for a brief period that spring. I wasn't surprised because water snakes in the area were drawn to limestone formations. She told me that the snakes had migrated indoors through a sump pump intake and wrapped themselves around the water heater for warmth.

I was apprehensive about what would greet us this time. Two months earlier, in March, when Carol and I arrived at the back door of her house, we saw a garter snake easing itself through a crack in the house's stone foundation. I had assumed that it would hide in the wall or slither down to the basement. But it was in the kitchen, head elevated and looking around. I rolled my overnight bag quickly past it and climbed the stairs, while Carol picked up a broom to brush it back outside.

This time there were no snakes inside. But on the front stoop I spotted a pale grey snake with dusty yellow and orange stripes and orange eyes, like a garter snake that had been washed with bleach. This fellow was happily coiled and gave no indication of wanting to come inside. But Carol, upon spotting it, took her straw broom from beside the fireplace and attempted to sweep it off the stoop. As she did so, the snake flipped around to face her—elongated, challenging. I would have stopped at that point. But she prodded him several more times with the broom till he landed in the adjacent flower bed. Carol had developed a hard shell where snakes were concerned. "Last week some snakes ate the eggs from the mourning doves' nest," she said, by way of explanation.

We brought out cold bottles of beer and salty snacks and eased into deck chairs to talk about the day's book club, the following week's visit of author Lawrence Hill to the women's prison at Grand Valley, the only federal institution for women in Ontario, and Carol's campaign to open book clubs at the final two federal institutions in the province: Fenbrook and Warkworth, both medium-security prisons. I admired her imagination and energy.

It was my chance to ask her whether she was just playing devil's advocate that day in the meeting, arguing that Grace was innocent, or whether she was trying to make a more subtle point. I had a feeling that she was encouraging the men to see that people on the outside are more inclined to assume that an individual is innocent, while the prison population is swifter to condemn.

"I'm always trying to bridge their inside world to the outside world," she said. "And I want them to realize that we on the outside are not all redneck types. They are acutely aware of the judgment of others." She said she would never forget an inmate at Beaver Creek saying to her once: "Carol, do they think we're all monsters?"

As the sun lowered toward the horizon, we prepared supper. I set out leftovers from the previous night's meeting of the board of Book Clubs for Inmates. Then I followed Carol to her vegetable garden, where purple-grey asparagus stalks were sprouting. She bent at the waist and snapped off a handful or two and snipped some daffodils for the table.

The lightly steamed asparagus was sublime. "What do you think?" asked Carol as we took our first bite. "You don't have to talk. Close your eyes." I tasted layers of green, like eating spring itself.

As we ate, we debated the merits of books to recommend the following week to the Beaver Creek Book Club. She told me about the previous week's book club meeting at Joyceville prison where she observed the men discussing Hemingway's *The Old Man and the Sea.* "The old man wins," she said. "He looks as if he's a loser, but he wins. They all love that. They talked about what it is to be a man. One aboriginal man talked about the fish he had caught and the fish his grandfather had caught." She wanted more books like that, more classics, for the book lists.

When we finished the meal, a look of distress appeared briefly on her face and she told me that the rapid expansion of Book Clubs for Inmates meant that she would have to surrender leading the book group at Collins Bay after the summer break. It had been her baby—the book group that had started it all. She had even invested personal time in helping many of the men by facilitating help with legal representation, marriage counselling and other supports. Now the demands of fundraising, running the charity and overseeing the other book groups left her no time. So she had picked a new person to lead the Collins Bay Book Club. The decision had been a hard one, given how much she cared about the men. "You know I'm really, really sad that somehow or other I can't be part of the book club at Collins Bay," she said. "I mean it absolutely breaks my heart."

Perhaps she would have felt differently if she'd known how lasting her impact was. Just downstream, Peter was in a cell at Kingston Penitentiary, possibly near Grace Marks's cell, writing a journal entry and reflecting on *Alias Grace:*

May 2, 2012

So here I am at the Penitentiary I just finished reading about.

I climbed the caged stairs to the level I was directed, the barrier opened to a long and narrow range with two tiers of cells down one side, 36 in all, and tall barred windows on the other side.

I was comfortable, in contrast, exact opposite, of what I was a few hours earlier while in line to get tea at Tim Horton's.

My cell is small but liveable for one (in my way), but has two bunks. It has been painted so many times that there are no longer any definitive edges left unrounded by the paint. The cell is barred, instead of the new style solid door barriers, so it has an open feel to it, seemingly less confined, but no good for noise.

There is a toilet paper shortage. People have been tearing strips off of sheets and stuff ... I lucked out as there was about 25% of a roll left in the cell. Not so lucky with soap though.

I am very tired.

It is only almost 5:30 pm.

... I now have a decent pair of shoes and a clean watch ... I smoked a cigarette. I saw my mother. I saw my sister.

20

MY LAST BOOK CLUB

Alias Grace remained on my bedside table because it was up for discussion just a week later at Beaver Creek. I was interested to see whether the men in the Beaver Creek Book Club would have a different gloss on the protagonist than the men at Collins Bay, and different reactions to the themes of criminality, conscience, prison life and gender.

It had been sixteen years since I had first read this novel and discovered the voice of Grace speaking so believably about her inner life as an Irish servant girl in Victorian Canada. I could never have imagined then that I would be looking forward to sitting down with men who had committed murder and other crimes to find out what they thought about this unforgettable character, with her practical world view, her sense of dignity and her lilting run-on sentences. And yet here I was on a beautiful May morning, certain that I would find the most insightful and unpredictable discussion of this book at Beaver Creek.

At the same time I had feelings of sadness. It was the season's final book club meeting before the facilitators took their annual summer hiatus. When meetings resumed in the fall, Frank would be out on parole, and Graham would likely be out as well. He'd been on so many Unescorted Temporary Absences, it was hard to imagine the Parole Board of Canada would turn him down at his hearing the following month. With both men gone, this was likely to be my last time to sit in on a book discussion at Beaver Creek because I had originally requested access at that prison primarily to follow Graham and Frank.

Just as I was about to leave home, my cellphone rang. It was Carol. She'd had word that there could be unrest in the prison that day—perhaps in all the federal prisons across the country. The federal public safety minister, Vic Toews, had announced a slate of cutbacks that were bound to make inmates angry: increases to the levy that inmates paid for room and board, the elimination of incentive pay for inmates working in the prison industry workshop, CORCAN, and new administrative charges for telephone use—on top of the toll that inmates already paid for telephone calls (which Graham told me was eleven cents a minute). Toews said the measures would save taxpayers more than ten million dollars each year and were designed to "hold criminals to account." It reminded me of the scene in *Alias Grace* when Grace hears talk that the prison might change the bathing rules so that female prisoners would have to bathe in groups, rather than in pairs, to save water and money. Carol and I conferred. We decided we would drive up to Beaver Creek and take our chances. After all, the cutbacks were not scheduled for implementation until the following year, so the inmates' reaction might not be immediate.

When we pulled in to the parking lot, everything seemed calm. I signed in and made my way to the chapel to meet Frank. He said the inmates at Beaver Creek were so happy to be in a minimum facility, they would be unlikely to create a disturbance to protest changing prison conditions. He himself was blasé about the proposed pay cuts. His job was shopping at the on-site grocery store for the other men on his unit. "I'm not worrying about my $6.90 a day," he said. "They could keep it for all I care." But he predicted that the changes would cost the government money because inmates in medium-security facilities would strike, forcing the government to hire contract workers at much higher rates to do the jobs the inmate workforce did: cleaning, cooking, electrical, masonry, garbage disposal and prison industries.

What was more on Frank's mind was the parole board's decision about his future. He'd just heard that he would be released in late May to a halfway house in Toronto, about five kilometres from his house, but not to his own house, which was what he wanted. I said that I understood how upset he was about the limitations on his freedom. It seemed a small consolation, but I told him that I'd heard that Gaston, another former Collins Bay Book Club member, might be billeted in the same halfway house. They could conduct their own mini–book club there.

Frank had one last batch of journal entries for me. Touchingly, he had devoted some of it to talking about a self-help book he was reading to brush up his parenting skills in preparation for going home. It was *Every Family Needs a CEO* by a psychiatrist named Reuven Bar-Levav. "'Cause my daughter's growing up," he said. "Like she's almost fourteen and she's talking about boys. The author says the father's attitude changes and these are subtle things that can balloon into big things." He wanted to be a good dad.

"It's important for her to know that she can talk to you," I said.

Eleven members showed up for book club: Frank, Tom, Doc, Earl, Jason, Raymond, Byrne, Bookman, Richard, Pino, Hal. It was too bad that Graham couldn't attend. He was in Toronto on an Unescorted Temporary Absence, staying with his mother. But I had plans to meet him for coffee in Toronto the next day to talk about the book. The windows were open and between the sounds of planes taking off from the small airport nearby, we could hear blue jays calling out: "Jay! Jay!" The atmosphere was relaxed around the table. By now, after eight meetings, the men knew each other pretty well and could even anticipate what each other might say about a book.

Carol was attending that day only to help pitch books for the next year's reading list, and so Phoebe moderated the discussion of *Alias Grace*. Although Phoebe suggested analyzing the book character by character, some of the book club members couldn't wait to deliver their overall reactions to the book.

Richard seemed to share my love of the novel. "I thought it was beautifully written," he said. "It was reminiscent to me of Dickens. I thoroughly enjoyed it."

Raymond, on the other hand, complained that the story left too many loose ends and predicted that Sarah Polley's anticipated film adaptation of the novel would be "a bore." It would, however, make a great opera, in his view.

Then Tom startled me with a sharp visceral reaction. "If I were to have any problem at all with this book," he said, "I hated the fact that it was in the first person for the most part. It's because as a prisoner and convict myself, I've had people telling me what I think for most of my life. 'This is why you did your crime,' or, 'This is what you're doing,' and I've looked at them my whole life and said, 'You don't know what you're talking about.'" In essence he was challenging Atwood's right to fictionalize Grace's motives and invent Grace's personality. "The audaciousness of thinking, 'I know what made Grace Marks tick'!" he said. He had raised an astute point about the limits of the imagination when dealing with an historical figure. Although Tom never told me why he was in prison, I learned from a newspaper report that a man with the same name was serving a life sentence at Beaver Creek for second-degree murder and had been incarcerated for more than a decade.

Byrne allowed that it was a bold move by Atwood to use the first person, but said she got one thing right about Grace: the lack of trust, which he said was pretty accurate for anyone who had been in prison.

With that, Phoebe directed everyone's attention to the deeply flawed Dr. Simon Jordan, the novel's would-be psychologist who employs free association to try to unlock Grace Marks's memory sixteen years after she was convicted. As a writer, I could see why Atwood invented him. He was a perfect vehicle for allowing Grace to tell her story, including the crossing from Ireland, during which her mother died, her earlier years in service, her fateful time at the Kinnear household and her years in prison and a lunatic asylum. But Atwood invented him as an equally good candidate for psychoanalysis. "A degenerate," was Frank's assessment. He pointed out that Dr. Jordan nurses sexual fantasies about his patient. "And he gets into this relationship with his landlady, who's a nut and wants him to kill her husband," said Frank. "I mean a guy in that position you'd think would go to the police."

Raymond found it unbelievable that the doctor would abandon his extensive work with Grace and run back to the U.S., especially since his psychological report on her could establish his credentials so that he could set up a clinic. Just like last month, when Raymond had argued passionately that the protagonist in *Ordinary Thunderstorms* was unlikely to shed his professional aspirations and his hunger for status, he was raising similar doubts about Jordan. And worse, in Raymond's view, Jordan's departure comes right after a hypnotized Grace seems to reveal that she has a second personality. "Just as it was reaching its crescendo, it completely fizzled," said Raymond.

"I don't find it all that surprising," said Richard calmly. "I think a lot of us fizzled when we were having our crescendo, or we wouldn't be here." Everyone laughed.

"It reflects life," said Doc. "Atwood created this huge void." He thought the doctor's decision to abandon his project was evidence of Atwood employing her literary tools to create character and successfully evoke an emotional response from the reader. It had worked on Raymond.

"I think it makes for a more believable character," agreed Earl. "Jordan had an idea to open an asylum and help heal the sick and it was all noble and everything, but then it turns out that he's just as human as everyone else."

"It's the Victorian era," said Richard. "It's hard for us today to imagine how people repressed their emotions and subscribed to this way of behaviour that was so puritanical." Jordan's decision to run away, he suggested, may have been a way to deal with underlying impulses.

Phoebe took that cue to ask what Atwood was trying to say about the Victorian era.

"I think she used Mary Whitney to put forth her critique of the era," said Tom. He talked about how limited Mary's aspirations were. "You sew your quilts and then you marry someone who already has a farmstead so that you can then hire another maid who will then do the exact same thing."

And then Doc skilfully summed up how badly it actually turned out for Mary: "She had sex with her employer's son, got pregnant for the price of a gold ring, went to get an abortion and bled to death and was buried in the backyard."

Mary and Grace represented opposite extremes of Victorian womanhood, according to Pino, an observation that made everyone's head turn to hear him speak. Without straightening from his habitual slump, he suggested that when they were young teenage servant girls together, Grace was repressed and uneducated while Mary was bold in ways that Grace longed to be. But if you accepted the theory that Mary was a secondary personality *inside* Grace, as Pino maintained, and not a separate character, then the dichotomy represented the self-denial that all Victorian women faced. His insight forced me to rethink everything about Mary, who, to me, had been so fully realized as a separate individual. "That's a classic multiple personality," said Pino. "Mary Whitney is Grace's other hidden personality. That's the way I saw it anyway."

And not just Victorian women. I thought about my own daughter's episodes of dissociation when her eating disorder was most intense. Imperceptibly to others, on some days there were periods when she blanked out while continuing to function on autopilot. For her, it wasn't a different personality emerging, but a numbness, because she was unable to tolerate being in her own body.

Raymond said that if it was a critique of the Victorian period, it wasn't Dickensian enough in its portrayal of prison conditions. But as Phoebe said, it was possible that the women's prison was less harsh than the men's. Even so, two of the men volunteered that they felt the book's scenes of prison guards' belittling treatment of prisoners reflected similar scenes in prisons today.

For Hal, it wasn't just the prison guards' conduct, but other things that hadn't changed significantly. "There's a lot of talk in the book about whether criminality is a condition from birth, a bad seed, the vapours," said Hal. "And once you're a criminal, you're a criminal forever and that stigma follows you. Again none of that thinking seems to have changed at all today and that's something that a lot of us have a direct kind of experience of." I reminded myself that Hal had been in prison for almost twenty years for killing his family. He sounded desperate for a chance to be believed that he had changed, but also hopeless.

Picking up on Hal's point, Pino noted that the doctors who came in to see Grace were interested in the shape of her skull. "That was a Spinoza theory," said Richard, saying that the phrenology in the book pointed to the ideas of the seventeenth-century Dutch philosopher. He tossed that off casually as though everyone in the room would know Spinoza. And sure enough, when I researched his point later, I found a book by the late philosopher H.S. Harris, who asserts that phrenology was inspired by Spinoza's theories.

We dissected the characters of the murdered housekeeper, Nancy Montgomery, and of James McDermott, Grace's co-accused. Tom's assessment that McDermott committed the murders for reasons of jealousy went unchallenged. However, Doc made one keen observation: that one of the reasons we can't fully penetrate McDermott's culpability is that we only see him through Grace's point of view.

I was itching for the discussion to finally come round to Grace. When it did, most of the book club members concluded that Grace was innocent of the murders of her employer, Mr. Kinnear, and Nancy Montgomery.

"I wholeheartedly believe that Atwood decided that this was a woman wronged," said Tom, arguing Atwood portrayed Grace as demure and introverted, even though somewhat calculating. Raymond agreed. Richard said he wanted her to be innocent. And

Frank said he felt sorry for Grace and wanted a good outcome for her.

But even though Frank was in the cheering section for Grace, he also planted a seed of doubt. He pointed out to us that when Grace and McDermott were on the run together after the crime, McDermott wasn't afraid of Grace turning him in. For Frank, McDermott's lack of fear indicated that she wasn't his hostage, which in turn spoke to Grace's complicity in the crime. In essence he was saying 'follow the fear' because fear can tell you a lot about a person.

Grace had given several accounts of the incident over the course of the novel. In the book club meeting it dawned on me that maybe the whole point of *Alias Grace* is to show how unreliable storytelling can be. Byrne asked us to turn to page 25 to consider a passage in which Grace is staring at a flowering tree design on a shawl from India. She stares at it so long that the branches seem like vines twisting in the wind. "I thought that was a pretty interesting little bit of symbolism," said Byrne. "So over a century and a half later, her whole story, we can twist those vines whatever way the wind blows." He wasn't trying to impress. He was just revelling in the beauty of literature.

Byrne wasn't the only reader who had appreciated Atwood's use of symbolism. Tom jumped in, observing that the names of the quilt patterns, Puss in the Corner, Pandora's Box and Solomon's Temple, that serve as the titles for each section of the novel, could generate a whole conversation. No one picked up on that point, but it would have been interesting to explore with him which quilt-pattern names were recognizable metaphors for chapter content.

I then asked the book club members the same question I'd put to Gaston and Dread at Collins Bay: given Grace's seeming amnesia in the book, is it true that perpetrators of a violent crime tend to blank out on the details of the incident, or do they recall everything vividly? Tom said that one man he'd done time with told him that he was in a fog after killing his wife. "He always used to talk to me about the fog of what happened and how he ended up sitting on the couch afterward in a daze and his dead wife sitting beside him," said Tom. The room fell silent at that.

I was glad of the direct answer, but also grateful when Raymond switched the topic to the hypnosis scene and how many questions it raised that Atwood never answered. "All these dangling participles over and over and if the author doesn't solve these issues, it drives me crazy," said Raymond. I could see from his smile that he was pleased with finding the phrase "dangling participles" to serve as a metaphor for loose ends.

"The novel leaves you with more questions," agreed Phoebe, who also admitted to disliking the loose threads in the tale.

Richard was okay with that feature of the novel, though. "There's lots of things in life we just don't get the answers to," he said.

"I tend to agree with you, Richard," said Carol. "As well, she was trying to be true to history."

Then it was time for some housekeeping. Frank announced that this would be his last meeting because he would be out on parole and another book club ambassador was needed to take his place. Earl volunteered to take Frank's place in the fall. I could see that Earl was already beginning to fill Frank's shoes. Phoebe told the men that Graham might also be leaving before book club restarted in the fall and that anyone willing to replace him should speak to him over the summer. All those who had participated since the beginning of the year received participation certificates, copies of which were provided to their parole officers for their case management files.

Finally we came to what many of the men had been waiting for: the vote on the books for the 2012–13 book club season. Carol had distilled the recommendations from our Book Selection Committee with requests from the men to come up with a long list of twenty books from which they had to choose nine for eight meetings. The extra book would serve as a backup in case one of the other books was out of print or hard to obtain. In deference to the men's request for the inclusion of sci-fi, I had added Kazuo Ishiguro's *Never Let Me Go* and Kurt Vonnegut's *Player Piano* to the list of options. And there were classics: Ernest Hemingway's *For Whom the Bell Tolls* and two novels by John Steinbeck: *Cannery Row* and *The Grapes of Wrath*. Also on the list was a book that Raymond had lobbied for at the last meeting: *Ragtime*, by American novelist E.L. Doctorow. Everyone voted by secret ballot.

Many of the men came up to me at the end of the meeting to say goodbye.

"Thank you so much, Ann," said Richard, taking off his black-framed reading glasses and shaking my hand. I thanked him for his comment on Spinoza. "Oh please," he said, and flushed slightly.

Then Byrne came up, his eyes alive with enthusiasm. He wanted to tell me about how the opening sequence in *Alias Grace* had triggered a strong memory of his own time at Kingston Penitentiary. "When it talks about the grey stone walls and plants growing up through the pebbles, I was there and picking up flowers thinking of my little girl," he said. The flowers were buttercups and chicory, not the peonies that Grace imagines in the novel. He had observed that moment in his life as a writer might do and was offering his observation as a gift. He also said he identified with the image of Grace's shoes as she walks. For him, it brought back memories of the shoes that inmates receive when they enter the federal penitentiary and his gratitude to get a new pair at that time.

Many of them asked hopefully if I would be back in the fall. I said it wasn't certain, but thanked them for making me welcome.

That evening I opened Frank's journals. He had lots more to say about *Alias Grace* and he described it as the best book he had read in the prison book clubs.

The next morning I was scheduled to meet Graham for coffee in Toronto. He suggested a local coffee shop in his mother's neighbourhood. It was my first time to meet him alone outside the prison and I was a little nervous, not knowing whether former gang members might be after him. He was already inside with a newspaper and a mug of coffee, looking out the window. We waved, and as I lined up to buy a bottle of water, I looked around. The place had a folksy log cabin decor and light-stained knotty pine furnishings, with branded coffees carrying backwoods names like "The Grizz."

When I sat down, Graham was full of talk about how the inmate pay cutbacks were lousy policy. On the subject of increasing inmate contribution to room and board, he said it would be like double-dipping, since the extremely low pay stipends already reflected amounts for room and board.

It sounded as though he would have very little time for reading if he were granted parole the following month. The John Howard Society in the area where he had requested a spot in a halfway house had asked him to address their general meeting to give them a briefing about the federal penitentiary system. He was writing a practical manual for criminology students and inmates in the federal system. And he was thinking of getting paid work with a moving company.

We were finishing up our drinks when a policeman walked by and took a good look at Graham. My reaction must have been transparent because he said, "I see them all the time. I'm used to them now." I felt very self-conscious. Was this just a chance encounter or did the police keep a close eye on parolees on their "unescorted" absences—especially high-profile offenders like Graham? I wondered whether my photo was now in a police file as an "unknown woman" or "associate." Were disgruntled Hells Angels members also likely to drive by? As I was mulling that over, Graham asked, "What time is it?" He had to check in with his parole officer at eleven. We hadn't had time to talk about *Alias Grace*. He gave me a big hug—by now his typical greeting and send-off for Carol and me whenever we got together. And he walked me to my car.

"Bye Graham," I said.

"Bye."

21

THE EXMATES

IT WAS CAROL who gave me the courage to meet with some of the book club members once they were no longer inmates and had become parolees. "Exmates" or "outmates" was her joking term for them. She dared them with her trust and referred to them as "graduates of the book club." They lived up to her trust, for the most part.

It had started months earlier with Vince, her special protege from the Collins Bay Book Club, who had left the prison before I even arrived. When he was transferred to a halfway house and found work with a moving company, she bought him some of the books that the men in his old book club were reading and urged him to read along. Because he had had an addiction, she deputized a Circle of Support for him, manned by volunteers who were friends of hers. Circles of that type were originally developed to support sex offenders as they re-entered the community, but a CSC community chaplain helped her adapt the program for other federal offenders like Vince graduating from her book club. And when Vince had trouble lining up housing after the halfway house, Carol and her husband acted as guarantors on his rental agreement. For other men, she supplied books, helped calm spouses and encouraged further education. None of this was part of Book

Clubs for Inmates. It was just her seemingly insatiable need to help and her desire to see her graduates succeed.

I was not as bold as Carol, but I was eager to see whether the men would sustain their reading habit after leaving prison. I began to find out on July 4, when my cellphone rang and an unfamiliar number appeared on the screen.

"Hello?"

"Hi, it's me, Frank."

"Hello, Frank!" I said. I had left my number for him at his new Salvation Army halfway house, a converted Victorian house with a wraparound porch in a downtown Toronto neighbourhood. He slept there and had a curfew, but was allowed to visit his home during the day.

"I'm calling you from a computer," he said.

"Voice over internet?" I asked.

"No, it's a phone. I just wanted a plain phone but my wife convinced me I had to be able to text as well." He had been in prison such a long time that he had missed how cellphones had evolved to include the internet, email and texting.

It was great to hear his voice. He told me that he already had a library card and a job on a landscaping crew. A library card! I told him that I was worried about him working in the heat that day. It was thirty-six degrees Celsius with 95 percent humidity and torpid air. The sky was grey with particulate matter. He said that the team had quit work at noon because it was dangerously hot.

According to Frank, his house had become chaotic in his absence. His mother-in-law had moved in, bringing her furniture with her, and the number of pets had spiralled out of control. "There are two dogs and a cat chasing each other and birds flying free," he said, complaining that the pets seemed to live forever. "It's like Tweety Bird and Sylvester." Now that he was back in town, the birds had to stay in their cages and his mother-in-law was moving out before Christmas.

"It must be great to see your family every evening," I said.

He said it was, but that he had eaten the previous evening's

Chinese-food dinner of duck and rice alone. His wife worked long hours and his son and daughter had numerous after-school activities. He had to weave himself back into his family's busy lives.

I was hardly surprised at what he told me next. He and Gaston were joining a book club that was just starting up at their halfway house, and Frank hadn't had to organize it. He had arrived just as someone else in the halfway house was hunting for a book club for herself—Renata, a staffer there. Frustrated by the waiting list at her local library's book club, Renata had persuaded her supervisor to let her start one at work, with parolees. Carol had offered resources from Book Clubs for Inmates, but Renata was determined to go it alone and buy the books at thrift stores whenever possible.

When the call ended I felt exhilarated. Finding time to read while in a halfway house was much harder than finding time to read in prison. As parolees, the men had multiple new responsibilities. Gaston and Frank both had to work, attend programs, observe curfews, see their parole officers and re-establish their lives with their wives and children. The fact that they had also made a commitment to a book club was an indicator that Carol's big idea was having long-term positive effects.

Three weeks later, I drove to meet Graham at his halfway house about an hour's drive outside of Toronto. Beaver Creek had released him a week earlier. As I was driving, a text came in from Frank. I pulled over and had a look at my phone. "The book group met," his text read. "Renata is not a bad facilitator. The group is small right now with six members. The book she chose is *Shutter Island* by Dennis Lehane. The movie bored me but maybe I will pay more attention to the book if I can find the time to read it."

I pulled back onto the road, enjoying the lushness of the roadside sumac bushes, their drupes the colour of dried blood. I was still a little nervous about meeting Graham outside of prison because I imagined that people from his past might want to target him. But I used the passing natural scenery to soothe myself, and Frank's news to give me confidence.

Graham's halfway house was on a dreary residential street in the city's downtown just five kilometres from a Hells Angels clubhouse. A broad-shouldered three-storey brick building, the halfway house was painted pale grey and had a wooden bench outside, presumably for smokers. The front door had been lowered to street level and there was no porch, only a tidy awning over the entrance door. What appeared to be a security camera was aimed at the entrance. Graham came out of the building wearing workout gear. I guessed that the staff inside were watching via the camera.

I suggested that we go to a café and then the library, since he was spending a lot of his time there. Halfway houses keep new parolees on a tight leash in the early days following release, so Graham had to go back inside to get permission for my suggested itinerary. And then it was time for me to take another brave step— unlock my car door for Graham and get into a car alone with him for the drive to the library. He lowered his towering frame into the passenger seat and used the mechanical lever to slide the seat back as far as it could go.

I asked if a ROPE (Repeat Offender Parole Enforcement) squad was following us, even though I knew that their focus was on parole violators. "Probably," he said. I looked over my shoulder as I guided the car to a parkade across from the library, but no one appeared to be tailing us.

"I have this niggling concern that we'll be gunned down," I said, thinking of his former gang members.

"No, the people who have a problem are the guys who are making up stories or who testified about people. I've got all the skeletons in the closet and they'll stay in the closet and they know that." I reminded myself that he'd left the gang on good terms. Nevertheless his parole restrictions required him to avoid a large area of the city around the Hells Angels clubhouse.

I was trembling in the parking garage, perhaps because of my difficulties with parking garages in London, and was relieved that Graham talked the whole time. I noticed he had sweat on his brow too.

We found a fluorescent bulb–lit café in the mall near the library and ordered coffee and pastries for him and water for me. I reached into my satchel and pulled out a used copy of *All the Pretty Horses* by Cormac McCarthy. "My husband and I have both read it and we thought you'd like it." He thanked me. I told him that Frank had joined a book club at his halfway house. "Is there potential that you could start a book club at yours?"

"It's possible. I'd have to get to know some of those guys a little better. Half don't intermingle with anybody, so I'd have only twelve guys to pick from. I think Frankie's in a bigger place." He said that if he couldn't start one himself, he would join a book club out of the public library. "A good way to meet people, right?"

I took a sip of my water. "What are your emotions now that you're actually out of prison?"

"It's anxiety probably. Your head's going in twenty different directions. It's almost like information overload for me." He hadn't said "a feeling of liberation," as I'd anticipated. He hadn't said "free."

"I know," I said. "Things are expected and yet there are so many limitations." He had ten more years until his warrant would expire. Ten years of parole. The authorities could impose restrictions on him for years to come.

He was aware that he needed to line up work and had already applied for two positions, including a job as a housing outreach worker for people coming out of jail. He'd included Carol as one of his references. "I could probably get a job doing grunt work right away, but I want to do something I like." For that job application, he was transparent about his time in prison. It was now his calling card.

Meanwhile, the local John Howard Society had invited him to appear at their Prisoners' Justice Day event, and a law professor at the University of Western Ontario had invited him to speak to his students in the fall. Graham was in demand.

As we talked in the café, his eyes occasionally looked over my shoulder or out the window. It made me a little more on edge about who might be following us. I asked him if he would show me his gang tattoo with the evidence of his withdrawal. He pulled the neck of his T-shirt to one side and there it was on his freckled skin, the logo of his street crew. The colours had faded but clearly etched were the year he joined, and the year he quit. The exit year was the year he joined the book club. He offered to show me another tattoo on his arm. An image of a man with pale eyes. "My buddy who was killed," he explained.

No matter how model a citizen Graham was now, his past was still etched on him.

When we had finished our snack, he gave me a tour of his favourite spot in the city's main library branch—a table on the third floor near the German literature and English literature stacks. We talked about *Alias Grace*, because he had been away on a UTA for that book club discussion. He had liked the story but was expecting Grace to fully assume the identity of Mary Whitney or some similar twist.

That table was where he would begin work on his next slate of distance university courses the following month, using a laptop that his wife had mailed to him from her base in Manitoba. And in a few months' time he would take part as a "human book" in the Human Library project. It was an initiative that aimed to dismantle stereotypes by asserting that each human being is like a book worthy of being discovered, and by inviting library visitors to sit down and talk with each one.

I drove him back to the halfway house, much calmer than when the visit started. His anxiety had matched my own. Anxiety was a great equalizer.

In the months that followed, Graham dazzled his parole officer and many others. After working briefly in construction, he started a successful painting company with one of his brothers. Several police conferences invited him to speak to their new recruits. And he became the star speaker at Carol's Book Clubs for Inmates fundraisers, often telling the story of how *The Boy in the Moon* reached one murderer who attended the book club, whereas the system's violence prevention programs had not. An engaging speaker, armed with a sense of humour and plenty of statistics, Graham captivated audiences. A rule preventing Canadian charities from having directors with criminal records meant that Carol couldn't install him as a director of Book Clubs for Inmates Inc., but he became an active member of the organization.

That fall I was dismayed to discover that Gaston was back behind bars. He had left the prison on May 10, shortly after the *Alias Grace* discussion. He had attended one meeting of Frank's halfway house book club, reading *Shutter Island*. Then in mid-August he was back in the slammer for having failed a random drug test. The test showed traces of opiates. Before returning to Collins Bay he spent fourteen days in the Don Jail in Toronto. "The worst fourteen days of my life," he told me. The Don Jail was what the men called a "bucket," a provincial jail that acted as a holding pen for individuals awaiting trial or convicted inmates en route to other facilities. During those two weeks he fasted for three days, ranted, yelled, screamed and banged.

The irony was that the trace opiates came from the poppy seeds on the bagels provided at breakfast by his Toronto halfway house, according to Gaston. He compiled documents reporting similar cases for his parole board hearing. A particularly compelling piece of evidence was the U.S. Federal Bureau of Prisons Form BP-S291(52), which acknowledges that poppy seeds may cause a positive drug test and that inmates on parole must agree not to consume them. While that seemed persuasive, in the ruthless court of the prison yard, the other inmates dubbed him "Bagel Boy."

That fall, the parole board agreed with Gaston's evidence about the poppy seeds and ordered his immediate release, this time to his home rather than a halfway house. A month later, I finally had an opportunity to meet him outside Collins Bay. It was on a day when he had just visited with Carol and she had given him one of her husband's suits to wear for a job interview at an addiction treatment centre. The interview opportunity itself was also thanks to Carol working her contacts. Inspired by Carol's generosity, I arranged to meet Gaston at the Royal Conservatory of Music café, and brought along three of my husband's silk ties to complete his interview outfit. It had been so long since Gaston had worn a suit, he was uncertain about the required components. "Is it just the jacket and pants?" he said, showing me Bryan's beautiful blue pinstripe jacket and trousers. I assured him that a vest was no longer necessary.

At the café I had a *prosciutto cotto* panini and he ordered the tuna wrap, though he was too busy talking to take a bite. Only now was he able to feel truly free, he told me in his usual rapid-fire nervous patter. During his three months at the halfway house, the burden of responsibilities was too great, he said. "Looking back now, I'm thinking, holy mackerel, how did I juggle it?" Back then, he had had to provide a complete itinerary of where he was at all times, and call the halfway house from a land line upon entering and departing a public building like a mall or library. The land-line number was proof of his location, but it meant scrambling to find increasingly rare public phone booths. When he found work on a landscaping crew, he had to phone in at the start and end of each shift. Whenever the crew drove near some of the banks he had robbed, he experienced an emotional jolt. "It brings you right back. Holy!" Once when he was late calling in, his curfew was moved up to seven o'clock as a penalty.

Gaston listed with exasperation all his other obligations from that time in the halfway house: attending weekly Community Maintenance Program meetings, AA and NA meetings, relapse prevention meetings, case management team meetings, urinalysis testing and parole officer meetings. His chores at the halfway house included vacuuming and yardwork. "Then of course my wife, my four kids, my job, my responsibilities to the church. Holy macaroni."

So when Collins Bay released him to his own home in Toronto, not a halfway house, it took him two full weeks to stop reaching for the phone out of habit, thinking he had to call someone to report in.

Gaston's cellphone rang during our conversation. It was his contact for the interview. He handled it professionally, and when the interviewer asked how he knew Carol, he said he had been in her book club in prison. After it was over, I told him how great it was that he had told the truth.

"I didn't want to, but when he asked me, I can't lie," he said. That was a change. I recalled another story he had told me about a different job interview back in the spring, several weeks before Collins Bay was about to release him for the first time. He did the interview by phone from prison with his parole officer in the room, and he told the potential employer a little white lie: he couldn't take up the job immediately because he had a "big project in eastern Ontario" and didn't want to leave his current employer in the lurch. He said his parole officer rolled her eyes.

"You know, Annie," he said, using a name I hadn't been called in more than thirty years, "if I had to tell you what my dream job was, it's to work in the addictions field. Not get calluses on my hands, but put on a nice suit and tie and help people. You know I like to talk."

As we finished our sandwiches and headed out, Gaston and I talked about his reading *Shutter Island* at the halfway house, then about his search for books that he and his wife could read together. "And you know what I want for Christmas?" he said, as we shook hands to say goodbye. "I told my wife I want a new reading lamp so I can read at night."

In the months that followed, Gaston enrolled in a two-year university program in addictions and mental health and began volunteering at the addictions centre. He left landscaping and began working in a sign business, making sales calls, driving a truck and organizing the warehouse. Like many former inmates, he remained on the police radar and wound up in jail twice more for brief periods though, to the best of my knowledge, he was never convicted.

Frank's life was so hectic that we didn't have a chance to talk at length until some nine months later. He and his wife spoke to me from an arena where their son was playing hockey. His son's team won the game but Frank observed that Malcolm Gladwell was right in *Outliers* when he said that hockey players born early in the year had an advantage over teammates born later in the same year. His son, born in November, was suddenly six inches shorter than his good friend on the team who was born in February. "He's disadvantaged," said Frank.

Lots had changed for Frank. He was working as a builder on a project to convert a six-car garage into a guest house on a property north of the city. It was a complete gut job and included elaborate reframing. During his six years on the lam, when he spent most of his time in the main branch of the Toronto Public Library, he had researched construction methods and materials at length.

He was still living in the halfway house and enjoying the book club there. Just like at Collins Bay and Beaver Creek, his new book club met about once a month, on a Wednesday evening after work, and they discussed books that many other mainstream book clubs were also reading, including Yann Martel's *Life of Pi* and Anne Michaels's *Fugitive Pieces*. They held their meetings off-site at a bubble-tea house or a donut shop. Because there were usually only about eight members, they could generally find a corner in which to talk. "It's a little diversion from everyday things, and it's interesting to hear those guys talk," Frank told me. He had no recruiting role in the book club. Renata ran it all, and did a good job, he said. He liked that she posted notices at the halfway house advertising each book club meeting, with accompanying blurbs from inmates who had read the book before. What a great way to promote a book in-house, I thought. Not quotes from Amazon or *New York Times* book reviews, but from the guys themselves. If there was a film associated with a book, like *Life of Pi*, the book club would screen it together sometime after the book discussion.

"*The Thirteenth Tale* is what we're reading now," he said. "It's pretty good. It's about a voracious reader. She was raised in a bookstore. Then there's a famous writer in England that's dying and wants her to do her biography. The problem is, she's had different biographers before and it's always a lie. This one's supposed to be the truth." Frank's mini-review made me want to read it.

"How would you compare your book club at the halfway house to the one at Collins Bay?" I asked.

"It's smaller. The Beaver Creek Book Club was probably the best one. You've got serious readers there, who've read a lot of books." As for the Collins Bay Book Club, "It gave me something to look forward to, 'cause I was bored out of my head there. At least once a month you could talk to normal people from the outside, not criminals." I recalled that he had once told me that the book club meetings were a respite from the prison yard, where most conversation involved boasting about crime.

Ben agreed to meet me several times, including one cool April day two years after he had left Collins Bay. I waited for him at a café near his halfway house in Toronto. When he walked in the door, he was almost unrecognizable, having shorn his dreads into a short head-hugging layer of hair, revealing his forehead. A curly moustache and goatee encircled his mouth and when he came toward me smiling, his teeth blazed white. He was wearing a black leather-sleeved hoodie with its hood down. I was only finally sure it was him when he removed his reflecting aviator sunglasses, revealing his familiar downward-slanting eyes with their heavy lids.

We took our coffees outside into the sunshine, grateful for our warm jackets. I knew Ben had had a succession of jobs since leaving Collins Bay, including warehouse work for a retail store and a pretty gruelling stint staining cabinetry, which had paid eleven dollars an hour. According to Carol, he had briefly run a Cash for Gold business until a customer conned him with a fake diamond ring, setting him back seven thousand dollars. That spring he was buying cheap cars at auctions, fixing them up and selling them, making two or three thousand dollars per car. And he'd been talking to a Jamaican coffee company about a business venture to sell their products in Canada.

"You know, Ben," I said. "I keep looking at these storefronts across the street and wondering which could be a bookshop café." I told him I'd always hoped one of the book club members might open a bookstore. The coffee tie-in sounded ideal to me. He looked dubiously at the row of two-storey brick shops. It would be all he could do to make the coffee deal work, he explained, because he had no capital up front to invest. There was also a sizable tax bill to pay first. He took a drink from his mocha coffee and wiped the whipped cream and chocolate syrup off his beard.

Ben had continued to write his journal regularly for about a month, recording all the happy reunions with friends and family. But his writing also contained descriptions of conditions in the halfway house that made him uneasy. His first roommate talked to himself, was heavily tattooed and wore white socks so dirty that they were black. The poor health and hygiene of some of his housemates made him fastidious in the kitchen and bathroom. "You have to clean, wipe, bleach, wash before you use anything," he wrote in his journal. As a result, he showered at the houses of family or friends.

Then we talked about books, how Carol had given him *Alias Grace* to read when he first entered the halfway house, and how he was now reading *And the Mountains Echoed* by Khaled Hosseini. He mentioned the scene where Abdullah was left behind as his father took his three-year-old sister to Kabul to be adopted by another family. It had stayed with him, he said. I told him it had lingered with me too, stirring up a sharp feeling of loss and confusion. I pulled a gift for him out of my satchel: my copy of Juan Gabriel Vásquez's novel, *The Sound of Things Falling*, which I had read with my women's book club. "We have to talk about it after you've finished," I told him. "One of the women in my book club identified something symbolic in the novel that the rest of us had missed and it's a thrilling insight."

Finally I asked him to tell me about the manslaughter charge that had landed him at Collins Bay and in Carol's book club. Ben told me his version of events. He said that people wearing courier uniforms attempted a home invasion at his townhouse. He was already suspicious about the delivery because he wasn't expecting a package. When they first knocked, he didn't answer the door. But when they rang the doorbell twice, he responded. He knew something was up when the courier driver didn't have a pen for him to sign the signature pad. As Ben went back into the house, a man came running through the door with a .380-calibre pistol. "My mistake was leaving the door open," said Ben. "So basically I had to shoot him." He used the Glock semi-automatic pistol that he kept in his house. He told me that the robbers knew he was involved in drugs and had assumed he had money and drugs in the house. The Crown acknowledged that there were elements of self-defence in the case, but Ben was nevertheless convicted of manslaughter.

I asked him about Dread. "All I know is that he was deported to Jamaica," I said. Ben said he had heard that Dread was building a house there and that his children were going to move to Jamaica to go to school. I remembered that Dread had once told me his dream house would have a "king's bedroom" for the man and a "queen's bedroom" for the woman.

"And his wife?" I asked.

He didn't know.

"Is he still reading?"

Again Ben didn't know. It was time to go, and we shook hands. I wished him well, as always, and reminded him to call me when he had finished the Vásquez book.

I first heard from Peter months later. He called me a couple of times from a halfway house, returned to prison for a while after what he called "a dirty piss test," and was then back out and keen to invite Carol and me for a coffee in his small town. We agreed to meet, but Carol had to cancel at the last minute. So I packed my copy of Lisa Moore's *Caught*, which I'd read in two days flat, and a copy of the children's book *Goodnight Moon* because he had a friend with a child who loved books, and I drove out of the city alone to meet him. As I drove I recalled my last visit with him, in which I'd asked him to describe the room in Collins Bay that we were sitting in from a writer's perspective. It was a different storage room from the one we usually used—one that also contained guitars, chairs and music stands but had no outside windows. Peter told me, "It's empty, even with stuff in it. Because it's jail." He had a writer's sensibility.

I arrived at the coffee shop first and found a booth by the window. When he walked in, it seemed to me that he had aged a decade beyond his thirty-eight years. His hair flowed almost to his shoulders and was significantly grey. He had grown bushy sideburns that mingled with his hair. His face was mottled—perhaps his old psoriasis problem—and he seemed a little confused. It was 11 a.m., so I had bought him a turkey sandwich and myself an egg-and-bacon bagel. Then when I only ate half of mine, he asked if he could finish it.

"Of course," I said.

He was not working and had no interest in looking for work, although he was a skilled millwright. He lived at no fixed address. And he wasn't reading, even though in the months after I'd stopped participating in the Collins Bay Book Club, he had been an outstanding ambassador for the group. Just as he had back at Collins Bay, he was up all night and asleep during the day. I was probably disturbing his schedule. Of all the men I had met in prison, he was the most promising writer, one of the most insightful readers, and yet at that moment seemingly lost. Music had become his main interest. He had played a few guitar gigs locally. He opened his phone and played me a few tunes that he was into. He looked so vulnerable and innocent as he stared down at the screen. I was very distressed to find out months later that he had been arrested and charged with first degree murder. His application for bail had been denied. At the time of writing he was awaiting trial.

As for Carol, her energy for expansion continued. She found it easier to open book clubs in more prisons when another charity called First Book Canada partnered with her to help reduce the cost of the books. That was in 2012. After she had complained to me about the many delays in opening a book club at Fenbrook, it finally happened that fall. And when Warkworth medium-security prison opened its book club also that autumn, Carol finally achieved the milestone of operating a book club in every federal prison in Ontario. The following year she added book clubs in Winnipeg at Stony Mountain Institution and at Bowden in Red Deer, Alberta. A memorial donation from the late Ontario court judge Madame Justice Joan Lax enabled Carol to open book clubs in all the remaining federal women's prisons in Canada, including her first francophone book club at Joliette Institution in Quebec. By the spring of 2015, she had seventeen book clubs in fourteen institutions and plans to open more in the fall of 2015. Among her many new book club members was a former Guantánamo inmate. She has also coached volunteers in New York and California in her model so that they could open book clubs in prisons there. Given her energy and drive, it's hard to imagine when Carol will finally feel satisfied that she has accomplished what she set out to do.

Although she has never claimed that the book clubs are designed to rehabilitate inmates, research continues to point to interesting links between reading literary fiction and the growth of empathy. One study by researchers at the New School for Social Research in New York City published in *Science* in 2013 found that study participants who read literary fiction, as opposed to non-fiction, genre fiction or nothing, performed better on tests that measured empathy and social perception. One hypothesis is that characters in literary fiction are less fully sketched and less stereotypical, requiring the reader to imagine some of their thoughts and thereby empathize.

A report on the U.K. project Prison Reading Groups sets out anecdotal evidence that fiction has played a role in nurturing empathy among their incarcerated readers and found that book discussions contributed to informal learning and pro-social behaviour. So it was surprising to witness new U.K. rules in November 2013 to stop family and friends of inmates sending books to their loved ones in prison. However, those provisions were overturned by a high court justice the following year after a sustained protest by many prominent U.K. authors and free speech campaigners. In Brazil and Italy, meanwhile, some prisons have experimented with reading programs that allow inmates to reduce their prison sentences by reading a prescribed number of approved books.

Since my time visiting the prisons in 2011 and 2012, both Collins Bay Institution and Beaver Creek Institution have changed substantially. Collins Bay, which was a medium-security prison at that time, has now opened a maximum-security unit and absorbed the adjacent minimum-security prison, Frontenac. Similarly, Beaver Creek's minimum-security facility has absorbed its adjacent medium-security prison, the former Fenbrook Institution. Regardless of those changes, the book clubs continue to thrive.

My stack of books from my time in the prison book club occupies a corner of my office reserved just for them. They fill one shelf, two rows deep, and then stack vertically on a lateral filing cabinet in five columns, each more than a foot high. When I look at them, my eye goes to the Dial Press edition of *The Guernsey Literary and Potato Peel Pie Society*, with its image of a vintage postcard postmarked from Guernsey; my Penguin trade paperback edition of *The Grapes of Wrath*, with the etching of an overloaded truck on the cover; and then of course *Alias Grace*, my old hardcover edition with the bars of a cell superimposed over a Rossetti painting of Elizabeth Siddal. Someday I will separate these books, but not yet. They belong together for now. They mapped my history with the men in 2011 and 2012.

When I began this journey in books with the guys and with Carol, I was encouraged by my father's voice in my head telling me to expect the best of people and they will rise to the occasion. Now all I have to do is look at that stack of books and the men's voices are in my head, offering surprising insights or making me laugh. One look at *The Zookeeper's Wife*, and I remember Peter saying that goodness is more contagious than evil. When

I pull *The Grapes of Wrath* off the shelf, I think of Ben's sweet observation about Rose of Sharon as she nurses a starving man after giving birth to a stillborn baby: "She fulfilled her purpose." With Frank, it was the way that characters stayed with him from book to book and entered his vernacular, like the Beggarmaster in *A Fine Balance*, or the father in *Angela's Ashes*, or Shackleton's men from *Endurance*. He made me think about the characters who have stayed with me since the prison book club: scrappy Tom Joad, elusive Grace Marks and bookish Dawsey Adams. And I can't look at the dust jacket of *In the Garden of Beasts* without hearing Graham laughing uproariously and saying "Fritz, count the cutlery," poking fun at the misguided priorities and parsimoniousness of U.S. ambassador William Dodd and the skulking of his German butler, Fritz.

Whenever I read a work of historical fiction, I'll think of Tom's passionate speech to the Beaver Creek Book Club about the audacity of any author trying to invent what Grace Marks thought. And then I'll picture Byrne telling me about walking the yard at Kingston Penitentiary, looking down at the chicory and buttercups growing between the stones and thinking of his daughter, and remarking on how the opening pages of *Alias Grace* echo that experience.

Someone once asked me what I would do with a spare evening, given the choice between attending a book club meeting with my women friends in Toronto or with the men at Collins Bay or Beaver Creek. I would choose the prison book clubs. I would give up the wine and beer, the hot pear-and-apple crumble and the unusual cheeses to sit without drinking or eating anything in a room with the prison inmates I knew. Why? Because so much more is at stake. Anything could happen there that could change their lives or mine. And I am sure that at least one of their comments would stay with me always.

EPILOGUE

Nᴏᴛ ꜰᴀʀ ꜰʀᴏᴍ ᴍʏ sᴛᴀᴄᴋ of book club books, in another section of my bookshelf, is an old red cloth-bound volume from my father's books of poetry, *The Collected Poems of W.B. Yeats* that came to me when we emptied my mother's bookshelves in late 2014. One day last spring I opened it for the first time and discovered that it was published in 1950 in London. I'm guessing that my father bought it during his trip to England that year when he went to Little Gidding for the first time. Several pages have the corners turned down and the book first fell open at the poem "Under Ben Bulben," revealing the lines that my father quoted so often:

> Cast a cold eye
> On life, on death.
> Horseman, pass by!

Those lines are the epitaph on Yeats's tombstone and they are the lines we said over my father shortly after he died. In my mind I was back where my own journey had started, by my father's grave in the cemetery where the sunken earth was awaiting a marker. I recognized the connections between Eliot's "Little Gidding" and this poem, with their ruminations on death and journeys. Until then, I had always imagined that the horseman was the horseman of death, and that the poet was asking to be spared. But another interpretation came to me that day: the horseman is fear. I had found some of the courage my father wanted me to find. I had created meaning with men who represented the very thing I feared. And, in a strange way, they had guided me back to a better understanding of my father.

READING LIST

A list of books and poems discussed or mentioned in *The Prison Book Club*:

Abella, Irving; Troper, Harold. *None Is Too Many: Canada and the Jews of Europe, 1933–1948*. Toronto: University of Toronto Press, 2012.

Ackerman, Diane. *The Zookeeper's Wife: A War Story*. New York: W.W. Norton & Company, Inc., 2008.

Adiga, Aravind. *White Tiger: A Novel*. Toronto: Simon & Schuster Canada, 2008.

Atwood, Margaret. *Alias Grace*. Toronto: Doubleday Canada, 2000.

Bar-Levav, Reuven. *Every Family Needs a CEO: What Mothers and Fathers Can Do About Our Deteriorating Families and Values*. New York: Fathering, Inc. Press, 1995.

Barbery, Muriel. *The Elegance of the Hedgehog*. New York: Europa Editions Incorporated, 2008.

Benioff, David. *City of Thieves*. New York: Penguin Publishing Group, 2009.

Boyd, William. *An Ice-Cream War*. New York: Penguin Publishing Group, 2011.

Boyd, William. *Ordinary Thunderstorms*. Toronto: Random House of Canada, 2011.

Boyden, Joseph. *Three Day Road*. Toronto: Penguin Group Canada, 2008.

Brontë, Charlotte. *Jane Eyre*. New York: Dover Publications, Incorporated, 2003.

Brontë, Emily. *Wuthering Heights*. London: Michael O'Mara Books, Limited, 2011.

Brown, Ian. *The Boy in the Moon: A Father's Search for His Disabled Son*. Toronto: Random House Publishing Group, 2010.

Brown, Margaret Wise. *Goodnight Moon*. New York: HarperCollins, 1991.

Caron, Roger. *Bingo!: The Horrifying Eyewitness Account of a Prison Riot*. Toronto: Methuen, 1985.

Cervantes, Miguel de. *Don Quixote, The ingenious hidalgo Don Quixote of La Mancha*. New York: Penguin Books, 2000.

Chapman, Gary D. *The Five Love Languages.* Chicago: Moody Publishers, 2009.

Conrad, Joseph. *The Heart of Darkness.* New York: Penguin Books Limited, 2007.

Conrad, Joseph. *The Secret Sharer.* New York: Penguin Publishing Group, 1960.

Crane, Stephen. *The Red Badge of Courage.* New York: Penguin Books, Limited, 2009.

Doctorow, E.L. *Ragtime.* New York: Random House Publishing Group, 2007.

Doyle, Roddy. *The Woman Who Walked Into Doors.* New York: Random House, 1997.

Eggers, Dave. *Zeitoun.* Toronto: Knopf Canada, 2010.

Eliot, T.S. *Four Quartets.* Boston: Houghton Mifflin Harcourt, 1968.

Eliot, T.S. "Journey of the Magi." *The Norton Anthology of English Literature, Revised, Vol. 2.* Ed. M.H. Abrams et al. New York: W.W. Norton & Company, Inc., 1968.

Ellis, Bret Easton. *Less Than Zero.* Toronto: Knopf Doubleday Publishing Group, 1998.

Fallada, Hans. *Every Man Dies Alone.* Brooklyn: Melville House Publishing, 2010.

Farjeon, Eleanor. *The Little Bookroom.* Toronto: Oxford University Press, 2011.

Findley, Timothy. *The Wars.* Toronto: Penguin Group Canada, 2005.

Foucault, Michel. *Discipline and Punish: The Birth of the Prison.* Toronto: Knopf Doubleday Publishing Group, 1995.

Fuller, Alexandra. *Don't Let's Go to the Dogs Tonight.* New York: Random House Publishing Group, 2003.

Galloway, Steven. *The Cellist of Sarajevo.* Toronto: Vintage Canada, 2009.

García Márquez, Gabriel. *One Hundred Years of Solitude.* New York: HarperCollins Publishers, 2006.

Gladwell, Malcolm. *Blink: The Power of Thinking Without Thinking.* New York: Little Brown & Company, 2007.

Gladwell, Malcolm. *Outliers: The Story of Success.* New York: Little Brown & Company, 2008.

Gladwell, Malcolm. *The Tipping Point.* New York: Little Brown & Company, 2002.

Goddard, Donald. *Best American Crime Reporting 2009.* New York: HarperCollins Publishers, 2009.

Goddard, Donald. *Joey.* New York: Harper & Row, 1974.

Golding, William. *Lord of the Flies.* London: Faber & Faber, Limited, 1958.

Gore, Al. *The Assault on Reason.* New York: Penguin Publishing Group, 2008.

Greene, Robert. *The 48 Laws of Power.* London: Profile Books, 2002.

Haddon, Mark. *The Curious Incident of the Dog in the Night-Time.* Toronto: Doubleday Canada, 2004.

Hemingway, Ernest. *A Moveable Feast: The Restored Edition.* New York: Scribner, 2010.

Hemingway, Ernest. *For Whom the Bell Tolls.* New York: Scribner, 1995.

Hemingway, Ernest. *The Old Man and the Sea.* New York: Scribner, 1995.

Henry, O. "The Cop and the Anthem." *The Best Short Stories of O. Henry.* Selected and with an introduction by Bennett A. Cerf and Van H. Cartmell. New York: The Modern Library, 1994.

Henry, O. "The Gift of the Magi." *The Best Short Stories of O. Henry.* Selected and with an introduction by Bennett A. Cerf and Van H. Cartmell. New York: The Modern Library, 1994.

Hill, Lawrence. *Black Berry, Sweet Juice: On Being Black and White in Canada.* Toronto: HarperCollins Canada, 2001.

Hill, Lawrence. *Dear Sir, I Intend to Burn Your Book: Anatomy of a Book Burning.* Edmonton: University of Alberta Press, 2013.

Hill, Lawrence. *Some Great Thing.* Toronto, HarperCollins Canada, Limited, 2009.

Hill, Lawrence. *Someone Knows My Name.* New York: W.W. Norton & Company, Inc., 2008.

Hill, Lawrence. *The Book of Negroes.* New York: HarperCollins, 2007.

Hirsi Ali, Ayaan. *Infidel.* New York: Simon & Schuster, 2008.

Hirsi Ali, Ayaan. *Nomad.* Toronto: Knopf Canada, 2011.

Homer. *Classics Illustrated No. 77, The Iliad.* Illustration by Alex Anthony Blum. New York: Gilberton Co., 1952.

Homer. *The Iliad.* New York: Penguin Classics, 1998.

Hosseini, Khaled. *And the Mountains Echoed.* Toronto: Penguin Group Canada, 2013.

Hugo, Victor. *Les Misérables.* New York: Penguin Books Limited, 1982.

Inwood, Brad. *Seneca: Selected Philosophical Letters.* Oxford: Oxford University Press, 2010.

Ishiguro, Kazuo. *Never Let Me Go.* Toronto: Knopf Canada, 2010.

Jansson, Tove. *The Summer Book.* Toronto: Knopf Doubleday Publishing Group, 1988.

Junger, Sebastian. *War.* New York: HarperCollins Publishers Limited, 2010.

Kershaw, Ian. *The End: The Defiance and Destruction of Hitler's Germany, 1944–1945.* New York: Penguin Publishing Group, 2012.

Kipling, Rudyard. "My Boy Jack." *100 Poems: Old and New.* Selected and edited by Thomas Pinney. Cambridge: Cambridge University Press, 2013.

Krakauer, Jon. *Three Cups of Deceit: How Greg Mortenson, Humanitarian Hero, Lost His Way.* Toronto: Knopf Doubleday Publishing Group, 2011.

Lamb, Charles. *Essays of Elia*. London: Hesperus Press, 2009.

Lansing, Alfred. *Endurance: Shackleton's Incredible Voyage*. New York: Basic Books, 1999.

Larson, Erik. *Devil in the White City*. Toronto: Knopf Doubleday Publishing Group, 2004.

Larson, Erik. *In the Garden of Beasts: Love, Terror, and an American Family in Hitler's Berlin*. New York: Crown Publishing Group, 2012.

Larsson, Stieg. *The Girl with the Dragon Tattoo*. Toronto: Penguin Group Canada, 2011.

Lawes, Lewis E. *Twenty Thousand Years in Sing Sing*. London: Constable & Co., 1932.

Lee, Harper. *To Kill a Mockingbird*. New York: Grand Central Publishing, 1988.

Lehane, Dennis. *Shutter Island*. New York: HarperCollins Publishers, 2009.

Levy, Andrea. *The Long Song*. New York: Penguin Publishing Group Canada, 2011.

Levy, Andrea. *Small Island*. New York: Headline Publishing Group, 2009.

Martel, Yann. *Life of Pi*. Toronto: Knopf Canada, 2002.

McCarthy, Cormac. *All the Pretty Horses*. Toronto: Knopf Doubleday Publishing Group, 1993.

McCarthy, Cormac. *The Road*. Toronto: Knopf Doubleday Publishing Group, 2007.

McCourt, Frank. *Angela's Ashes: A Memoir*. New York: Scribner, 1999.

McEwan, Ian. *Saturday*. Toronto: Knopf Canada, 2006.

Michaels, Anne. *Fugitive Pieces*. Toronto: McClelland & Stewart, 2009.

Mistry, Rohinton. *A Fine Balance*. Toronto: McClelland & Stewart, 1997.

Mistry, Rohinton. *Such a Long Journey*. Toronto: McClelland & Stewart, 1997.

Mnookin, Seth. *The Panic Virus: The True Story Behind the Vaccine-Autism Controversy*. New York: Simon & Schuster, Incorporated, 2012.

Montefoschi, Giorgio. *Lo Sguardo del Cacciatore*. New York: Rizzoli, 1987.

Moore, Lisa. *Caught*. Toronto: House of Anansi Press, 2013.

Moore, Robin, with Barbara Fuca. *Mafia Wife*. London: Macmillan Publishing Co. Inc., 1977.

Mortenson, Greg. *Stones into Schools: Promoting Peace with Books, Not Bombs, in Afghanistan and Pakistan*. New York: Penguin Books 2009.

Mortenson, Greg, and David Oliver Relin. *Three Cups of Tea: One Man's Mission to Promote Peace ... One School at a Time*. New York: Penguin Books, 2007.

Nafisi, Azar. *Reading Lolita in Tehran: A Memoir in Books*. New York: Random House Publishing Group, 2003.

Nafisi, Azar. *Things I've Been Silent About*. New York: Random House Publishing Group, 2010.

Nordhoff, Charles, and James Norman Hall, adapted by Kenneth W. Fitch. *Classics Illustrated No. 100, Mutiny on the Bounty.* Illustration by Henry C. Kiefer and Morris Waldinger. New York: Gilberton Co., 1950.

Nordhoff, Charles, and James Norman Hall. *Mutiny on the Bounty.* Boston: Little, Brown and Company, 1932.

Obama, Barack. *Dreams from My Father.* New York: Crown Publishing Group, 2004.

Orwell, George. *Animal Farm.* New York: Penguin Books, 2008.

Portis, Charles. *True Grit.* New York: The Overlook Press, 2012.

Rice, Connie. *Power Concedes Nothing.* New York: Scribner, 2014.

Robbins, Harold. *A Stone for Danny Fisher.* New York: Touchstone, 2007.

Salinger, J.D. *The Catcher in the Rye.* New York: Little Brown & Company, 1991.

Setterfield, Diane. *The Thirteenth Tale.* Toronto: Doubleday Canada, 2013.

Shaffer, Mary Ann, and Annie Barrows. *The Guernsey Literary and Potato Peel Pie Society.* New York: Random House Publishing Group, 2009.

Stegner, Wallace. *Crossing to Safety.* New York: Random House Publishing Group, 2002.

Steinbeck, John. *Cannery Row.* New York: Penguin Books, 1992.

Steinbeck, John. *Of Mice and Men.* New York: Penguin Books, 1993.

Steinbeck, John. *The Grapes of Wrath.* New York: Penguin Publishing Group, 2006.

Steinberg, Avi. *Running the Books: The Adventures of an Accidental Prison Librarian.* Toronto: Knopf Doubleday Publishing Group, 2010.

Stevenson, Robert Louis. *Dr. Jekyll and Mr. Hyde.* New York: Penguin Books, 2012.

Stevenson, Robert Louis. *Treasure Island.* New York: Penguin Publishing Group, 1994.

Swarup, Vikas. *Six Suspects.* New York: HarperCollins, 2011.

Swarup, Vikas. *Slumdog Millionaire.* New York: HarperCollins, 2008.

Swift, Jonathan. *Gulliver's Travels.* New York: Penguin Publishing Group, 2003.

Tolkien, J.R.R. *The Hobbit.* New York: HarperCollins, 1991.

Twain, Mark. *The Adventures of Huckleberry Finn.* New York: Penguin Classics, 2002.

Vásquez, Juan Gabriel. *The Sound of Things Falling.* London: Bloomsbury Publishing, 2013.

Vonnegut, Kurt. *Player Piano.* New York: Random House Publishing Group, 1999.

Walls, Jeannette. *The Glass Castle: A Memoir.* New York: Scribner, 2006.

Wells, H.G. *The Island of Dr. Moreau.* New York: Dover Publications, 1996.

Wells, H.G. *The Time Machine*. Eastford: Martino Fine Books, 2011.

Wurtzel, Elizabeth. *Bitch: In Praise of Difficult Women*. Toronto: Knopf Doubleday Publishing Group, 1999.

Yeats, W.B. "Under Ben Bulben." *The Collected Poems of W.B. Yeats*. London: Macmillan and Co., Limited, 1950.

ACKNOWLEDGMENTS

M Y FIRST ACKNOWLEDGMENT goes to the men in the prison book clubs at Collins Bay and Beaver Creek for their warm welcome and for putting me at ease. It was a privilege to have spent time with them. I am particularly grateful for the trust and generosity of those who agreed to be interviewed and who kept journals about their reading. Thank you above all to Ben, Dread, Frank, Gaston, Graham and Peter. I hope we will continue our journey in books together.

This book could not have been written without the equally generous access provided by Correctional Service Canada. Thanks especially to Kevin Snedden and Charles Stickel, who were the wardens at Collins Bay and Beaver Creek, but also to officials at the regional and national levels who approved access. I send thanks, as well, to the chaplains in each institution, for cheerfully hosting the space for my interviews, which meant additional administrative work for them, and to the Collins Bay prison librarian, who gave me insight into the prison book culture.

My Toronto women's book club granted me permission to write about three book club meetings in which we read the same books as the men in the Collins Bay Book Club, for which I am very appreciative.

I am also deeply indebted to my writers group, The Ridge Group, now celebrating its tenth anniversary: Brigid Higgins, Peggy Lampotang, Mike MacConnell and Susan Noakes. When I was writing four chapters a month they agreed to read along at that pace, and their comments helped me to apply the techniques of fiction to a non-fiction book.

I consider myself very fortunate to have as my agent and mentor the smart and very capable Hilary McMahon, at Westwood Creative Artists. She supported the project at its earliest stages and challenged me to move beyond my training as a journalist to express my reactions to experiences in the prisons and incorporate more elements of memoir. The agency's Lien de Nil worked through a terrible cold following the Frankfurt Book Fair to orchestrate the initial sale on the international rights side. I am incredibly grateful to them both.

I am thrilled to have found a home with the great publishing teams at Penguin Canada and Oneworld, in the U.K. Diane Turbide, my wonderful editor at Penguin, offered invaluable editorial advice early on and solid support throughout. Oneworld publisher Juliet Mabey has been an inspiring collaborator whose early interest in the project encouraged me to tell the U.K. part of the story more fully. Copy editor Chandra Wohleber's detailed read helped immeasurably. Also vital at Penguin were publisher Nicole Winstanley, publicist Emma Ingram, senior production editor Sandra Tooze and many others. I am fortunate as well to have in my camp Oneworld publicist Lamorna Elmer, a poet in her own right, and the rest of the team at Oneworld.

Many thanks to the author Roddy Doyle, for permission to use his emailed answers to the inmates' questions about *The Woman Who Walked Into Doors*. Thanks too to Lawrence Hill, for allowing me to cover his author visit to the Collins Bay Book Club and agreeing to be interviewed afterward.

I would like to thank Carol Finlay for inviting me to participate in the prison book clubs she organized at Collins Bay and Beaver Creek. She and her husband, Bryan, hosted me with great warmth at their Amherst Island home on numerous occasions during the research for this book so that I could combine my visits to the book club with follow-up interviews with the men and with Carol.

My parents encouraged me to write and nurtured my love of books and nature. They also taught me invaluable lessons about trust. I am grateful to them and to my brothers, who took on additional family duties during the period when I was writing intensively.

To my precious children, you are my best cheering section, and offered great insights into the universal themes in this book. You also have my back and I love you fiercely.

My beloved husband, Bruce, made the manuscript many times better. He was my first and most dedicated reader. In the final editing stages, we sat across from each other at our dining room table, reading each chapter aloud and discussing it line by line. His constant love and support gave me the time I needed for research and writing. Without him, this book would have been impossible.